THE SUSSEX SPANIEL

THE
SUSSEX SPANIEL

Peggy Grayson

THE BOYDELL PRESS

© Peggy Grayson 1989

First published 1989 by The Boydell Press, Woodbridge

The Boydell Press is an imprint of Boydell & Brewer Ltd
PO Box 9, Woodbridge, Suffolk IP12 3DF

ISBN 0 85115 528 6

British Library Cataloguing in Publication Data
Grayson, Peggy
 The Sussex spaniel.
 1. Sussex spaniels
 I. Title
 636.7'52
 ISBN 0-85115-528-6

The paper used in this publication meets the minimum requirements
of American National Standard for Information Sciences – Permanence of
Paper for Printed Library Materials, ANSI Z39.48-1984.

Printed in Great Britain by
The Camelot Press PLC, Southampton

Contents

Acknowledgements

The author would like to thank the following for their kindness in allowing her access to family records and photographs, and for permission to quote and reproduce from these:

The late Sir George Meyrick, Bt,
Francis Drewe, Esq., JP,
Charles Clarke, Esq.

She also wishes to thank the following:

Mrs Mavis Lancaster, Miss Mary Harris and Mrs Ann Findlay, for the loan of pedigrees and photographs;
Mrs Mavis Lancaster, for her chapter on the Sussex Spaniel Association;
Mrs Lancaster and Mrs Faith Gilham, for their advice on the breeding and rearing of Sussex Spaniels;
Miss Theresa Slowik and the staff at the Kennel Club Library, for their manifold help and kindness;
Mr Martin Sinnatt, Secretary of the Kennel Club, for permission to include the new breed standard;
Sue Robinson Tye, for her painstaking Fuller research;
the archivists of West Sussex and Anglesey for their efforts on her behalf;
George Warley, Thomas Fall and Mr William Moores of *Our Dogs*, for the provision of photographs;
John Quelch, for his many hours of work producing the manuscript in such good order;
members of the Sussex Spaniel Association for their kindness in supplying photographs and details of their dogs.

To all these she gives her grateful thanks; without their co-operation her task would have been impossible.

Author's Note

Our spaniel breeds have a long and fascinating history. The more one delves into the past, the more intriguing the story becomes. This work is an attempt to set, in fairly easy-reading form, the history of the Sussex breed and of the people who have owned, bred and exhibited it through the past 130-odd years. A history of the dogs without the owners is like apple pie without the cream. The style of living of the owners, the numbers of dogs they were able to keep, the staff employed and the reason why such a complex and rather difficult breed should have inspired such enthusiasm in so small a number over so long a period are all worth recording. Not every Sussex Spaniel of the past can be examined in detail, but the dogs and bitches to whom the present-day Sussex can claim lineage have all been faithfully recorded. This may not be a very erudite book, but I hope that it will prove readable and interesting, and provide an insight into the Sussex Spaniel and his adherents.

Peggy Grayson

Kennel Names Used in Sussex Spaniels, 1874 to 1987

The author hesitates to call this a list of affixes/prefixes, and prefers to use the term, 'kennel names'. At one time the Kennel Club allowed breeders to use a kennel name on three different dogs before he or she had to register the name as an affix/prefix, and therefore many of the names used as an affix or prefix were never in fact registered as such. In seeking to give the reader as much information as possible, the author has listed the names in the order in which they appear in the Kennel Club Stud Books rather than alphabetically, as with the latter method the reader has no means of determining when the name-holder first had dogs in the KCSB.

1874 to 1900		*1901 to 1918*	
Bradley	J. Hooker	Newbarn	Mrs F. Woolland
Bridford	M. Woolland	Harviestoun	J. Kerr
Rosehill	Campbell Newington	Beechgrove	F. Winton Smith
Hoyle	Mrs Maw	Oldship	Mrs R. Bayley
Heather	R. Chapman	Langrish	Col. Talbot Ponsonby
Alsagar	F.C. Wade		
Celbridge	Col. Claude Cane		
Carntyne	A. Miller		

1920 to 1939			
Broadhurst	J. Stevenson Clarke	Westmark	F. Blagg
Leetside	R. McDougal	Oakerland	Miss F. Reed
Primax	S.C. Mitchell	Agrivista	Mrs M. Bower
Earlswood	Mrs C. Youell	Newburie	Capt. N.W. Tredinnick
Stonecourt	S.C. Batcheller	Hornshill	Miss L.N. Wigg
Ladbrooke	Miss B.A. Warren	Trinity Chest	Mrs A. MacArthur
Fourclovers	Miss J. Scholefield	Kemsdale	Miss D. Neve
	(later Mrs J. Freer)		

1946 to 1987

No new prefixes in the 1940s. The pre-war prefixes Agrivista, Fourclovers and Hornshill were revived.

	1950s		*1960s*
Tarbay	Dr E. Rickards	Sunreef	Miss M. Scarr and Miss M. Harris
Montgarvey	Mrs Manley Cooper		
Penruddick	Mrs D. Peck	Weiden	Miss D.P. Dodson and B.J. Dyson
Buxton	Mrs Merridrew and Miss E. Gregory	Patmyn	Miss J. Collings and Mrs Eysemount
Framsden	Mrs R. Johnstone	Chesara	Mrs J. Elsden
		Sedora	Miss E.M. Adams
		Creswelshaw	Miss M. Clarke ((later Mrs Lancaster) and Mrs M.W. Brookes
		Sharland	Mrs J. Munday
		Kilcoram	G.P.D. Avis
		Treherne	Mrs J. Harvey

	1970s		
Shipden	Mr and Mrs Muirhead	Bryntonian	Mr & Mrs I.G. Williams
Oakmoss	G. Lancaster	Corraline	Mr and Mrs Townsend
Oldholbans	Mrs A. Findlay	Maidenbower	G.T. Candler
Elmbury	R. Hall Jones	Novacroft	Mrs D. Gardner
Penygader	Mrs E.J. Moore	Quintic	Mr and Mrs J. Perkins
Pitchill	Mrs C. Spooner	Topjoys	Mrs F. Gilham
Invermay	Mr and Mrs Gilmour		

	1980s		
Risdene	Mrs and Miss Leslie	Norris	Mr and Mrs C.B. Wakefield
Trovilea	Mr and Mrs Learmouth	Jezemay	Mrs C.D. May
Gemrocks	Mr and Mrs J. Almond	Oldfield	Mr and Mrs C. Bexon
Loweview	Mr and Mrs C.P. Jackson	Daelyb	Mrs D.E. Bailey
Nordhal	Mr and Mrs M.T. Dalebo		
Chilsham	Mrs B.A. Purkiss	Pedlarmans	Mrs S. Palmer
Maladetta	L. Cox	Walkers	M. Corby
Northerwood	Mrs S. Tiller	Karmar	Mrs M.G. Newbold
Serendel	R. Goodwin	Kincaspa	Mr and Mrs Roberts
Forestdown	Mr and Mrs C.B. Wakefield	Rangitara	Mr and Mrs C. Brown
Scotshill	Mr D and Miss M. Fox	Upend	Mrs B. Butler

Some of these kennel names only appear once in the Stud Books; others appear for a number of years. It is interesting to note that the dogs in the early books were mainly owned by gentlemen, then after the First World War the lady owners gradually took over, and today we see many husband-and-wife partnerships.

Augustus Elliot Fuller Esq. of Rosehill, Sussex. 1777 to 1857

1

The Fuller Connection

The beautiful county of Sussex and the western parts of neighbouring Kent have one thing in common: thick, heavy clay soil. Two hundred or so years ago much of the area was wooded, with thick undergrowth and strong, deep fences. Where the Downs roll down to the Weald it is steep, with heavy oak and beech woods known as 'the hangers' clinging precariously to the hillsides. Small, deep ravines bottomed by strange dark pools are everywhere; it is a country that calls for a sturdy horse, a fleet hound and a strong and untiring gundog.

The men who peopled this wild and beautiful landscape so long ago were all sportsmen, from the cottager who sneaked out on a moonlight night to catch a few rabbits for the pot, aided by his terriers and ferrets; through the boys who delighted in the rat hunt round the stockyard; to the rough shooter, the huntsman, the fisherman, the gentleman in his large mansion who invited guests for shooting parties, the gamekeeper, the wildfowler and, indeed, any man worth his salt who could handle a gun, ride a horse or train a dog. Sport in the true sense of the word, involving horse and hound, dog and gun, hawk and net, rod and line, did not involve activities such as football or running which are, today, erroneously dubbed as sport. It is difficult for the urban-dwelling people in this highly mechanised and technological age to imagine the scene. The horse was not only a source of pleasure but also the only means of transport; the countryside abounded with game, pheasants, partridge, duck, woodcock, snipe, hares and deer, and there were large colonies of badgers, warrens full of rabbits and foxes in profusion; and rats multiplied in every barn, stack and hedgerow. The possession of good horses was a priority; the packs of foxhounds, harriers, beagles, bassets and otterhounds were highly prized, the best greyhounds were destined for the slips, and perhaps most highly prized of all was the good dog for the gun, one of the most coveted being the good spaniel.

There were spaniels for working on land or water, cocking spaniels to rustle up the wily woodcock, and spaniels to spring the game for hawk and net and later for the gun. Apart from spaniels, there were larger gun-dog breeds, setting and pointing dogs for the moors and open spaces, and retrieving breeds of several kinds.

In those days, long before the setting up of the Kennel Club, there were no official records or pedigrees of the dogs bred for all these various purposes. Gentlemen kept their own personal records, most meticulously in some cases, and a few, though not nearly enough, have come down to us today. They recorded matings: when Bess went to Bob, how many pups she had, their sex and colour, how many went in the bucket, and which were sold, exchanged or given away; and they kept a record of the training of those that were retained as they grew up.

Small or weakly pups were put down at birth, and dogs were culled from kennels if they showed cowardice in the field, were unbiddable, savage or wild. Various scourges, such as distemper, carried off the sickly or unthrifty ones or any suffering from an inherent disease, making a race of strong hardy dogs and keeping numbers well in check. Most country gentlemen bred their own line of gundogs – setters, pointers and retrievers as well spaniels – and many were named after the person who developed a particular breed or after the place where they were bred. There was the Gordon Setter bred by the Dukes of Gordon; the Clumber Spaniel named after Clumber Park; and the Sussex Spaniel, so named because a number of landowners in that county developed, bred and perfected a type of spaniel capable of working heavy clay soil and the dense undergrowth through a long day without tiring.

These dogs were deep through with well-sprung ribs, longer in the back than the cocking spaniels, short and strong in the couplings, with great hindquarters and wide, thick thighs, strongly boned legs and big feet. The head was large but without coarseness. The strong sloping shoulders and the large muscular thighs drove the dog through the heavy going, and his babbling voice told his owners in which part of the wood he could be located. The coat too was different, very thick and dense with a seal-like feel and shine, and completely waterproof. The sportsmen of the area swore by this dog for work in the county where he was bred, although many disagreed about his colour. Some maintained that he should be liver and white; some that he should be liver with white chest, paws and blaze; and, as time went on, some that he must be liver with no markings and, later still, that the liver must have a golden tinge. The latter colour was, as old books tell us, bred into the strains by Dr Watts of Battle in the early part of the last century. He had a stud dog at the time who threw pups 'of a sandy hue'. At first they went into the pail, but they were later saved and bred from. The colour became the norm for the breed and is greatly prized to this day.

The reason for the sandy liver has not been explored, but the explanation seems fairly simple. That part of Sussex was rich in iron ore, which is said partly to account for the colour of the Sussex cattle, a red-gold. On the Sandlings in Norfolk, with similar soil, they breed the chestnut

Suffolk horse, which has the same golden highlights. The breed or strain of Sussex Spaniels in those early days no doubt contained the blood of many kinds of dogs until the right mixture had been obtained. Then inbreeding took place, brother to sister, father to daughter, mother to son, to set the type for all time, and this ploy succeeded well. In those days if a sportsman saw a good working dog belonging to someone else which had a characteristic he desired in his own strain, he would use it and then inbreed again. By culling the puppies that showed breed characteristics of the outcross which were not wanted in his line, and by careful inbreeding and line-breeding again for several generations, he could incorporate this new characteristic in his line. There was no registration, no Kennel Club to say 'no'; the man was free to develop his strain for his own purposes. The black and tan cocking spaniels that appeared were accounted for by a cross with the old English black and tan terrier by men who wanted a keener, faster spaniel; they bred out the terrier characteristics after a bit, keeping the characteristics for which the cross was made.

The Sussex Spaniel is undoubtedly one of the early recognisable breeds of spaniel. It is mentioned in all the old books on dogs of the late eighteenth century and on throughout the nineteenth century. As one browses through these books it is interesting to note how the canine historians faithfully copied from the past. Few, if any, conducted any research, and much of what was set down had reached them by word of mouth. No doubt the stories differed according to who told them. The claims grew more extravagant as the years passed. Much of what has been claimed has proved on closer investigation to be nonsense, and all of us who have written on spaniels over the past hundred years − right up to the present day − have set down incorrect information simply because we took it for granted that what was written in a past century was totally correct. Now is the time to set the record straight. However, before giving my findings, based on a line of research undertaken recently, it will be of interest to look at what old books on sporting dogs have to say about the Sussex Spaniel.

The Sportsman's Cabinet, produced by John Smith in 1803, says of spaniels, 'the largest and strongest are common in most parts of Sussex and are called Sussex Spaniels'. The author reiterates this in the 1820 edition. John Scott, also writing in 1820, said, 'The largest springers were some years since and probably may at present be, found in Sussex.' So there is good evidence that a breed of large working spaniel was evolved and pioneered in Kent and Sussex. Youatt in *The Dog*, published in 1845, says under the heading 'The Springer' (a general term for all spaniel breeds that sprung game, such as the Norfolk, Clumber and Sussex, and not to be confused with the modern springer breeds), 'This dog is slower to range than the cocker, but it is a much safer dog for the

Early Sussex Spaniel. 1800s. 'An old, short legged, strong-loined Sussex.' Dog Breaking. Gen. Hutchinson. pub. 1856

shooter and can better stand a hard day's work. The largest and best springers are said to be in Sussex, and are much esteemed in the Wealds of that county.' A piece in a spaniel magazine of 1833 written by 'A Quartrogenarian' says of the Sussex, 'a large brown and white Springer chiefly used in the large, wet, clayey woodland coverts of Kent and Sussex'.

In General Hutchinson's *Dog Breaking*, written in 1856, only one mention is made of the Sussex Spaniel. The author says he was told of a farmer in Kent, 'one of the fine yeomen of whom England has such cause to feel proud', who was out shooting with 'an old, short-legged, strong loined Sussex Spaniel'. Idstone instances paintings he has seen by Landseer and Abraham Cooper featuring spaniels which answer the description of the breed: 'In Cooper's picture the dog is represented with white toes.'

Stonehenge (J.H. Walsh), editor of *The Field*, has this to say in his work The Dog, published in 1859:

George and Romp. Property of E. Soames, Esq. Circa 1850. Bred by A.E. Fuller, Esq. of Rosehill. 'Stonehenge on the Dog.' Pub. 1859.

The Sussex differs from the Clumber in shape as well as colour, as well as in his 'questing', his note being full and bell-like, though sharp. In height and weight there is not much difference, nor is the general character of the head very distinguishable from that of the Clumber, but in length of leg he is not nearly as remarkable as that dog, though still long and low, the body being very rounded and full, indicating great power. The coat also, is pretty nearly the same in quality, being soft and silky, though thick and free from distinct curls, and this dog is also beautifully feathered. The head is not quite so heavy about the muzzle, but very square above the eyes, and with an expression of exceeding gravity and intelligence. The ears are full in length and not very thickly covered with hair. Muzzle broad, with the underjaw receding more than in the Clumber, and the point of nose of a liver colour. The whole body is also of a decided liver colour, but with rather a golden shade, not so deep as that of the Welsh or Devon Cockers or the Irish Water Spaniel. Legs and feet very strong and well feathered. Tail generally cropped and well clothed with wavy hair. The bitches are usually smaller than the dogs. All this breed throw their tongues, and when kept to cocks or pheasants, they readily indicate their scent by a sharper note than usual.

Idstone, writing in the 1870s, gives a chapter to the Sussex breed and says, 'The Sussex is nearly, if not quite, extinct, and I have not seen a first class one for years', and, later:

Good spaniels may be obtained in any colours, but the true Sussex is a golden liver. The dog has never been produced in great numbers, nor has he ever been common. He has been in the hands of a few families, and the late Mr. Fuller was a celebrated breeder and for the breaking and discipline of his team. For the patient, genuine sportsman there is no better dog than the short legged, thick set and low spaniel, which ought to down-charge, to retrieve and swim well and cheerfully. The Sussex possessed all these accomplishments and he was a capital dog to go through thick covert or woodlands, being able with his formation, to burrow under gorse and tangle and to rouse fur and feather in situations impossible for his master. For this purpose he should have a thick, straight, voluminous coat, such as shall protect but not impede him, and ears of a moderate size, or what a judge of exhibition Spaniels would pronounce small.

Idstone then goes on to say that the dog, being of uniform colour, may be indistinct in beechwood and similar country, and says no such objection can be levied at a dog with white on him. He says he saw spaniels at Devon shows with a tendency to the Sussex colour, but with white blaze, throat, neck collar and feet, and was struck with the idea that these spaniels had been produced by a cross with the Sussex. Idstone goes on to say of the Sussex that he saw they:

were of the following form . . . . The forehead marked with a decided brow and deep dent or stop between the eyes, the nasal bone was long, nose liver coloured, nostrils well developed, mouth very large, the corners loose and rather heavy, the ears level, the eye bold, large and hazel in colouring but not protruding, neck long with no loose skin, shoulders powerful with short joints, the tail thick and strong. The colour is a mark of great purity being golden or orange and not blue or puce like M'Carthy's Irish Water Spaniel.

The coming of dog shows brought an entirely new element to the world of sporting dogs: the exhibitor. Prior to the show scene, the spaniel had been bred solely for work, and although gentlemen were proud of good-looking dogs, it was for their prowess in the shooting field that the dogs were most esteemed. Then the scene changed and over the first ten years of shows, from 1859 to 1869, the trend was slight but discernible. However, with the formation of the Kennel Club, the registration of dogs and the regulation of shows, needed − we are told in old books − to 'stop all the cheating', a dramatic change took place. Shows began to attract a large number of exhibitors, entries rose, more show societies were formed to cope with growing demand and breed clubs began to make their appearance.

With all this activity, the need to produce something novel was as fierce then as it is today; but whereas in the 1980s people have to import some obscure breed from overseas, the men of the 1870s had plenty of home-grown material to work on. Some concentrated on producing the first strain of all-black spaniels, to be called the Black Field Spaniel; others took roughly the same foundation stock and set about producing a Sussex Spaniel for the bench. Why a Sussex? You may well ask. Well, it had been a breed about which a good deal had been written in old books, notably about its handsome looks, its working abilities and, above all, its distinctive colour; and there was the additional fact that it was practically extinct. One can understand the ambitious would-be exhibitors of the time getting excited and becoming enthusiastic to revive such a paragon. But where were they to start?

In 1859, when Mr Walsh (Stonehenge) published his first dog book, he used in it an illustration of two spaniels. The caption to the picture reads as follows: 'George and Romp. Property of E. Soames Esq., of London.' A footnote read, 'Bred by the late A.E. Fuller Esq., Rose Hill, Brightling, Sussex, and descended from the stock of Mr. Moneypenny of Rolvedon.' That is the very first reference in any book to Mr Fuller of Brightling, to George and Romp and, indeed, to Mr Moneypenny.

The whole story would appear to hang on that one picture in Stonehenge's book, printed in 1859. It establishes the fact that Mr Fuller of Rose Hill had Sussex Spaniels and, not only that, the drawings in the book show that they were handsome dogs. It is from the mid 1870s that the stories about Mr Fuller really start, and they become more significant as the years go on. The first author to write about Mr Fuller was Idstone, who in 1879 wrote that, 'Mr. Fuller was a celebrated breeder'; he also affirmed that the Sussex 'was nearly extinct'. It seems, however, to have been in *The Sporting Spaniel* that Col. Claud Cane declared:

Mr. Fuller is said to have kept his strain for 50 years, which takes us back into the eighteenth century, as Fuller's death did not occur until 1847, when his famous kennel was dispersed by auction. In consideration of his long and faithful service, Relf the head keeper was allowed to select a dog and a bitch and from these two, George and Romp, most of the Sussex Spaniels that have attained celebrity are descended. Relf survived his master by 40 years, dying in 1887 at the patriarchal age of 87 and kept up to his last his interest in the breed.

In 1904 Herbert Compton published *The 20th Century Dog*. He copied Cane's story, adding his own embellishment, that:

on Mr. Fuller's death Mrs. Fuller allowed Relf the head gamekeeper to select a couple of spaniels by way of a legacy and from these emanated the pure bred specimens that existed 35 years later. The rest of the kennel was sold and reached fabulous prices which serves to show what high esteem the strain, confessedly local, was held. Descendants of the keeper's dogs passed into Mr. Campbell Newington's and Mr. Moses Woolland's hands.

Robert Leighton's two-volume work, *The New Book of the Dog*, published in 1907, also gives Cane's version of the story. In *Hutchinson's Dog Encyclopaedia*, published in parts in the years between the wars, Mrs Youell, who then owned the Earlswood Sussex, wrote the Sussex chapter. She once again reiterated the story that Mr Fuller died in 1847, but she went further and said, 'there were supporters who carried on the strain'.

In the sporting section of Herbert Compton's *The 20th Century Dog*, published in 1904, the author claims that Campbell Newington made the extraordinary statement, 'My old dog Laurie, a son of Hudson's Dash, was considered by the late Dr. Williams the handsomest spaniel he had ever seen. I mated him to a beautiful bitch called Lady Rosehill, which came direct from Mr. Fuller's kennel.' Mr Newington did not come into possession of Laurie until the early 1880s, when he founded his kennel; this was twenty-three years after Mr Fuller's death, so Lady Rosehill could not have come direct from the kennel. Recourse to the records shows that Mr Newington never owned a bitch called Lady Rosehill, and that a bitch with that name was half-Field Spaniel and bred on the Isle of Wight. He did, however, own a Countess of Rosehill and she was indeed mated to Laurie. This does show that one should never take statements in the old books too seriously. It is always wise to dig back as far as possible when attempting to discover the true facts about a breed.

It is noticeable when reading the books on dogs published over the past hundred years that neither Vero Shaw nor Theo Marples propound the

Fuller myth; perhaps they were doubtful of its authenticity even when they were writing.

The facts regarding Mr Fuller, his family and his spaniels, are quite different from the story peddled down the years. The true facts are now set out.

Augustus Eliott Fuller died in 1857, not in 1847. He did not inherit Rose Hill until 1834, and therefore lived there for some twenty-three years. There is no written reference to a keeper called Relf in any of the family papers still available. It is extremely doubtful that this man ever existed. The dogs George and Romp appear in the 1859 edition of Stonehenge's book, and are listed as the property of Mr E. Soames. Given that publishing was a much slower process than today, this book must have been in the course of compilation around 1857 to 1859, at the time of Mr Fuller's death, which must have been when Mr Soames (not Relf), came into possession of the two Sussex Spaniels. As for Mrs Fuller giving spaniels to Relf, that worthy lady predeceased her husband by twelve months.

The story of the kennels being struck by dumb madness may be true, as most kennels suffered this form of rabies at one time or another, and this probably accounted for the fact that only six spaniels appear in the inventory at the time when Mr Fuller died. Presumably Mr Soames took two of these. I imagine that Mr Fuller's son retained a pair, because of the entry in the Stud Book for 1876 for the Rev. Shields's dog Bras, the first entry under 'Sussex Spaniels'. He is recorded as being bred by Mr Caple Hanbury in 1874, KCSB 5244. His sire is Rag and his dam Maud 2219. The footnote reads: 'Rag, bred by Mr. O. J. A. Fuller Meyrick of Brightling, Sussex.' Mr Fuller Meyrick was the only surviving son of Mr A.E. Fuller. Mr Hanbury had by then apparently acquired Maud from Dr Spurgin. If, as it is claimed, she was descended from the Rosehill blood, then so maybe was Rag, and that is why Mr Hanbury chose to use him. Although Bras does appear as the sire of a couple of dogs in later Stud Books, they do not appear in the pedigree of today's dogs – unfortunately, as this line was possibly the only true line to the original Rosehills.

Much stress has been laid in books over the past century on Mr Fuller's connection with the Sussex Spaniel. As you may have read this and much of it is either incorrect or misleading, it seemed to the author of this book that a chapter on the Fuller family, with an investigation into the actual proof of their connection with the breed, was essential.

Far from being a modest country gentleman whose sole occupation was sport Augustus Eliott Fuller was an extremely wealthy landowner. By the time he died, he had several estates in Sussex and Surrey, a house and offices in London and business property and large holdings in Jamaica.

How and why he came to inherit Brightling Park in Sussex makes fascinating reading.

The Fuller family, who were ironmasters, lived originally in Uckfield, but moved to Waldron, where Samuel Fuller built Tanhouse or Tanners Manor in the early part of the seventeenth century. It appears that Samuel's grandson, Thomas Fuller, purchased the original house at Brightling in 1697 from the Collins family. It was then known as Brightling Park. He apparently put his nephew John Fuller in possession of it. Either Thomas Fuller or his nephew rebuilt it, and this is the house that stands today. This nephew, John, married Elizabeth, daughter of Fulk Rose of Jamaica, and thus the Fuller connection with Jamaica began. In recognition of the large fortune brought to him by his wife, John re-named his residence Rose Hill, after his wife's maiden name. The first Fuller of Brightling died in 1745 and was succeeded by his son, John, who never married and died ten years after inheriting the property. During his life he made many alterations to the house, including building an egg-shaped bedroom and dressing-room – which later had to be demolished because of settlement – and a drawing-room where a relief of a large cannon was set in the plasterwork over the fireplace. This was a reference to the major source of the fortunes of the Fullers, ordnance. Much of the building the second John Fuller undertook has vanished, but he is remembered in the plantations and parkland that he planned, much of which still survives, and which can be seen in a large Turner painting still in the family's possession.

Following John Fuller II's death, the property passed in 1755 to his brother, Rose Fuller, a remarkable man who was squire of Rose Hill for twenty-two years. Much of his early life was spent in Jamaica looking after the plantations, but he came back to England in August 1755 to look after the London office of the family firm in Gerrard Street, Soho. While in Jamaica he was appointed Chief Justice by George III, and on coming home to live he became Deputy Lieutenant of Sussex in 1757 and Member of Parliament for New Romney in 1761. From family papers it appears that he was a close friend of Sir Francis Dashwood, Hell-Fire Francis of the Hell Fire Club.

His colleague in all his business activities was his younger brother Stephen, and together they actively pursued the gunfounding industry at Brightling. Rose Fuller was also a charitable man. He was keenly interested in the Foundling Hospital in London, and was responsible for several clauses in an Act to correct abuses there. He was also active locally and dealt with petitions for the repair of roads and for the removal of turnpike gates and with scores of begging letters. Rose Fuller, after a busy life during which he, too, remained unmarried, died on 7 May 1777.

'Rosehill'. A modern photograph of Brightling Park, known in the 19th century as Rosehill, home of the Fuller family from where their business in ordnance was carried on.

The estates at Brightling and Rose Hill itself passed to his nephew John (Mad Jack) Fuller, a son of his brother Henry, Rector of South Stoneham in Hampshire. Mad Jack's mother was Frances Fuller, a cousin, daughter of Thomas Fuller of Park Gate, Catsfield. Mad Jack found himself a wealthy man, and he indulged in some more building in and around the Park and in the acquisition of other property. One acquisition was Bodiam Castle: he was interested in preserving the ruin. He also erected a temple in the Park and, it is said, a charming little summer-house. Later the architect who designed those, Sir John Smirke, built an observatory at his instruction. Smirke was also responsible for building the mausoleum in Brightling churchyard where the mortal remains of Mad Jack were laid to rest; he was yet another Fuller to die unmarried. However, the Fullers who embarked on wedlock had large families, and Rose Hill passed to Mad Jack's cousin Augustus Eliott Fuller, son of the John Trayton Fuller who had married as his first wife Eleanor; she brought the Trayton fortune with her and was responsible for the Trayton name coming into the Fuller line. John Trayton Fuller was married a second time in 1776, to Ann Eliott, the daughter of Baron Heathfield of Brayley Park (later re-named Heathfield Park). It was at

The grave of Lucy Fuller's spaniel at Bodorgan in Anglesey. The home of A.E. Fuller's son, Owen Putland Fuller Meyrick, where Mr Fuller and his family spent a good deal of time.

Heathfield Park that Augustus Eliott was born in 1777. Brayley Park was sold in 1791 and John Trayton Fuller moved his family to his newly built mansion, Ashdown House, in East Grinstead. Augustus Eliott inherited Ashdown House on the death of his father in 1811, and in 1834 he inherited Rose Hill, Brightling, Bodiam Castle and the Waldron estate from Mad Jack.

Augustus Eliott Fuller was married on 5 September 1801 to Clara, one of the three children of Owen Putland Meyrick of Bodorgan in Anglesey. This was a very old Welsh family whose pedigree went back to Cadfael Ynad, Lord of Cydewain. Their ancestor Meyrick ap Llewellyn was Captain of the Guards to Henry VIII and it appears that it was around that time that the Bodorgan estates came into the family. The couple had nine children of whom the eldest was Clara, born in 1802; there were four other survivors, Lucy Anne, Augusta Maria, Catherine Sarah and Owen John Fuller. Of the four who failed to reach maturity three were sons: Richard Garth, who died at 16 days of age in 1812; John Francis, died aged 16 in 1822; William Loundes, died aged 15 in 1825; and Mary, died aged 14 in 1831.

On the death of Owen Putland Meyrick, the Bodorgan estates passed, through his daughter (her only brother being dead), to Augustus Eliott Fuller's only surviving son, Owen John Putland Fuller. He then took the surname of Meyrick. Owen was only in his early 20s when he took over Bodorgan, but he proved to be a wise and dedicated owner, not only preserving the estates but improving them and building a billiard-room, aviaries and other additions to the mansion. His sister Clara married William Tapps of Hinton Admiral in Hampshire, and this family also took the name of Meyrick as Clara had been another heir of her grandfather. Clara died at the age of 29, and when her brother Owen died unmarried at Bodorgan in 1876, the whole of the Bodorgan estates passed into the hands of Clara's descendants.

Owen took up residence at Bodorgan in 1827 at the age of 23. His parents, who were still living at Ashdown House, spent much of their time at Bodorgan, and Owen had kennels built to house several packs of hounds for his father to hunt. Part of these kennels are still intact. The brick building at the end of one of the long fields, where the carted stag lived, is also still standing. This animal's name, Rob Roy, was given to the wood that adjoins the building and yard. There are records of quite large payments being made annually to Augustus Eliott Fuller from the Bodorgan estates. It is apparent that even after inheriting Rose Hill in 1834 the Fullers spent a large part of their time at Bodorgan. Their residency at Rose Hill lasted twenty-three years, until Mr Fuller died in 1857.

In his nine-page will made before the death of his wife in 1856, Mr

Fuller left everything (bar legacies to his surviving children) to his part-ner of fifty-five years, but after her death he wrote two long codicils. The will mentions the large amounts of land owned by Mr A.E. Fuller: 'the mansion called Rose Hill, and all my manors, messuages, farms, lands, tenements and hereditaments situate in the several parishes of Brightling, Burwash, Dallington and Mountfield, and all and similar my marsh lands in the several parishes of Pevensey, Hailsham and Westham'. Mr Fuller also left Ashdown Manor (sold in later years; it is now a school), his Lon-don house in Clifford Street, and 'all sugar works, lands and hereditaments in the island of Jamaica'. These last properties remained in the family for two more generations before being sold, the family house on Barbados being the oldest on the island. The will also lists paintings, books, etc. Mr Fuller left substantial fortunes to his daughters, but the bulk of the estate passed, with the lands, into the hands of Owen, already owner of Bodorgan.

There is no mention of any bequests to any retainers at Rose Hill, and no mention of any animals, bar the asses and cattle in Jamaica. It is only the inventory made after his death that notes the fact that he left ten beagles, three pointers, two retrievers and six spaniels. This list was drawn up in 1857.

Besides being a great landowner at the time of his death, Mr A.E. Fuller had, all his life, extensive business commitments both in this country and Jamaica. He was Member of Parliament for the Eastern Division of Sussex, and so must have been a very busy gentleman, not the quiet country squire who spent his time breeding spaniels at Brightling, as past writers would have us believe. All the family at Bodorgan were keen sportsmen, and there is evidence of large shooting parties back in the early 1800s in which, no doubt, Mr Fuller was a keen participant. He might even have taken his spaniels there from Sussex. Did he in fact give one of these to his daughter, Lucy Anne? In the grounds of Bodorgan there is a 10 ft by 8 ft grave, surrounded by black-painted gold-tipped railings, and inside is an oval stone bearing the inscription: 'Trim. A favourite spaniel of Lucy Anne Fuller. Died May, 7th. 1840 aged 17 years.' Is this really one of the famous Rose Hill spaniels? Or was it perhaps a Welsh Cocker, or even a toy spaniel, much favoured by ladies of that period? We shall never know. I think this is possibly the nearest anyone will ever get to the Fuller spaniels from Rose Hill, Brightling.

A large part of Augustus Eliott Fuller's life was undoubtedly spent at Bodorgan, and presumably his children lived there over fairly long periods; if not, why was Lucy's pet spaniel buried there and not at Rose Hill? Certainly he was either married there, or at a church chosen by his bride's parents, and not in Sussex. I have been unable so far to discover where he died but, wherever that was, he is buried at Bodorgan with his wife. The church of St Cadwaladr at the tiny village of Llangadwaladr is the resting-place of the Meyrick family. To the left of the altar is the Meyrick Chapel, where many generations lie in the family vault. Under the splendid stained-glass window is a black marble tomb; inscribed round the edge, the letters incased in finely carved leaves, are the words 'In memory of Augustus Eliott Fuller Esq. and Clara his wife'. On the wall to the right of the tomb is a white marble memorial to their children who died so young, and also to Clara, who died aged 29. Their son, Owen John Putland Fuller Meyrick, died in February 1876 aged 72; he was succeeded by his nephew – son of his sister Clara – Sir George E.W. Tapps Gervais Meyrick, Bart, of Hinton Admiral, Hampshire. Sir George inherited the Bodorgan estates, and is the great-great-grandfather of the present Sir George Meyrick, who can therefore claim Augustus Eliott Fuller as his great-great-great-great-grandfather. Sarah Fuller, also unmarried, died aged 43 in 1858; she was the last of the combined Fuller-Meyrick family to be buried in St Cadwaladr's churchyard, beside his sister Augusta Maria Fuller, who died in 1871 aged 53, unmarried, as was her brother. There is no record of Lucy's death, but as she had married presumably she was not brought home to lie with the family but was buried with her husband's people.

The history of the Fuller family is full of interest, all of it well documented, all, that is, except the spaniel. This leads one to believe what one has always suspected, that Mr Fuller kept and bred his own strain purely for his own use, for shooting over both in Sussex and Anglesey. If he could come back, no doubt he would be highly amused at the tales that have been told and the claims that have been made for the spaniels from Rose Hill. His portrait, in water-colours, shows a tall, spare man; a handsome man of fair complexion with a high forehead and wispy blond hair. The blue eyes look steadily at you out of the painting, and there is a hint of a smile about the corners of the mouth. Truly Augustus Eliott Fuller would have enjoyed his posthumous fame as a breeder of Sussex Spaniels.

2

Developing the Breed

One of the first of the men to bring out a 'Sussex' spaniel in the early 1870s was Phineas Bullock, who kept the Bull's Head Tavern at Bilston in Staffordshire. Mr Bullock had a large hand in spaniels, keeping several varieties and being in the van of all Cocker, Field and Sussex breeding and showing activity of the time. Mr Bullock showed a liver dog called George as a Sussex; his sire and dam were Bob and Nellie, two blacks who featured in the pedigrees of the black Field Spaniels which Bullock was promoting at the time. George met with some success in the rings, but was eventually objected to by Mr Thomas Bowers, who averred that no dog bred from two blacks could be a true Sussex. George was quickly sold by Mr Bullock. Although the new owner showed him a few times, it was with little success, and George disappeared from view. In a short time a rule was made that all liver spaniels being shown as Sussex should come from liver parents. This rule was a rather toothless affair, and although it may have worked for a year or so it certainly did not apply for long. A large number of Sussex who had a least one black parent, or indeed one coloured parent, won prizes over the next fifty years of the breed's history, and indeed this did not cease until the 1920s!

Another keen breeder of the new Sussex was John Hopcroft, who also supplied his liver and white and black and white Norfolk Spaniels to those trying to breed the black Field, as well as those gentlemen reviving the Sussex. Dr Spurgin, a great spaniel man of that time whose interest in and association with several varieties of spaniel stretched from the 1860s to around 1912, took an interest in the Sussex, but one of the chief architects of the breed was Mr Thomas Bowers, whose name loomed large in Fields, Sussex and Cockers from the 1870s to the 1890s. Another gentleman early on the scene was Mr T. Burgess, but he did not live long enough to enjoy the fame which undoubtedly awaited him. The Rev. Shields of Kirkby Lonsdale in Cumbria was another keen spaniel breeder and exhibitor. He had all three breeds but leaned heavily on his Cockers to supply foundation stock for both Sussex and Fields. The only gentleman who possibly had Sussex Spaniels from the old stock within the home county was a Mr Saxby of Lewes, and if there were any of the old working Sussex blood in the new Sussex of the 1870s then it was through his dogs that it came. There were two Saxby families living near Lewes in the 1870s but no records remain of any involvement of them with spaniels.

The Saxby blood was said to be mixed with that of 'Mr Marchant's strain', but apart from knowing that this gentleman came from Kent, we can only hazard a guess that here again might have been the blood of the old working spaniel used by yeomen in the Weald of Kent. Reference to the Stud Books shows a number of gentlemen claiming to have dogs from 'pure Rose Hill stock'. How much truth was there in all these claims? Precious little as far as one can judge, because by the time these claims came to be made, Mr Fuller had been dead for nearly twenty years.

In the first Stud Book, published in 1874 and containing names and details of dogs from the commencement of shows in 1859 until 1874, there is only one claim that a particular dog came from Rose Hill blood and that is Maud 2219: 'Property of Mr. (Dr.) H. B. Spurgin. Bred by Saxby in 1871, by Marchant's Rover x Saxby's Fan, both Rose Hill breed.' But in later volumes every Tom, Dick and Harry claimed their dogs went back to the Rose Hill dogs, and there is nothing to prove or disprove their statements, no pedigrees or other proof being given.

Mr Walsh (Stonehenge) writes in his *Dogs of the British Isles* that:

> until the year 1873 Sussex Spaniels were never distinguished as a separate class at any of our shows, being admitted only as 'other than Clumber' or as 'large spaniels'. In that year however, the committee of the Crystal Palace Show instituted a special prize for the Sussex breeds, and this example was followed in October by Nottingham where the puce coloured Rufus bred by Mr. Beeley defeated Mr. P. Bullock's George.'

Mr Walsh goes on to say that Bullock's George was so named 'for his resemblance to Mr. Soames' George, selected by me in 1866 as the type to breed. Mr. Soames' George has yet to be surpassed, as far as my opinion and observation go, and I shall therefore retain his portrait as efficiently representing the true type of Sussex Spaniel.'

So was Mr Walsh referring to the George of the pair 'George and Romp' shown in his 1859 book, or did that pair beget another George? In 1866 the George of the picture must have been an oldish dog as his breeder had then been dead for nine years. Mr Walsh does not say that he actually judged George in 1866, and if he did the dog was unplaced; there is no George owned by a Mr Soames in the first Stud Book, and Mr Walsh does not, unfortunately, tell us anything about this Mr Soames or where he lived. Mr Walsh goes on to say that it was impossible to criticise the various liver coloured spaniels exhibited, except generally;

but as soon as the opportunity was given it was taken advantage of. A whole host of spaniel men leapt into print declaring that not only must the Sussex possess a proper liver colour but it must also be descended from parents of similar hue. Even Phineas Bullock took pen in hand, although at the time he was showing George (so admired by Mr Walsh) from the two blacks. Later he had to withdraw George from the ring following Mr Bowers's complaints.

Vero Shaw speaks of the 'gentlemen of the 1870's taking on a self-imposed task of endeavouring to resuscitate the "old Rose Hill type"'. He goes on to speak of a 'large number of spaniels in whom the blood of the old Rose Hill spaniels ran, but they bore the taint of foreign crosses', which is a polite way of referring to the black and coloured blood in use at the time.

It is difficult to pin-point exactly who first started the Fuller myth, which crept into dog literature, each writer copying from those who had gone before. It was left to the writers of the 1890s to concoct the story which readers have accepted and writers have copied up to the present day, and which has been detailed in the previous chapter.

So the revival of the Sussex Spaniel in the 1870s was undertaken by a group of men headed by Phineas Bullock, which included Dr Spurgin, the Rev. Shields, Mr A.W. Langdale, Mr J.A. Salter, Mr T. Bowers and Mr Saxby. It seems clear that the black and tan spaniel dog Frank owned by Mr Frank Burdett – the promoter of the first dog shows at Birmingham – and black Cockers from Mr Footman's original strain, together with Mr Hopcroft's black and white and liver and white Norfolk Spaniels, had a little to do with the revival. Idstone has written that he had not seen a specimen of a Sussex Spaniel for some time, and Youatt calls them rare, so base stock had to be arrived at from somewhere. In the first Stud Book, Fields, Cockers and Sussex are lumped under one heading. Some are stated to be 'under 20 lbs – these were the Cockers; others have 'Sussex' in brackets beside them; some are just down as 'liver'. By comparing the early dogs with those in later volumes one builds up a picture of how the new Sussex was arrived at.

Already we have spoken of Maud, bred by Mr Saxby and sold to Dr Spurgin, as being one most likely to carry the old blood from Rose Hill. She had a brother called Buckingham, who does not appear until KCSB 1875. Buckingham was owned by Mr Bowers. All today's Sussex can be traced back to these two through the tenuous threads surviving after the First World War.

Going back to the first Stud Book, we have Mr T. Burgess, who showed two dogs at Birmingham and won first prizes with them as Sussex Spaniels. These two, Sam 2171 and Flora 2204, were by Hopcroft's Dash 2133, born in 1860 by Old Dash out of Nell, born in 1865.

Both these liver spaniels had white markings, not surprisingly as Mr Hopcroft was a breeder of Norfolk Spaniels, although he claimed that Sam and Flora were both descended from an old Sussex breed. Both dogs were shown and won at a number of shows and their appearance and origin caused long discussion in the canine press of the day; it is said that 'great rancour was engendered'. A long-drawn-out investigation purports to have proved conclusively that even if Mr Hopcroft had a strain of pure Sussex, some cross had been introduced: hence the liver Sam and Flora with their white markings. However, let us remember that liver and white Sussex had appeared and been mentioned at the early part of the century and a piece which appeared in a magazine of 1833 speaks of 'a large brown and white springer chiefly used in the wet, clayey woodland coverts of Sussex and Kent'.

Mr A.E. Langdale's thoughts on Sussex appear in Stonehenge's 1879 work. He writes as follows:

There is a notion in Sussex, especially round Brighton, that liver and white is the orthodox Sussex Spaniel colour, but such an idea is ridiculed when we get further in to the county. Old specimens are very bad to see and worse to obtain. I have searched all over Sussex and Kent in search of a bona fide specimen, and although I have been favoured with a view, have never yet been able to obtain one to call my own.

Later on in the piece he goes on:

The breed since Sussex classes have been established [1872], has brought out a number of different types such as Bullock's George, Langdale's Lawyer, Salter's Chance, Spurgin's Bebb, and Pratt's General Prim, to say nothing of Max, Sweep, Buckingham, Rover 3rd., Ladysmaid, Maud etc. Now of these George, Chance, Lawyer, General Prim, Rover 3rd. and Bebb are as different in their respective points as it is possible to conceive. Buckingham (late Mat), is called pure, and claims his descent from Rose Hill, the place of all others where this particular breed of spaniel is worshipped [note, this was written in around 1874, eighteen years after Fuller's death[, taking him for a pure specimen we cannot for one moment believe Bebb, Lawyer and George can be in the hunt.

He then goes on to quote from a report in the *Live Stock Journal* for 4 July 1874 in which Lawyer, shown under the name of Nep, was, as he puts it, 'lauded to the skies'. The report goes on: 'Nep appears to be good in all points, golden liver in colour, with rare coat, good frill in front, and a head so characteristic of his breed that he must prove a very dangerous rival to Bebb when they meet in the ring.'

Mr Langdale, in describing Buckingham, says he was, 'a dog decidedly dark in colour and very Pointer coated. Maud, his sister in much of the same stamp and if she were a little longer in the head I don't know of one to beat her. Max, although having liver and white blood in him, is decidedly the most typical dog of his day.'

A draft of Sussex Spaniels sold at this time by Mr T.B. Bowers, then living at Woolton near Liverpool, consisted of Max, Rover III, Bustle, Bess, Duchess III, Lizzie and Beatrice and fetched 420 guineas. Mr Bowers averred that the best Sussex were still to be found in their home county, notably at Squire Edgerton's of Hawkhurst.

Dr J.A. Salter of Tolleshunt D'Arcy in Essex was the owner of Chance 2119, shown in Volume 1 as a Sussex and bred by a Mr Bradfield of Sussex. Chance was born in 1865 and was liver with a white frill.

This breeding tells us very little, but Mr Cox bred quite a number of dogs registered as Sussex, and Chance was well thought of by breeders of the time. Dr Salter also owned Chloe, and both dogs are down as being 'of good old Sussex blood'. It is in the first volume that we find the name of Bebb 2101, born in 1866 and destined for a fame that has survived down the years. Mr Bullock's George is down, as is the Hon. Capt. Arbuthnot's Dash, who was bred the same way as Bebb. As the Captain was a dedicated Cocker breeder from Scotland, Dash undoubtedly had a larger hand in promoting that breed than any other. Mr Burgess's Sam and Flora appear in Volume 1 and there too is Maud. That appears to be the sum total of Sussex in Volume 1. However, in Volume 2 the Rev. Shields's Rex turns up as Sussex although he was almost all Cocker breeding, and also a dog called Rufus who owes not a little to Field and Irish Water blood and is spoken of in show reports of the time as 'puce coloured', the Irish Water colour. Then there is Mr Langdale's Sweep, who was out of a liver and white bitch of Hopcroft's Bess, who was by the aforementioned Sweep out of Maud. Bustle, owned by Mr T. Bowers, is down as having been bred by a 'Mr. Smith' with unknown parents of Fuller's (of Brightling) breed! If they were unknown one wonders how it could be stated they were of Fuller's strain. But this Bustle was used a great deal for breeding later, and one supposes that there were gullible people around who actually believed in the Mr Smith and the doubtful claims of blood.

Although the gentlemen who headed the revival of the Sussex Spaniel in the 1870s managed to produce a large number of winners despite the scarcity of material to work on, few of them appear in the ancestry of today's Sussex. Tracing the breed back thirty generations to this era, it is noticeable how few of the famous names of the 1870s figure in the story.

Three names do occur again and again: they are Bebb 2101, Buckingham 4400 and Bachelor 6287.

James Farrow, writing on the Sussex breed, recalls that in the year 1874 he visited, as he puts it, 'poor Phineas Bullock, I well remember his telling me that the greatest mistake he ever made was selling a spaniel named Bebb'. He goes on:

Why did Bullock regard the sale of this spaniel as the mistake of his life in Spaniel matters? For this simple reason. Jealous in the extreme of his beauties, he quickly found he had sold a trump card, and that Bebb was, as a stud dog, open to the world, and as a pillar of the Stud Book. This spaniel, has not, in my humble opinion, had an equal from the commencement of dog shows up to this date. It matters not what prominent spaniel's pedigree, Field, Cocker or Sussex, we unravel, Bebb's blood turns up in 80 per cent of them.

At the time Bebb was only 8 years old, and since that time it can be said that Bebb's blood turns up in 99% of the spaniel breeds named. I leave 1% unaccounted for; there is always the exception that disproves the rule, although I have not yet found it in my researches! In a later passage Mr Farrow continues his thoughts on Bebb: 'Right glad I am that my old friend Bullock made the mistake which in after life he so bitterly regretted. I have said sufficient to show Bebb a champion of champions!' He gives a long list of spaniels winning top honours who owned this remarkable chameleon of a dog as a sire. He was a chameleon indeed, for what other dog has there ever been who could claim to be the sire in three different breeds and whose name appears as an ancestor of every Sussex, Field or Cocker Spaniel in the world over a hundred years later?

Mr Farrow goes on to give his own opinion of the remarkable Bebb, and this is what he wrote:

Now for a few words about Bebb's points as a spaniel. He is entered in Volume I of the Stud Book as a liver coloured Sussex. Well, as a matter of fact he is no more like a Sussex than I am like a black man. Indeed the only point about him, including his pedigree, that could be called Sussex, was his colour. In Bebb's day many men called every spaniel that was liver coloured a Sussex. As a Field Spaniel Bebb had a really very grand head, a head that would fit in with the particulars given in the standard of points issued by the Spaniel Club for Field Spaniels as near as any dog I know today [He was writing this in 1897.] He had very long ears, too long, I used to fancy a little, wonderfully low set, tail action good, in outline, of course, very different to the typical dog of today [1897], nevertheless what in those days was considered long and low, when I tell your readers that he weighed, in show form, 38 pounds, and stood 18½ inches high.

Bebb was entered in the first volume of the Stud Book and his particulars are given as follows. '2101. Bebb. Mr. T.B. Bowers. Mollington, Cheshire. Breeder: Mr. Phineas Bullock. Whelped 1866, liver coloured Sussex. Late property of Mr. T. Burgess. Weight 38 lbs. Height 18½ inches. Pedigree: by Bullock's Old Bebb out of Flirt.' A list of winners by him follows, as does a list of his wins, such as Birmingham, first and Elkington Cup for the best spaniel in ten classes, 1870; Glasgow, divided first prize, 1871; Islington Dairy Farm, first prize, 1869; and about thirty other prizes at local shows. Old Bebb is listed as 'Lord Derby's breed', said to be Water Spaniels; he was presumably of the English variety, and possibly liver and white.

As the reader can see, this remarkable dog carried no Sussex blood at all, and after 1872, when the rule was made that all liver dogs being shown as Sussex Spaniels had to have had liver coloured parents, he ceased to appear in the show rings.

Buckingham 4400 first appears in the 1875 KCSB, as follows: 'Owner Mr. T.B. Bowers. Br. Mr. H. Saxby. Wh. 1871. Colour, golden liver.' There is a note after this information stating that, 'Mr. Saxby and Mr. Marchant had the same breed as that belonging to Mr. J.[?] Fuller of Rosehill, Brightling, Sussex.' How much credence one places on this is difficult to say; for instance, Mr Fuller's initial is wrong.

In the first Stud Book there is an entry for Buckingham's own sister, Maud 2219, owner Mr Spurgin. She has shorter particulars. Her pedigree simply states: 'By Marchant's Rover out of Saxby's Fan, both Rosehill breed.' Maud appears prominently in Field Spaniel pedigrees of the time. Claims that this or that dog is descended from Rose Hill dogs abound but are impossible to authenticate. The foundation for the future of the Sussex lines was laid by the breeding of Buckingham to Bebb's daughter Peggie 5255 by her owner Mr H.B. Spurgin. This union produced the dogs Bachelor 6287 and Rover III and the bitch Duchess III in one litter. Peggie's dam was a bitch called Ruby (one of several of this name, some with and some without Stud Book numbers), by Salter's Chance 2119, a dog bred by a Mr Bradfield of Sussex but owned by J.H. Salter of Tolleshunt D'Arcy in Essex. Chance was whelped in 1865 and was out of two livers, Lightfoot Bounce – said to be by Eyton's Tipoo Sahib from the Sherwood Kennels – and Lightfoot's Belle. Chance's dam was Bradfield's Spot, said to have been bred in Berkshire by Mr Cox. He is given as a liver with a white frill. An interesting item came to light during my researches. There is a dog's grave at Hinton Admiral, where Mr Fuller's daughter Clara lived. It is thought to be dated around 1850 – 60 and the inscription on it reads simply 'Tipoo Sahib'. Is this just coincidence?

Of Chance, Mr Farrow has this to say:

I have very little doubt myself, that the very first spaniel to be exhibited that can claim in anyway to be a fairly typical and of something like a reliable pedigree as a Sussex, was Dr. Salter's Chance 2119, born 1865 and entered in Vol.1 of the KCSB as a Sussex, and often quoted in show catalogues as of pure Sussex pedigree. This dog can fairly claim to be one of the pillars of this variety of Spaniels, and he did a lot to fix the type at earlier dog shows. I remember this dog quite well, and although I firmly believe he was as pure in pedigree as could be obtained in those days, he was not of the type that a few years after we were introduced to as the absolutely pure article in type and pedigree, i.e. Buckingham.

(One must remember that Mr Farrow was writing some thirty years later.)

Chance only appears in Volume 1 and is credited as winning at the Crystal Palace in both 1872 and 1873, as well as winning local prizes. It is, however, as Peggie's grandsire that he is of interest.

Bachelor 6278 was whelped in May 1875 and first appeared in the Stud Book for 1877; he was then owned by Mr Saxby of Lewes. He did a considerable amount of winning for this owner, including firsts at the Agricultural Hall, but in 1876 he was sold to Mr A.W. Langdale of Scarborough, who had not had him long before he sold him to Mr T. Jacobs of Newton Abbot in Devon.

On looking back over the years since Mr Bowers lodged his famous complaint about Mr Bullock's George – and had him banished from the ring by helping to form the rule that those shown as Sussex must have liver parents – it is ironic that we find that he rose to fame on the possession of Bebb. This dog was out of George's sister, and so carried the black blood to which Mr Bowers so strenuously objected! Perhaps if Mr Burgess, to whom Mr Bullock originally sold Bebb, had not died so suddenly, Mr Bowers might never have been able to possess him. The relevant dates are imprecise, but one supposes that Mr Bowers's complaint against George was made before he came to own Bebb; he would hardly have complained against a dog if he was campaigning another out of the sister of the dog objected to – or would he? George, by all accounts, was a good specimen and was winning well; maybe it was a good way to remove a rival from the ring. Who knows? There is no date to suggest when Bebb passed into Mr Bowers's hands.

Before one leaves this particular period to follow the fortunes of Bachelor, it would be as well to glance over other Sussex Spaniels of the time and their owners. The Rev. Shields of Kirkby Lonsdale was a great spaniel man and had more than a little to do with setting a type for the Sussex. His dog Rex 2167 appears in Volume 1 and was a son of Bebb 2101 and out of Fuss 2213 who was owned by H. Shields of Northampton, probably a relative. Fuss was said to be 'under 20 lbs.' which means she would have been called a small Field or a Cocker. These two breeds often appear in one litter, those over 25 lb being classed and shown as Fields and those under as Cockers. She was whelped in 1867 and her colour is unknown. She was the proud possessor of a long pedigree which is printed in Vero Shaw's *Book of the Dog*, published 1879, and is all Cocker breeding back to Footman's Jet and Burdett's black and tan Frank.

Mr Fletcher of Stoneclough, Manchester, claims attention as the owner at that time of George 2146, to whom Mr Bowers objected. He also owned several more spaniels at the time which he claimed to be Sussex: Dash 2132, born 1869 and by Old Dash out of Nell; Bell 2185, born 1869 and bred by Bullock; and Flo 2203, of whom little is known. Later he owned Major, a Bebb son out of Maud 2219, Buckingham's sister.

Mr A.W. Langdale of Bishops Stortford in Hertfordshire bred a dog called Lawyer, said to be a bad-tempered dog, who is listed as 'breeding unknown' in the 1875 KCSB, in which he appeared by reason of wins at Hull and Manchester which earned him his number, 4401. Lawyer is listed as 'late Vicar, also called Nep or Ness'. It is strange that his owner-breeder could give no details of his breeding. Lawyer was sold to Mr Fletcher who won quite well with him, but he soon returned to his breeder who continued his show career. Mr Langdale also owned Sweep 2177, bred by Dr Spurgin in 1871 by Bebb out of a liver and white called Fan. It was in 1875 that Dr Spurgin bred his notable litter containing Bachelor. Mr Langdale bought another Bachelor sister and shortly after acquired Bachelor, bought from Mr Saxby. It is notable that the five members of this litter, shown as having the same parents and year of birth, all have different months of birth recorded, demonstrating how inaccurate and doubtful many of the early records are. Buckingham, the sire of Bachelor, was a dog much used to produce both Sussex and Fields as Bachelor was to be in his turn. Notes in the Stud Book say he was a descendant of the Rose Hill dogs; indeed, as the years go on the claims get more extravagant. By 1881, under Mr Bowers's Bob 9264, a note reads 'Mr. Marchant kept the Rose Hill strain pure from the year 1851 down to Old Rover'; the latter dog is listed as the sire of Bounce, father of Bob; while Bob's dam is Bess, listed as a pure Rose Hill Sussex Spaniel obtained direct from the Rose Hill kennels, but with no details to substantiate the statement. As Bob was whelped in 1879, and Mr Fuller had been dead for twenty-two years, Bess must have been a great age when she produced her litter! The more one reads of these claims, the more one comes to the conclusion that most must be taken with a grain of salt.

Mr Langdale's involvement with the Sussex continued with Laundress 7263, whelped in June 1877 and by Lawyer ex Ladies Maid; and Laura 7366, bred by Mr J.M. Smith in May 1875 by Buckingham out of Smith's Bessie; and another purchase from Dr Spurgin, Progress 7367, whelped in 1876 by Monk 5248 ex Bachelor's dam, Peggie 5255. Monk, who appears for the first time in the KCSB of 1876, appears with the following particulars: 'Bred and owned by Dr. Spurgin, whelped 1874, by Bebb 2101 ex Bess (late Moss) 2150, Vol.1.' On looking this up one finds that there is indeed a Moss bearing that number, but it happens to be a dog!

Mr Langdale was also the breeder of Ladygirl 10427, who appears in 1881 as owned by a Mr Bates, but, once again, she has no breeding. However, she was said to be a liver with white feet and a white chest, so up to then the contentious colour issue had still not been resolved.

Mr T.B. Bowers was active in spaniels over a long period and he had a great involvement with the Sussex, notably as the owner of Bebb 2101 but also for owning and breeding many more, some of whom possibly owed more to the Sussex breed than his most famous stud dog. In 1875 we find Young Bebb 4398, bred by S. Lord but owned by Mr Bowers and by Bebb – as one would expect – out of Dunce by Old Sam 2171 and ex Fan. Old Sam was the same Sam who had won as a liver and white and precipitated a storm in 1867. Bishop 4399, bred by Dr Spurgin and born in 1872, was another Bowers buy, by Sweep 2177, ex Maud 2219, Sweep being a son of Bebb. Mr Bowers's next coup was to purchase from Mr Saxby Buckingham 4400, a dog claimed to be directly descended from the Fuller Rosehills, and with none of the Bebb blood. And then came Bustle, the one bred by Mr Smith, who in 1875 was put to Buckingham and produced Bute 5245. In the same volume we come across Rover III 5249, bought from Dr Spurgin and a brother to Bachelor; and Beryl 5250, born 1868, another with no pedigree – but the claim was that she was a direct descendant of the 'Rose Hill strain'. Belle 6294 was whelped in 1876 by Rover III ex Maud 2219, and Jewel 6297, whelped 1876, was the result of a union between Bustler and Beryl. An interesting entry in the 1877 Stud Book is May 6299, bred by Dr Spurgin and bought by Mr

Bowers, who sold her to Navun Duhany Effendi, of Malta. She is one of the many spaniels sold overseas to various potentates and other rich men in that era. Ruby 6301, whelped 1872 – although this date is qualified by the word 'believed' against it – was by Chance out of the black bitch Pop.

A footnote in the Stud Book for 1875 under the Sussex entrants reads: 'The dogs in this class (classification) are registered as Sussex Spaniels solely because they have won classes for Sussex Spaniels at dog shows.' Obviously the editor did not give a lot of credence to the claims of the exhibitors and breeders of the time!

In 1886, the KCSB classification for Sussex Spaniels was withdrawn, and a new classification for Sussex and other 'liver coloured spaniels' was introduced. It would be interesting to know the thinking behind such a move. One wonders if it was done in an effort to stop all the extravagant and often untrue claims of the time. When Sussex Spaniels got their own register back eight years later, the new pedigrees were by then beginning to show some uniformity.

This, then, is the background of the modern Sussex Spaniel. All today's dogs trace back through the handful kept by Mrs Freer in the 1940s to the beginning, although the threads are tenuous and much outside and unknown blood has been used over the past hundred years to keep the breed alive. But when looking back, one cannot escape Bebb. Even if you grant that Bachelor's sire went back to Mr Fuller's Rosehill stock, the Bebb blood is carried by his daughter who was Bachelor's dam, and nowhere can one escape Bachelor.

3

The Jacobs Intervention

Dr Spurgin's litter born in 1875, containing Bachelor 6287, Rover III 5249 and Duchess III 5252, had far-reaching effects on the development of the Sussex breed. Bachelor is the dog that everyone knows about, but his brother and sister were also used for breeding and appear in several places in the extended pedigree I have made out. Rover III, like many dogs of that time, had several owners: he was sold by his breeder to Mr Bowers; then went to Mr Brandreth of Bromborough in Cheshire; the following year he was transferred to Mr Hawkins of Preston and from there he went on to Messrs Parkinson of Macclesfield, a kennel that also held a big stake in the Field Spaniel scene of the time. His last appearance in the KCSB is in 1882.

Rover and Bachelor often met in the rings and each won in turn: Major Willet, a noted judge of the time, was said to have preferred Rover to Bachelor. A description of Bachelor is as follows:

Weight: 46 lb. Height: 15 in. Length from nose to tail set: 32 in. Girth of chest: 25 in. Girth of loin: 23 in. Girth of head: 17 in. Length of head 9¼ in. Girth of muzzle: 9¼ in. Length of forelimb from elbow to nail: 9 in. Ears, tip to tip: 22 in.

It is said that Bachelor had a superabundance of feathering and was a much more golden liver than either his brother or sister. There is no list of measurements of Bachelor's sire Buckingham, but he is spoken of as 'a longish bodied dog, short on the leg, with a heavy type of head and golden liver coloured'.

Bachelor makes his debut in the KCSB for 1877 in the ownership of Mr Saxby, having won a first at Maidstone and seconds at Crystal Palace and Manchester. The following year, still in the same ownership, he won at Alexandra Palace and at the Agricultural Hall. He was then bought by Mr R.W. Langdale, who showed him and won at the Crystal Palace, Alexandra Palace and Bristol – although there is a note by these wins to the effect that at two of them he was shown by Mr T. Jacobs, who had then purchased him and who continued winning firsts with him the following year at Alexandra Palace, Brighton, Bristol and Birmingham.

THE CANINE WORLD
SPORTS AND SPORTSMEN.

Vol. I.—No. 17.]   FRIDAY, SEPT. 12, 1890.   REGISTERED AS A NEWSPAPER AND FOR TRANSMISSION ABROAD   [PRICE TWOPENCE.

The Canine World and Sports & Sportsmen.

Dr. J. H. SALTER.

Dr J.H. Salter of Tolleshunt D'Arcy, Essex. Owner of Chance.

28

Mr T. Jacobs of Newton Abbot, pioneer of the long, low spaniels. Owner of Bachelor.

His wins at Crystal Palace and Bristol in 1880 were to be his last as he was killed in a kennel fight at the age of 5 years. In the *Kennel Gazette* of December 1880 the following appeared: 'Death has been very busy with some of our best known prize dogs of late. Bachelor, the well known Sussex Spaniel met his death a week after Bristol Show in much the same manner as Bristle and Little Badger, killed in the kennel.' Kennel fights were quite usual in those days; dogs tended to be kept as a pack and were not housed in pairs or individually as they are today.

He had been extensively used at stud and if his end had not come so suddenly, who knows what further influence he might have had? Some of his best-known get were Chance II 12691 and Guy 8352 (out of Chloe 5251); Caistor 9265, Swaby's Bounce, Fan VII and Bachelor II. Another, Rover III, was the sire of Bridford Brida (originally Brida II), one of the foundation bitches of Mr Woolland's kennel and of Countess 9269, the dam of Bachelor II.

It is interesting to read some of the reports of shows at the time when Bachelor and Rover were in the ring. At the Crystal Palace show in 1880 the following appeared in the *Kennel Gazette*:

> Sussex Spaniels were good but still not up to the standard of two or three years ago, when such dogs as Mr. Salter's Chance, Mr. Langdale's Lawyer and Mr. Bowers' Buckingham and Maud were on the benches. It is generally considered a toss up between the two sons of Buckingham, Rover and Bachelor, on this occasion the former won, but we prefer the latter. The only pure specimen of this grand old breed was Dr. Williams' Laurie and he was passed over altogether! Certainly the dog was looking his worst and was badly handled in the ring, but he is a most typical dog and should certainly have received some notice. Six entries were made in bitches but only three put in an appearance one of which was suffering from acute chorea, and so Mr. Bowers had an easy win with Romp, a half sister to Buckingham and Maud.

Certainly the writers were more outspoken in those days! It is of interest to note that Dr Williams's Laurie had no papers of any sort.

Here is a report of 1880: 'At Stratford-Upon-Avon the spaniels were divided in 4 classes, over and under 35 pounds in weight. We hardly think this is a good thing as Sussex, Clumber and Fields had to compete together.'

A report of the 1880 Bristol show read:

> Bachelor and Rover III had another good tussle for supremacy in the Any Variety class. Both dogs have their admirers and their

merits are very evenly divided. On this occasion Bachelor won, if anything, he has the advantage of condition. In bitches, Mr. Bonner's Nellie II a good sort of bitch came second. Nellie was originally from a home for lost dogs and her age and pedigree are of course unknown.

Of the Birmingham Show of 1880 we read:

First prize to Rover, second to Max. The pair were in splendid condition and never looked better in their lives, their grand condition bringing out the golden tint. Guy was passed over, not looking at all fit. Guess had an H.C., Bachelor was absent. With an entry of but three bitches, there was only one prize which was old Maud in blooming condition who carried off the prize with great ease. Merrythought is spoilt by white on head and feet, and that successful brood bitch Peggie, as she ages, shows more and more of the Water Spaniel blood which she gets from her sire Bebb.

Peggie was, of course, the dam of Bachelor and Rover III.

Bachelor's stock accounted for a large number of winners, his son Swaby's Bounce siring Ch. Baryta, and his son Guy accounting for Bridford Maud 20595 and Naomi 20596.

Bachelor. KCSB 6287. Whelped 1875. Appears in all Sussex Spaniel pedigrees today.

Rover III. KCSB 5249. Brother to Bachelor.

But it was Caistor, originally known as Guess, who was to prove the greatest sire of all Bachelor's sons; some twenty dogs and bitches by him achieved a place in the Stud Books. Caistor was bred by Mr H. Green of Downham Market in Norfolk. He was born on 27 September 1877 and was said to be 'whole golden liver'. His dam was Chloe 5251, the daughter of Chance and Salter's Chloe. Caistor sired Young Wallace 20594, used in the production of Mr Campbell Newington's line; mated to Countess of Rosehill 20598 he bred the influential Rosehill Reine 24769, grandam of Bridford Giddie.

Caistor, shown as 'Guess', won for his breeder at Essex County and at the Alexandra Palace in 1879, and at the latter again in 1880 when he was awarded the champion prize. In 1881 he took second at Margate. He does not appear in the Stud Book again until 1886, when he is under his new name of Caistor and in the ownership of Mr J.J. Pollock of Strathblayne, for whom he won a first at Glasgow in 1885. Presumably this was his last home, and he lived to a good age: there is Caistor II by him, whelped in 1887 when Caistor himself was 10, this young Caistor being bred by Mr London.

The time has now come to bring in the man who was to alter the

Sussex Spaniel to suit his idea of the breed, as he did with the Field Spaniel, Mr T. Jacobs of Newton Abbot. Mr Jacobs was, from all accounts, a self-opinionated man who when set on a course of action was not easily put off. His acquisition of Bachelor in 1878 came a few years after he had established his kennel of black Field Spaniels, and from then on he proceeded to mate Sussex to Field, producing, at times both breeds from one litter. If they were liver they were registered as Sussex; if they were any other colour and over 25lb they were Fields; if they were under 25lb they were Cockers. Mr Jacobs had two black bitches, Smutty and Negress, bred from a union of two blacks, Rolfe 5264 and Belle 2184. Negress was bred to Bachelor and in April 1879 bred a litter containing the Sussex bitch Ferryside (originally called Bee), sold to Mr F.T. Rees of the Barley Mow, Cardiff, and re-purchased by her breeder in 1881; Lass o' Devon, a liver and tan Field Spaniel; and one of Mr Jacobs's most famous black Field bitches, Ch. Squaw.

Mr Jacobs also purchased the bitch Russet, registered as a Sussex, from Mr Martin Pate of Ely, Cambridgeshire; she was daughter of Shields's Cocker Rex 2163 out of Ruby 6301, and bred by Mr Pate in 1875. Ruby was bred by Mr Handy and had passed through Mr Bowers's hands on her way to Mr Pate; she was by Chance 2119 out of the black bitch Pop. Jacobs changed Russet's name to Ladyship, and by mating her to Bachelor in 1880 bred Sport 14619, a liver dog with white on chest, Brunette 15906 and Lady Russet, all registered as Sussex. However, in 1881 Ladyship was mated to Mr Jacobs's black Field dog Kaffir and produced Black Knight 12707 and Ben d'Or, both registered and winning as Fields.

Mr Jacobs, writing in the early 1880s, defined his ambitions thus: 'to improve type in both [Fields and Sussex] I wanted to get more bone, longer bodies, and shorter legs in the blacks and longer heads in the Sussex'. A writer of this time, commentating on this statement, said, 'Neither his method or object was commendable, and the desire for more bone etc. is an unwholesome craze of the modern fancier.' However, Mr Jacobs, despite his critics, had a big following and many breeders followed slavishly in his footsteps, resulting in both blacks and Sussex becoming so long, low and cumbersome as to invite heavy criticism from the men who still liked their spaniels to be useful in the field; and leading to both breeds attracting a great deal of ridicule.

Mr Jacobs continued with his breeding programme, however, to suit himself. After a few years there is very little to distinguish the Jacobs black Field Spaniel from the Jacobs Sussex apart from their colour, as can be seen in the illustrations. The involvement of the Sussex with the Field shows in pedigrees.

Apart from Mr Jacobs's efforts, there are some doubtful dogs in the

Stud Books of the time under the heading 'Sussex Spaniels'. The most amazing appears in the KCSB for 1883. Mr Harry Green, of Caistor Hall near Norwich, had a dog from his breeder G.H. Peck. Born on 16 May 1881 and a golden liver, he was called Glance 12693 and he was by Guess 9265. Guess was by Bachelor out of Chloe 5251, but Glance's dam was Gipsy Bang 12700, a liver bitch with a white star on her chest who was by the Sussex Spaniel Guy 8252 out of Mr Green's black, white and tan Field bitch, Go Bang 28998. Go Bang, with another of the same colour, unusual for this breed at that time, had caused a sensation when shown in the Field rings and had some considerable wins. The breeder of Glance, Mr Peck, has two sisters to him in the same volume: Princess Gracey 12703, also liver with a white spot on chest, and Glimpse 12714, the colour down as liver and tan. It was in 1886 that the Kennel Club abolished the Sussex register and substituted one for Sussex and all other liver coloured ones, which means that unless one knows the classes in which the dogs were shown in those years, it is almost impossible to decide whether dogs were being shown as Sussex, Field or Cocker. That must have been very useful to Mr Jacobs.

The 1870s had proved to be a great period of change for the Sussex Spaniel; many well-known spaniel men of the time were showing one or two specimens and winning well, and then dropping out, possibly in favour of some other breed. Others in the news at the time include Mr Bowers's Bishop 4399 (Sweep 2177 x Maud 2219), golden liver; Mr H. Green appears again, this time as the owner of Chancellor 5247 by Change 2119 ex Salter's Chloe; and there are Beau 6288 and Beaver 6299, bred by Mr Brandreth and owned by Mr E.V. Richardson of Dunmurray. Others of note are Mr Brandreth's Punch 6292, another of the Chance x Chloe litter; Ladysmaid, bought from Mr Langdale and renamed Baroness (quite a step up) – 6293 in the KCSB, she is down as golden liver, age and breeder unknown; Mr Bowers's Belle 6294, by Bachelor's brother Rover III out of Maud 2219, and Jewel 6297 by Bustler out Beryl. Dr Spurgin won with Pilgrim 8254, a liver, by Monk 5248 out of Peggie 5255 while his sister Pop 8357 was taking a lot of prizes in the hands of Mr J. Taylor of Rochdale. An interesting entry is Bob 9264, owned by Mr Bowers and bred by Mrs Parks, the first lady mentioned in the breed up to that time. Whelped in July 1879 he is by Bounce out of Bess, and so is a brother to Swaby's Bounce out of the Bess classed as pure Rosehill! Mars 9266 appears this year; owned by Mr J. Freme, but bred by the redoubtable Dr Spurgin, he was a golden liver by Bebb out of Maud. A Rover III son came into the limelight in Major Ireland's Rupert 9268; there is Mr Barton's Countess, bred by Mr Hawkins in 1878 by the brother and sister mating of Rover III to Duchess III; and there are two bitches: Ruby 9275, bred and owned by the Rev. Shields by the Cocker Rex 2163 out of Speck – who is by Rock by Prentice's Rover out of Rose. The name of Ruby crops up in many Sussex pedigrees at that time. It is difficult to know exactly how many bitches of this name were used for breeding, and it is possible that there were only one or two at the outside and that this Ruby could well be one of them, given that the breeders did not always state a KC number. The last interesting Sussex of the 1870s is Mr Bowers's Romp 9274, a golden liver bitch bred by Mr Cox and whelped in 1874 by Marchant's Rover out of Bustle 4405. The owners of the time used a very small number of names and repeated them over the years: Sam, Dash, Rover, Bustle, Ruby, Romp, Fan or Fanny, Flirt, Flo and Rose are some which one finds over and over again, with or without a number after them and sometimes prefixed by 'Young' or 'Old'.

The start of the 1880s finds new names cropping up in the breed, but also some old ones. In 1881 there is Jug 10430, bred and owned by Mr W.E.M. Watts of Battle, a 'pure liver with a few grey hairs' whelped in 1877 by Dash out of Romp by 'Rose Hill'. The latter statement is difficult to interpret; was this Watts the same person as Dr Watts whose dog sired the original sandy puppies? If so, he must have been very old. More likely Mr. W.E.M. Watts is Dr Watts's son, and if so perhaps he did indeed have some of the old line to Rose Hill. Jug 10430 does not appear in the extended pedigree of today's dogs. In this same issue of the Stud Book, one finds Smutty II, Mr Bulled's bitch whom he bought from Jacobs. Smutty II, 10441 was by Bachelor ex Smutty, born in 1879 and black! I think she should have been in the Field register.

In 1881 the first of the Sussex bred by Jacobs out of the black bitches appear. There is Flirt II, said to be 'about 3 years' owned by Mr A Phillips of Newton Abbot; she is by Bachelor ex Negress 2184 – this is an older bitch of the same name as the one which produced Ferryside and Squaw. This older Negress was bred by Mr Boulton, one of the early pioneers of both Sussex and Field, and his Field dog Rolf was the sire of the second Negress. However, the first Negress, originally named Belle, was a black whelped on 10 August 1873. She was by Boulton's Boss out of Nellie 2221, the key bitch in the original Field pedigrees, who was thought to have Irish Water Spaniel blood in her. Boss was by Powley's Ben out of Boulton's Fern, while her grandmother Jet went back to the original black Cockers used to evolve the black spaniels later known as Fields. A bitch who was to figure largely in the Sussex foundations of the important Bridford Kennel was Brida II 11623. She was bred and owned by Mr J. Partridge of Barnstaple, born 19 September 1878, colour golden liver, by Bachelor's brother Rover III out of Brida I by Bachelor out of one of the Rubys. Bachelor III comes on the scene in 1883 as does Baryta, owned and bred by the Holley brothers, who owned a large kennel near Basingstoke. Born in 1882, he was by Chance II 12691, bred in 1880 and owned by Dr J. Salter. Over the next few years other breeders joined in. Councillor 14204 was owned by Mr T. Codling of Spalding and had passed through the hands of Mr Dexter, having been bred by a Mr Ogle by Rover III out of a Field-bred bitch. Mr W.E. Eastern owned Councillor's brother, Eastern's Rover, in the Sussex register although he was liver and tan. This dog had previously been shown as Rover IV and also as Lawson's Rover. Horatio 13625 makes his debut; a brother to Baryta and also owned by the Holleys, Horatio was to become the sire of two well-known Bridfords, Dallian and Maubert. Mr Campbell Newington has his first entry in the Stud Books in 1884: this is Laurie 14209, bred by Mr Hudson in 1877. The details of his breeding mean very little; none of the names is in the Stud Books and therefore it is impossible to authenticate them, but for what it is worth I repeat them: 'by breeder's Dash out of his Romp, by Edgerton's dog out of a Rose Hill bitch. Dash by Mr. Watts' Dash, out of Curties Bess.' 'Watts' Dash' is presumably the same dog that is down as the sire of Jug. Bismark, owned by E.T. Smith of Colchester, was doing well in the Sussex rings although his sire was the black Field Kaffir, and his dam was the liver and tan Field Lass o' Devon from Mr Jacobs's litter which contained both Field and Sussex. Voisine 14213, breeder and pedigree unknown, was a liver with a white star on the chest. Owned originally by a Mr Jacquet, she had been sold to Mr J. Whittle's veterinary establishment in Reading. Welsh Harvester 16293 was an interesting dog owned by Dr Parry Thomas of Pontypridd, who bought him from Mr James who had originally procured him from his breeder, Mr R.P. Morgan. Born in August 1882, he was by the Field Spaniel Tancred 10555 – belonging to Mr Bowers – who was a son of Freme's Little Bob and out of Busy 10465, another Field.

It is of interest to note that the poisoning of dogs at shows is not a new thing. The *Kennel Gazette* for 1891 runs this story:

The analyst who examined the Sussex Spaniels that died at Birmingham Show, has reported that the deaths resulted from strychnine. A mistake however, seems to have arisen as to the name of one of the dogs. We may therefore state that Mr. Phillips' dog Chester, and Messrs. Gamon's Rover 4th died, and not Messrs. Gamon's Guy as stated in 'The Field'. Rover died early in the morning before judging commenced, whereas Chester we hear, was quite well at 1.30 and was suddenly taken ill and died by 2.0 p.m. The Committee are doing their best to trace the mystery.

Judges in the early 1880s were not over enthusiastic about the breed.

At the Crystal Palace in 1881 it was said: 'Sussex were not very numerous, Ch. Rover 3rd defeating Guy easily, and Lawyer VHC looked stale and in poor form. There was nothing special in this class and really new stars are wanted in the Sussex division. The bitches were a bad lot and Mr. Lort did not consider them worth even a mention.'

A report of 1881 on Woodbridge said: 'A very fair Sussex called Dash 5th was shown by Mr. Campbell Newington and was somehow passed over. He should have, without doubt, been noticed, although he is a little too dark in colour and a little rough about the muzzle, he has plenty of spaniel points, good flat coat, bone and length of body.'

Of Alexandra Palace in 1882 we read: 'There would seem to be great difficulty in breeding Sussex, why, we know not and we cannot help thinking with ordinary attention good specimens might be brought forward.'

So the early enthusiasms of the gentlemen who sought to revive the breed in the 1870s had somewhat evaporated. No doubt having to breed from stock of such mixed ancestry produced problems, and many thought it easier and more prudent to go over to other breeds of spaniel where colour was not so important. Indeed, many of the names connected with the Sussex revival were still active and successful, but that was in the popular Field or the Cocker, whose star was then in the ascendant.

Those who bemoaned the decline of the Sussex in the early part of the 1880s had their prayers for a saviour answered in good measure. Not one but two men of wealth took up the breed, and each in his own way contributed to bringing the Sussex back to some credibility after the damage done by Mr Jacobs and his breeding programme. Mr Moses Woolland and Mr Campbell Newington founded their kennels at roughly the same time, and from then on Bridford and the second Rosehill line were to dominate the Sussex Spaniel scene for some time to come.

4

The Bridford Empire

MR MOSES WOOLLAND OF BRIDFORD

Mr Moses Woolland, whose Sussex Spaniel breeding programme under the Bridford prefix was to have such a far-reaching effect on the breed and its future, hailed from the village of Bridford in Devon, ten miles from Stover, the country seat of the Dukes of Somerset, and eight miles from Exeter. Mr Woolland was one of a large Victorian family, and he and two of his brothers, all bachelors, founded Woolland Bros drapery shop in Knightsbridge, London. This drapery shop became in time the great Woollands' department store, a Mecca for wealthy shoppers until the development of the area in recent times. However, Mr Woolland's family had not planned this kind of enterprise for their son. He was in fact articled as a young man to Mr William Rowell of Torquay and Newton Abbot, surveyor to both the Earl of Devon and Lord Haldon, for whom he later acted as draughtsman. Mr Woolland became interested in spaniels following a visit to Stover House, where he made the acquaintance of Hooker, head gamekeeper to the Duke of Somerset. Mr Woolland's visit had been for the sole purpose of seeing the large kennel of spaniels kept at that time by the Duke.

Hooker spent a quarter of a century at Stover and before that had been for a similar period in the employ of the Earl of Chichester, where he had learned his spaniel lore. By the time Mr Woolland met Hooker, that worthy's career in spaniels spanned half a century, and he was known all over Devon for his shrewdness as a breeder of spaniels. In his early days, Mr Jacobs of Newton Abbot had also taken advantage of Hooker's experience, and he gleaned much knowledge to help him establish his kennel of spaniels.

Mr Woolland, it is said, had many meetings and discussions with Hooker on the subject of spaniels and the science of founding a good line and following it through. In consequence of these meetings and discussions, Mr Woolland bought two Sussex Spaniel puppies from Stover, to be known as Bee and Belle of Bradley. With these two Mr Woolland made his first tentative steps into the new world of dog shows, exhibiting at the Crystal Palace in 1883 under no less a spaniel personage than Mr

Mr Moses Woolland, owner of the Bridford Sussex Spaniels. This kennel was dominant from 1882 until 1905 when all the dogs were sold by auction.

Reproduced by kind permission of *Our Dogs*.

T. Bowers himself, who owned the mighty Bebb. Although Bee, the dog, was unplaced, Belle was awarded a VHC. The winner of her class was a bitch called Brida II. The dog class was won by Horatio, and to this dog Mr Woolland mated Belle, this being his first effort at breeding Sussex Spaniels. The mating produced two famous dogs, Bridford Dallian and Bridford Maubert. Two other specimens, said to be even better, died as a result of distemper caught at a show where Mr Woolland, full of fire and enthusiasm for his new hobby, exhibited a litter with disastrous results. The indiscretion was never repeated!

By now Mr Woolland was thoroughly bitten by the spaniel bug and determined to found as good a kennel as possible. His next purchase was Battle from Mr Sutton: he paid £8 to secure what was to be a most valuable foundation bitch. Battle was one of those spoken of as 'pure Rosehill', but for that there is no evidence and as twenty-five years had passed since Mr Fuller's death the claim is fairly spurious. However, from Battle, renamed Bridford Battle and mated to Capt. Moreton Thomas's Guy, a big winner of the time, Mr Woolland bred Ch. Bridford Naomi, Ch. Bridford Laddie and Bridford Maude.

Mr Woolland, over the few years since his debut in the rings, had nurtured a certain regard for Brida II and managed to buy her when she was 8 years of age. He tempted her owner, Mr Partridge, with an offer of £45, quite a sum in those days for an ageing bitch and one whose show days were long past and whose record as a brood bitch had been a dismal failure. However, Mr Woolland, buoyed up with the successes he made in a short space of time, and full of youthful enthusiasm and (no doubt) help from the redoubtable Hooker, was convinced that, properly mated, Brida II (renamed Bridford Brida 11623) would prove a jewel. He was right: her union to Dallian produced Ch. Bridford Brida II at the first attempt. Brida's chief attribute was said to be her colour, 'a beautiful gold', and Mr Woolland always gave her credit for bringing the true Sussex colour into his strain. Mr Woolland then purchased, again for the sum of £45, the dog Bachelor III from Thomas Jacobs, spoken of by his contemporaries as 'that wily Newtonian'. Brida was next mated to this dog and the union produced one of the most famous bitches from the kennel, Ch. Bridford Dolly.

Mr Woolland's purchase of Bachelor III was a surprise for some of his contemporaries. In an article in the *Kennel Review* of 1885, a writer signing himself 'T.H.' (who could have been Mr Handy or Mr Holley, both active in the breed at the time) describes Bachelor III, who was bred by Jacobs in 1881, as 'a coarse cross-bred dog'. If the original Bachelor had not succumbed in the kennel fight in 1880, Mr Woolland would possibly have opened his purse to Jacobs and secured this jewel for his crown. But it was not to be: Bachelor died the year Mr Woolland bought his first two puppies. No doubt the Bridford owner wanted a stud carrying as much of the old Buckingham lines as he could get. The critics were envious, which would explain their damning criticism of Bachelor III when Mr Woolland prevailed on Thomas Jacobs to part with him in 1886 when the dog was 5 years old. In fact, as Mr Jacobs had used Bachelor III extensively at stud to produce Field Spaniels as well as Sussex Spaniels, he probably had no further use for him. Unlike Mr Woolland, he was only too ready to part with any of his dogs, although the price had presumably to be right!

Show reports of the time give several views of this controversial dog. At Sheffield Show in 1882, the report on the Sussex classes reads thus: 'Bachelor III won. He has not the grand head of old Bachelor and he shows the haw too much and his lip is too pendulous. Dash 5th. (Mr. Campbell Newington) is much too dark in colour and it shows the scarcity of the breed to see him placed so often.'

At Alexandra Palace in the same year the report was:

Sussex dogs, only four. Bachelor III won, a dog of fair colour but his head is short and his forelegs crooked. Quince property of Mr. Bishop [the half Field dog later purchased by Theodore Newington] altogether too leggy, carries his stern badly. Laurie was right in colour but wrong everywhere else. Bridford Brida 2nd. a very nice specimen, excellent colour, inclined to be a bit throaty, won easily. Second Busy Busy, a small Cocker-like bitch with an indifferent head, belonging to Mr. Jacobs.

A report from Bristol was: 'In Any Variety, Mr. Jacobs' Sussex Bachelor III won but he is not a very wonderful specimen.' An advertisement placed in the stud columns of the livestock journals reads thus: 'Bachelor III. Golden Liver. Born 1881. By Bachelor 2nd. ex Brunette. Weight about 38lbs. Fee 4gns. 1st. Eastbourne. 1st. Frome. 1st. Sheffield.'

Whatever they said about him, Bachelor III lived it down, for he was a prolific sire of winners in both Fields and Sussex and had one of the most complete pedigrees on paper of the time.

As can be seen from this, Bachelor III had four lines to Buckingham and also to Salter's Chance, and one has to go back four generations to find any black blood; this is in Ruby's dam, Pop. Bachelor III sired, among other Sussex, Ch. Bridford Dolly, Newton Abbot Russet, Newton Abbot Blossom, Freefolk Russet, Lady Falmouth and Dick of Arvon 29104. Dick was out of Bridford Maud, sister to Naomi. Maud had been sold to Mr Maw of Chester, was renamed Hoyle Maud and became the dam of Hoyle Prince and Princess. Dick of Arvon goes down in history as the sire of Futurity, the dam of Ch. Rosehill Rush; this was achieved by mating him to a Field Spaniel, Fidelity II, whose pedigree went back, however, in the fourth generation to Bachelor. Born in September 1889, she was bred by Mr F. Scholfield, a keen Field Spaniel breeder who had a finger in the pie of several spaniel breeds; he was responsible in part for the sudden arrival of coloured Fields in quantity on the scene in the 1890s. In one entry she was said to have been bred by Mr A. Fletcher, but she was actually by his Field dog Candidate, a popular sire in his own breed. No doubt Mr Fletcher acquired Fidelity II from her breeder. She comes under that ambiguous heading 'Sussex and other liver coloured ones', which included several spaniel varieties.

Candidate was a liver dog of all-black breeding, being by the well-known black stud dog Sterling out of the best-known black Field bitches of the time, Vinci. Fidelity's dam was a bitch called Stubley whose sire and dam were Zanzibar and Countess. Zanzibar appears several times with no particulars, but in the extended pedigree of Belton 20603, who is said to be by Mr Greenwood's Zanzibar, Zanzibar's sire is given as Rap 2159, a dog of Mr Boulton's in Volume 1 who has no fewer than three KCSB numbers. Zanzibar's dam is given as Bessie, with no further particulars. Stubley's dam Countess was bred by Mr Jacobs, and is by Smutty II (black), a Bachelor son, out of Negress 7385. Ch. Rosehill Rush has much bearing on the future lines of Sussex Spaniels, and it is well to bear in mind that his grandmother was a Field Spaniel of very mixed ancestry. Fidelity was later purchased by Mr Moses Woolland and renamed Bridford Fidelity. She was used to produce Field Spaniels, her most famous son being Moston Lord by Ch. Bridford Shah, a dog who was bred by Jacobs and was 60% Sussex.

In the *Kennel Gazette* for January 1892, the writer of the Sussex column speaks of Fidelity II, who was second at Birmingham and a winner at Liverpool, Bath and Manchester, but, 'has not, in my opinion, the beautiful colour of the typical Sussex, nevertheless she is quite a useful sort but will never be able to beat our well known Sussex specimens'. Considering Fidelity was half-Field, it is not surprising that her colour failed to please this writer!

Bridford Infidelity ended her days in the possession of Mr C.P. Johnson in Ireland, where she was shown considerably, winning, says Col. Cane, 'sometimes in Field classes and sometimes in Sussex', as did many of the liver spaniels of that time.

Shortly afterwards Mr Woolland decided to add black Field Spaniels to his kennels. For this he leant heavily on purchases from the Jacobs kennels, and his name was for a time bracketed with the man who sought to make Field and Sussex Spaniels so long and low as to be virtually useless. Mr Woolland must have seen the light as the later Bridford dogs were in truth a little shorter in the body than those of the Jacobs period.

Newbarn House, Freefolk with Whitchurch, Hampshire, home of the Bridford Sussex Spaniels.
Photograph reproduced by courtesy of *Our Dogs.*

They were, however, long by the standards of Mr Campbell Newington, whose main object was to breed good spaniels for work first and show second, whereas at Bridford the idea seems to have been the other way round.

Mr Woolland moved himself and his kennels from Devon to Hampshire, to Newbarn House, in the parish of Freefolk with Whitchurch. There he established a fine kennel and he persuaded Hooker to come with him as kennel manager. An article of the time says, 'what these two shrewd spaniel experts did not know about spaniels is, we would say, scarcely worth knowing'. The new Bridford domain was bounded on one side by Lord Portsmouth's famous Hurstbourne estate and on the other by the equally famous River Test. The shooting available covered 3,000 acres with some 600 acres of cover, including the celebrated Freefolk Wood with the Ladies Ride through the centre, down which the Duke of Wellington had been known to take exercise from his seat at Stratfield

Saye. It was altogether a most admirable place to found a spaniel kennel. The shooting must have been superb; it was said to yield some 7,000 head of game in a season.

A note about the Bridford spaniels written at the time says, 'we must point out that all Mr. Woolland's spaniels are more or less trained for the gun', a pretty ambiguous statement! Mr. Woolland was fortunate in his henchmen. He had not only prevailed on the ageing Hooker to leave the Duke of Somerset's employ and come to Whitchurch as manager of the kennel, a post of which it was said 'Hooker is in sole control'; but he also employed Hooker's eldest son as head keeper; and Hooker's daughter held a position on the indoor staff. Miss Hooker was at times called on to assist in the kennel to the extent that it was said:

> but for this lady's fostering care in times of sickness and other occasions when only a woman's feelings could meet the necessities of the case, the spaniel world would have been bereft of some of its Bridford Victors or Brilliants and other pillars of the breed who have done so much to build up the kennel which is at once the admiration and envy of the spaniel world'.

Mr Moses Woolland's views on his spaniels, and his determination to keep his lines entirely for himself wherever possible, is well summed up in an unsigned profile of the man by a writer of the time in 1895. This is what was written:

> It is an old saying that 'every man has a right to do as he likes with his own', and although this axiom does not always apply, it at least holds good in the case of Mr. Woolland and his famous sires, whose stud services he has hitherto kept almost entirely for his own kennel requirements not allowing many of the public the use of his stud dogs. Although the services of Mr. Woolland's sires cannot be procured, his surplus stock can, which owing to this protective policy have, naturally, a high market value.

Indeed, a few of those highly priced Bridford puppies did go into other hands, but only a few, and to breeders with notably long pockets. Later in the article Mr Woolland is spoken of as being a very generous man in all matters, a stalwart supporter of the Spaniel Club, where he held the office of treasurer, 'a genial man, a crack shot and no mean wielder of the willow'. Mr Woolland's services as a judge were in demand, but he 'resolutely refused all invitations until he was thoroughly convinced within himself, that his experience sufficiently extended to warrant him in undertaking such an onerous post'. Mr Woolland's first appearance in a judicial capacity was at the Kennel Club's Crystal Palace Show in 1893, when he drew, according to the writer of the time, 'a large and representative entry, as indeed he has commanded on all occasions since, when he has officiated'.

Returning to the breeding programme formulated by Mr Woolland with the help and advice of Hooker, it should be noted that Mr Woolland's first bitch, Belle of Bradley, was by Hooker's Sport (by Bachelor) out of Hooker's Flirt, and so was not actually purchased from the Duke but from Hooker himself. The bitch Battle 19249 was whelped in 1883 and was by Chance II out of one of the Bustles of the time – none of these had any papers and how many or how few there were is anyone's guess; it is possible there were only two, but as no particulars of any sort are given their number and origin remain, as do many others, a mystery. Renamed Bridford Battle, this bitch after her litter by Guy 8352 – which produced Naomi 20596 – was then mated to Dallian and produced Bridford Victor 20589. These two, Bridford Victor and Naomi, were mated together to produce one of the best of the Bridford Sussex and a most influential sire, Bridford Giddie 26957. Bridford Brida (formerly Brida II), was by Bachelor's brother, Rover III and out of Brida I, a Bebb daughter. Apart from her new-found success as a brood at the age of 8 plus, she is credited with being mated to Giddie at the age of 12, a union that resulted in Bridford Minnie 33937.

Having achieved four generations of his own breeding based on the two foundation bitches, Bridford Brida and Bridford Battle, Mr Woolland mated their descendants together, providing the most perfect example of properly conducted scientific breeding to set the type required. The exercise resulted in, among others, the notable Ch. Bridford Mocky, whose pedigree all students of line-breeding to secure type should study.

Being a very wealthy man, by then married and a partner with his brothers in the thriving Woolland Bros store, Mr Woolland also owned an imposing town house in Lowndes Square as well as the Whitchurch estate. He was able to purchase, sometimes at a very high price, any spaniel he fancied and was not obliged to sell anything or allow anyone to use his dogs if he did not want to. Recourse to the Stud Books shows how few Bridford-bred dogs and bitches came into other hands, and how seldom anyone outside was allowed to use his dogs. This was a matter of considerable sorrow to the authors of *The Sporting Spaniel*. No doubt the co-author Claud Cane, who had the not inconsiderable Celbridge Kennel of Fields and Sussex in Ireland, had tried to buy Bridford dogs without a great deal of success. However, he managed over the years to winkle at least two out of the Bridford fortress and he should have been satisfied as this was far more than most achieved.

Mr Jacobs, meanwhile, continued to mix his Fields and Sussex,

Ch. Bridford Giddie. KCSB, 26,957. Wh: 1888. By Bridford Victor. 20,589 ex Bridford Naomi. 20,596

Ch. Bridford Bredaboy. KCSB, 671A. Wh: 1892. By Ch. Bridford Giddie x Bridford Brida. 22,555

Ch. Bridford Mocky. KCSB, 745D. Wh: 1897. By Bridford Prince. 796C ex Bridford Minnie. 33,937

Hooker and his charges

From these pictures it is possible to observe the low to ground dogs in favour at that time, but to note that the Bridford dogs after Giddie have become shorter in the body.

producing in several litters a mixture of black, black and tan, liver and tan, and liver puppies, the latter going in the Sussex register while the rest were registered as Fields. His main concern with Sussex, however, seems only to have been to mate them to Fields in order to obtain his ideal black spaniel.

At the start of the 1890s Thomas Jacobs, 'the wily Newtonian' – in a fit of pique, it is said, because of all the unfortunate comments about his long dogs, which were likened to 'cucumbers' and 'fenders with knobs on' in the sporting press of the time – sold his entire kennel. Mr Woolland, who had heard of the intended sale, was swift off the mark. He went to Devon and purchased the black Field Spaniel bitch Bridford Perfection for the then enormous sum of £380. Perfection is of interest to us as she was a granddaughter of both Bachelor and Bachelor III, and therefore contained more than her fair share of Sussex blood. She was also the last of the four generations of Newton Abbot-bred spaniels to find fame. Mr Jacobs had done, in a comparatively short time, what he set out to do and made no bones about: to produce a line of black Field Spaniels and liver Sussex Spaniels of a standard size and type, each, apart from certain head properties, indistinguishable one from another. It was a pity that he wasted several good Sussex in the process.

At the Jacobs sale, Moses Woolland, with his long purse, was able to snap up the best spaniels on offer, most of them being black. How closely Mr Jacobs had intermingled the two breeds can be shown by the pedigree of the black Ch. Bridford Shah (formerly Newton Abbot Shah), who was one of Mr Woolland's most important Field Spaniel studs.

5

The Rosehill Name Revived

CAMPBELL NEWINGTON (1851–1929)

The fact that there were two lines of Sussex Spaniels referred to as Rosehill has confused writers, and therefore readers, for well over a century. Mr Fuller's working spaniels were simply known as 'Fuller's strain from Rose Hill'. The line that has most to do with the breed from 1880 onwards relates to the kennel of the name of Rosehill owned by Mr Campbell Newington of Ticehurst in East Sussex. The Newington family, like the Fullers before them, are a fascinating family and rich in wonderful characters. The Newington dynasty stretches far back into history. The pedigree starts with Sir Adam de Newington, Knight of Withernden, back in 1481; so far it has not been possible to take the line back further. Withernden is a village in the parish of Ticehurst, and it was here that the Newington family settled. Our story is best started with Samuel Newington of The Vineyard, Ticehurst, born in 1739. He entered the medical profession and started a practice from his home, which has been described as 'a perfect English rural retreat with its lawns and spreading trees'.

In the rate books of 1792, Samuel is described as an apothecary, a term then used not only for purveyors of drugs but for any general medical practitioner. He devoted particular study to the treatment of the insane. Samuel Newington had a large house erected in the grounds of The Vineyard for use as an asylum. So successful were his treatments that he became very celebrated and prospered as a result. He had fifteen children, and when he died in 1811 aged 72 he was succeeded by his sons Jesse and Charles. His wife Martha lived on until 1831 and died at the great age of 91.

The sixth and seventh sons, Jesse and Charles, took over the running of the asylum. In 1802 Charles had become a Member of the Royal College of Surgeons. When he married, in 1812, Eliza (a daughter of the Rev. William Hayes, a priest of the Royal Chapel), he built a residence on the land adjoining the asylum and called it The Highlands. Jesse died in 1819; and on the death of his mother in 1831 Charles purchased the asylum and became the sole owner.

Mr Campbell Newington of the Rosehill Sussex Spaniels at Ticehurst, with some of his winning dogs. 1908.

Davis, one of the Rosehill keepers, with the Sussex Spaniels and a Flatcoat Retriever in 1901. All the Rosehills were broken for work with the gun.

From these two pictures it can be observed that Mr Campbell Newington had brought the breed up on the leg, shortened the backs and improved coats.

Pictures reproduced by courtesy of Frances Drew Esq.

Charles was a large man, by all accounts, in frame, energy and nature. He was very highly thought of both as a physician and surgeon and as a person. He enlarged and improved the asylum, making it into a model for the time. He too had a large family, six sons and a daughter, and two of the sons embraced medicine as their chosen career. It was sad that such a good man who had worked so hard for so many people should have his life's work ruined by a fire, but such was the case. As he lay on his death-bed, a fire broke out in the main building of the asylum and the whole edifice was reduced to ashes. Fortunately his bedroom in his own house was situated on the side facing away from the asylum, so he never knew of the disaster. He died on 27 April 1852.

The next two Newington doctors were Charles's sons, Charles Edmund, LRCP, and Samuel, who obtained his MA at Oxford and was a Member of the Royal College of Physicians. Between them the brothers rebuilt Ticehurst House. A large mansion, it can be seen today on the left as one approaches Ticehurst village from the west. The brothers restarted the asylum on the same sound lines of their forebears. In 1841 Samuel married Georgina, sixth daughter of Major General Boatson of Frant, at one time Governor of St Helena. They lived at The Ridgeway, Ticehurst, and this house stood intact until it was demolished by a flying bomb in the 1939–45 war.

Samuel had another large family, seven sons and six daughters. The fourth son, Alexander, MA (Cantab.), MRCS, carried on the family medical work in conjunction with his cousin Dr Herbert Francis Hayes Newington, a son of Charles Edmund. Dr Alec, as he was known, was a greatly loved figure in the neighbourhood, a first-class sportsman, a great rider to hounds and an excellent shot. He was a pioneer of motor cars and was killed in January 1914 at an early age when the car he was driving overturned on a bend approaching his home. Campbell Newington was a brother of Dr Alec, the seventh son and one of a pair of twins born to Samuel and Georgina. He had no bent for the medical life, but his twin brother Theodore studied medicine and became a doctor. Theodore never went into practice, but spent his life quietly in his house at Ticehurst.

Campbell Newington was a great sportsman, countryman, landowner and breeder of pedigree animals: his herd of Sussex cattle was world famous. He was born on 19 March 1851 and educated at Cheltenham College and Caius College, Cambridge, later studying land agency on the estate of Lord Fethersham in Yorkshire. He was, from a boy, keenly interested in nature and anything to do with the countryside. He lived with his mother at The Ridgeway until his marriage to Margaret Holgate Foster of Regent's Park, London, on 21 October 1896. The Campbell Newingtons bought a large house called Oakover in extensive grounds in

Oakover at Ticehurst in Sussex. The home of Mr Campbell Newington's Rosehill Sussex Spaniels. Mr Newington used the Rosehill name as a compliment to Mr A.E. Fuller. These Rosehill Kennels were founded in the 1880s. The last of the Rosehills appear around 1918.

Ticehurst, and at once started on a building programme to enlarge it. Their only child, Beatrice, was born in London on 6 August 1897, and it was at that time that the renovations and alterations were carried out. In a short but wonderfully descriptive autobiography written in late middle age, Beatrice says that she has 'no remembrances of coming back to Oakover when the additions were complete or of any time when it was not my permanent home'.

Here Mr Campbell Newington lived for the rest of his life, and here his famous Rosehill Spaniel Kennel was founded and flourished.

Campbell Newington was a sportsman first and an exhibitor second, so all his dogs had first to be of use with the gun. This left him at a slight disadvantage in the rings, for, as everyone who has worked spaniels knows, they get lean and hard and pull out a great deal of hair working in heavy cover. Also, for work they needed a little more length of leg than the Sussex then fashionable in the show rings of the time had. At first Mr Newington's Sussex, although pre-eminent in the field, were often outclassed on the bench by long, low dogs popular with some judges. But by keeping to an ideal, Mr Newington, more than anyone else, showed the breeders of the long, low dogs the folly of their ways. He became not only one of the most successful breeders of the dual-purpose Sussex but

Mr Campbell Newington's only child Beatrice with Ch. Rosehill Rock. 1904.

also one of the most successful exhibitors and certainly the most consistent winner with Sussex at field trials. After a few years anyone interested in breeding good Sussex desired to own a Rosehill in order to achieve success. Unlike Mr Woolland, who shunned those who wanted to share in his success, Mr Newington sold a number of good dogs and bitches to other breeders, including Mr Woolland, and allowed others to use his studs.

Apart from his own considerable acreage at Oakover, which included a farm, Mr Campbell Newington rented the shooting for many miles around. The head keeper in Beatrice's childhood was a man named Coley, who lived in a cottage on the Hurst Green road just beyond Singehurst, where the birds were reared. In her memoirs Beatrice recalls halcyon childhood days in the woodlands of Oakover, picking primroses, wood anemones and bluebells, and she recalls that 'it seemed as if the sun shone all the time'. The most interesting part of Beatrice's writings, to my readers at least, will be this reference to the Rosehill dogs:

At the time [she was then a schoolgirl] my father's great interest was in breeding pedigree Sussex Spaniels, a beautiful race of golden brown dogs which is now practically, if not entirely, extinct in this country [she was writing in the mid 1960s]. The kennels were on the far side of a small valley below the stables, now Sheepwash Farm, and here there were always thirty or forty spaniels and their litters. In those days there was no innoculation against illness, and every year the deadly epidemic of Distemper swept through the kennels taking its toll of puppies and young animals. Only the strongest recovered, and they were, of course, immune for life. My father was a genius for choosing and combining the best strains to produce the desired results, be it in poultry, dogs or cattle. In consequence he swept the board at Crufts, and Ladies' and Kennel Club shows, and also at Field Trials, and his Rosehill strain of Sussex Spaniels were much sought after and well known all over the county and beyond. Ch. Rosehill Rock and Ch. Rosehill Rag were two of the most famous, and their portrait still hangs at Oakover. When he had got all the prizes and championships that were to be won, he began to lose interest a little, especially when the show authorities started to encourage points which they considered would improve the breed. He was strongly opposed to these alterations, and when the last of his veterans died, he gave up spaniels and turned his attention to Sussex cattle.

Ch. Rosehill Rock. KCSB 856G. By Bridford Bibelot 77OE ex Rosehill Rhonda. Taken in 1904 when Rock was four years old.

Beatrice Newington was a pretty child who grew into a very lovely woman. She was also highly talented as an artist and many of her paintings are retained by the family. She married, and I am indebted to her son Francis Drewe for permission to reproduce extracts from her memoirs. Mr Drewe, a JP like his grandfather, now lives at Oakover with his wife. He remembers the last of the Sussex, a very old dog, sleeping in front of the drawing-room fire in the mid 1920s. That place is now occupied by an elderly and friendly Springer. The original painting of Mr Campbell Newington's two champion Sussex Spaniels now hangs on the wall of the billiard-room.

The prefix 'Rosehill' is credited as belonging to Mr Campbell Newington up to his death, when it was transferred to his daughter, Mrs B. Drewe, and it is in her name until 1958. It is credited in the KCSB from 1959 to a Mr W. Crawford. However, in the directory of affixes published by the Kennel Club in 1986, the name 'Rosehill' is shown as belonging to Mrs Drewe. I asked Mr Francis Drewe if the name of W. Crawford meant anything to him; he told me it did not and that he had no idea why anyone else should have been able to use the Rosehill prefix. As Mrs Drewe is still credited with the prefix today, it seems likely that Mr Newington compounded it for life.

Mr Campbell Newington's brother Theodore's name appears earlier than his own in the Stud Book with a Sussex Spaniel, which surprised Mr Drewe; he said he had no idea that Theodore ever had an interest in spaniels. However, the history of the breed shows that initially he did have Sussex. He and his brother exchanged puppies, but his interest in showing appears to have waned after a few years and, apart from a few dogs, all the entries are under Campbell's name. Certainly Theodore did not use the Rosehill prefix although a number of dogs in the Stud Book show Theodore as breeder. One of the most interesting is a bitch called Bonny Beauty 40627, owned by Mr Boniface of Uckfield. Beauty has a most complete four-generation pedigree.

Theodore Newington appears first in the Stud Book as the owner of Dash V, by the unidentified Scrub out of Cyprus, down as a Bachelor daughter out of Bustle (although in an earlier mention she was listed as 'pedigree unknown'); and as the owner of Quince, an interesting dog who appears far back in present-day lines. Quince 12695 was a son of the black Field Spaniel Boscoe 10444, who in turn was by the liver, roan and tan Field Alonzo, one of the most famous studs of his era, who − like his contemporary, Bebb − appears in the pedigrees of all today's Sussex, Fields and Cockers. Boscoe was out of Blanche 8367, whose sire was Mars, a Bebb son and out of Maud, the litter sister to Buckingham. The dam of Quince was Fan VI 12735, by Bachelor out of the black bitch Negress 8373, so there was a good deal of alien blood in his lines. Quince was mated to Cyprus and produced a bitch, Wanda, who became the property of Campbell Newington; mated to Young Wallace she produced in one litter two sons named Rosehill Ruler and Rosehill Ruler II, which has proved rather confusing.

Mr Campbell Newington's first entry is Laurie in 1884. Laurie 14209 was bred by Mr Hudson in 1877 and is by Hudson's Dash out of Hudson's Romp; this bitch is said to be 'by Edgerton's dog out of a Rosehill bitch'. Mr T. Newington acquired a bitch, Romp 9274, from Mr T. Bowers, who had bought her from her breeder, a Mr Cox. She is down as by Marchant's Rover out of Flirt, yet another bitch said to be 'pure Rose Hill'. Romp is reported as having won seconds at Saffron Walden and Henley in 1884 when she was 10 years old.

The first Sussex Spaniel to bear the revived name of Rosehill was Countess of Rosehill, who was whelped in 1883 and bred by H. Sutton. Countess of Rosehill 20598 appears in the Stud Book for 1887 and was by Chance II out of Bustle, another with the tag 'pure Rose Hill'. Chance II was by Bachelor and out of Chloe 5251, a sister to Chancellor 5247, who was bred in May 1875 by Mr H. Green of Fincham, Norfolk. Countess of Rosehill and Wanda formed the base of Campbell Newington's Rosehill Sussex Spaniels.

Mr Campbell Newington (centre) at the Maiden Stakes, Kimbolton, home of the Duke of Manchester. December 16th 1904. Rosehill Rag and Rue are pictured with the keeper. On the left Mr F. Winton Smith's Clumber Spaniels.

Photograph by courtesy of Francis Drew Esq.

Ch. Rosehill Ruler II. KCSB 36,391. Br. Mr T. Newington. Owner: Mr Campbell Newington. Wh: 1889. A key dog in the pedigrees of the time.

There are many unexplained items in the KCSB and none is more puzzling than the identity of the dam of the two bitches sold by the Newingtons to Lt.-Col. H.C. Leigh of Knutsford, Cheshire. Flush II and Nell VII are in the Stud Book for 1888 as being whelped in April 1886, and said to be by Lord Rosehill and out of Countess of Rosehill. They have a brother in the Field Spaniel register, a liver and tan owned by Mr Cox of Clayhanger in Somerset, who possibly was the same Cox who had bred Romp. Mr Newington, no doubt, also had trouble in producing a litter of whole livers from the suspect lines of the times. Mr Cox also used Lord Rosehill, and his Jubilee Jack by that dog appears in a later volume, 'his dam being Fiddler, by breeder's Shot out of his Jill' – there are no further particulars.

In the *Sporting Spaniel*, published in the late 1890s, Col. Cane, the author of the Sussex chapter, gives a totally different pedigree for Flush II and Nell VII. He says they were bred from a bitch called Lady Rosehill, who was by Edgerton's Bounce out of Perk's Bess who was by Dr Watts' Jock out of Flush 'a bitch from Rose Hill'! He also says that Lady Rosehill was from very blue blood indeed and was descended 'from the dogs carried off from Rose Hill by Relf', a story that must be taken with more than a grain of salt. Col. Cane then goes on: 'Mr. Newington says she was his finest worker and had the best nose of any Sussex

57

Spaniel he had seen. He bred some good pups from her, two of which were sandy and went to Col. Leigh. He only kept the strain for work and has now quite lost it.'

There was indeed a Lady Rosehill 38601, but she was not born until 1894, eight years after her alleged daughters. Lady Rosehill appears in the KCSB for 1895, being then owned by a Mr E.S. Taylor from Ryde, Isle of Wight; she had been acquired on the death of her owner/breeder, Mr F. Stamp. Her sire is given as Wheatley Rufus, a son of Rosehill Ruler 33934 and out of Rosehill Russet 29111; her dam was a Field Spaniel, Mr Miller's Fen or Fidelia, by CSI and out of Belle of Rossett who was also the dam of a very influential black and white Field Spaniel stud dog, Welsh Harvester.

Mr T. Newington used Young Wallace on Wanda to produce Ruler and Ruler II. Young Wallace had been bred in Scotland by Mr J. London of Kilsyth, and was by Caistor (late Guess) 9265, and out of an unidentified bitch, Flirt. Laurie does not appear in the future pedigrees of the Rosehill line although Mr Handy, writing at the time, states, 'Laurie is the only pure Sussex living'. Mr Handy went on: 'every spaniel that can be bred with a golden liver flat coat is now called a Sussex without being any such thing as the real article is as scarce as the Dodo'. Col. Cane of the *Sporting Spaniel* claims that Mr Newington's dogs were 'less in-bred to the Jacobs strain than others, as nearly all went back to Cyprus and Bustle two beautiful bitches of pure Rose Hill descent'. Col. Cane conveniently overlooked all the black blood in the early Rosehills and the facts that Cyprus was by Bachelor and that Bustle had no pedigree of any sort!

From the start of the new Rosehill line to the end of the 1890s, a very commendable breeding programme had been undertaken in order to stabilise a type, although the dogs used to do this had very mixed ancestry. One can only conclude that Mr Newington, like Mr Woolland and the redoubtable Hooker, had a very strict policy of culling the poor specimens and keeping, breeding and showing only those that came up to his ideas of what a good Sussex Spaniel should look like. At this time the first of a large number of Newington Rosehills that were to appear in the Stud Books, getting on for fifty, were making their mark: Rambler 29155, Rustic 29106 and Russet 29111 – these by Candidate 22548 and out of Reine 24769 (Caistor x Countess of Rosehill); Royal and Rachel – out of Restless, a sister to Russet; Ranger 33932 and Rosebud 33944 – by Ruler 33934 out of Russet; Rita 38603 – sold to Mr Woolland; Rebel 38595 – by Ruler II out of Ruby (Ruler 33943 x Russet); Rush 40625 – who was by Rebel out of the half-Field Spaniel bitch Futurity; Rutland 803C; Rosette 751D; and the interesting Rue 1051H – who was by a Field Spaniel called Duckett 790E, out of the bitch Rhonda who was formerly named Beauty and bought from a Mr F. Still and renamed (she has no pedigree).

In 1897, the year after his marriage, the *Kennel Gazette* records, 'Mr. Campbell Newington has sold his kennel of Sussex Spaniels to Mr. Luxcombe'. I think the statement is erroneous, and that it is more probable that Mr Newington – who by then had bought Oakover and was in the process of re-building and adding to the house, and who with his wife and newly born daughter was living in London while the work was completed – had leased some of his stock to Mr Luxcombe. Mr Luxcombe lived at Ashbrook Hall, Middlewich, Cheshire. Only three dogs seem to have been involved, Roland, Rutland and Rush; these all appear for two years in Mr Luxcombe's ownership and were extensively shown under his name. In 1898 at the Crystal Palace it is reported that: 'the Sussex class was quite robbed of its interest by the absence of Mr. Luxcombe's entries'. A short while after this appeared, the Rosehill trio were transferred back into their breeder's ownership, presumably when Mr Newington took up residence in the completed Oakover.

Mr Woolland, judging in 1897, had noted: 'What to say about the Sussex I hardly know, the colour was shades too dark and most specimens were on the small side. It is a curious thing that I feel more dissatisfied when judging this variety than any other, tho' it is well known that I have bred them successfully for years.'

Critiques for shows in the 1890s record, to give one example: 'Rosehill Royal, good in bone, crooked in leg, good stern action, wanting in quality of head and with too much haw'. Another report read:

> In open dog or bitch Mr. Campbell introduced a nice young dog in Rosehill Ruler 2nd. Looking in splendid condition he won easily. He has a good head and ear, is very low, but too short in body. Coat fairly good colour, but feather too profuse for a Sussex and I did not like the light hair on his ears, chest and between his toes. Rosehill Rosebud 2nd has a good head and nice set on ears, she is on the small side but showing a lot of quality.

Rush was one of the early Rosehill champions. There were to be many more, including Rangi and Rock. The latter was Mr Campbell Newington's especial pride.

6

Two Powerful Influences

Mr Campbell Newington, writing at the end of the century, said:

> I am satisfied with the type of the present day but would like to see
> them higher on the leg, this would render them much more useful
> for work. I think Mr. Woolland's Bridford Bredaboy and Bridford
> Daisy the most typical dogs of the breed but I must say their coats
> are not as hard as my old Rosehill strain. Sussex Spaniels have been
> my only breed for 22 years, I use them for shooting over and for
> field trials and consider they have better noses and are better
> scented than any other spaniel provided the strain is right. They are
> hardy, good retrievers and stand the wet and cold, provided they are
> not bred from parents with silky coats.

Col. Cane professes himself as 'satisfied with the type of Sussex that
exists today. I prefer the breed to others as it is an older and purer breed
[!] and on account of its beautiful colour, also because it is scarcer. In
characteristics and temperament it differs little from other spaniels.' I am
afraid other breeders of the time would not agree with him on this point.
   Mr F.E. Schofield said he was satisfied with the type of Mr Woolland's
dogs; while Mr F. Winton Smith said he considered the winning dogs too
heavy, long and low to ground and preferred Mr Newington's dogs as
being more workmanlike.
   The *Kennel Gazette* correspondent, writing of Sussex Spaniels in the
1900s, says:

> This variety is down the line, probably because of undue encourage-
> ment given by some judges to the caterpillar type and the con-
> genital idiots. Mr. Campbell Newington has turned out some nice
> specimens from the Rosehill kennels and Mr. Woolland has held
> his own with Bridford Queenie, a bitch that is possibly of very high
> pretensions but which never gives one the chance of even guessing
> whether she can walk, let alone display spaniel character or activity.
> I most emphatically protest against any spaniel being awarded a
> prize, that lies prone in the ring and cannot be induced to move!

It seems that Mr Moses Woolland could do no wrong in the eyes of the judges with whatever dog he took into the ring, and writers were not slow to pin-point that kind of thing in those days. In January 1904 under 'Sussex Spaniels' the *Kennel Gazette* writer states:

This breed is, I am afraid, almost at a standstill, at least at present, as it is impossible to predict what newcomers may be placed on the bench in 1904. Mr. M. Woolland, who for many years has held the strongest hand in Sussex won 1st and 2nd in the Open class at Crufts with Bridford Bredaboy and Mocky, 1st Limit with Daisy and 2nd Novice with Roger . . . Mr. Campbell Newington who probably has the next most important kennel won with the following dogs. Rosehill Rhonda 3rd Open and Limit at Crufts [this is the bitch with no papers], Rosehill Rock, 3rd Kennel Club show, Ranji 1st Novice at Crufts, Rag 1st Novice at Kennel Club show Rush 2nd Novice Kennel Club show . . . . Col. Cane had a first in the Open at the Kennel club show with Ch. Celbridge Eldorado.

The last-named dog was a son of Jonathan Swift and out of Celbridge Stella (Bridford Prince x Bridford Minnie). To return to the *Gazette*, the writer further states: 'It is gratifying to note that although Sussex have practically stood still as regards shows, the breed acquitted itself well at our Field Trial Meeting. Mr. Campbell Newington's Rosehill Rag won second in both Maiden and Novice Stake, and his Rosehill Rue was awarded a Certificate of Merit in both these stakes'.

These two rivals, Mr Moses Woolland and Mr Campbell Newington, were in part responsible for the decline in the Sussex breed, for when two powerful kennels monopolise the rings other breeders tend to become discouraged and cease to show. In many cases they quit a breed altogether. Another reason was the scarcity of stock to breed from that did not all come from the same lines. Mr Newington partially solved this by using two bitches of unknown pedigrees, while Mr Woolland bought one of these two later and also had his Sussex-bred blacks to call on if necessary.

The number of top winners produced by these kennels in the 1885 to 1905 period is prodigious. Among many, the winners the Bridfords could claim were Giddie, Maubert, Maubert II, Victor, Maud, Naomi, Brida II, Fidelity II, Minnie, Dolly, Leopold, Queenie, Bredaboy, Mocky and Daisy, many of whom were champions. Some of Campbell Newington's were Rosehill Rush, Rock, Ruler, Ruler II, Romulus, Reine, Rue, Rag and Ranji, and after Mr Woolland's departure from the scene there were Rashleigh, Rosie, Rattler and Ruce.

Ch. Bridford Bredaboy was voted the most typical Sussex Spaniel living. He was described as a 'golden liver weighing 42 pounds'. His owner wrote of him as:

having a beautiful head, well balanced and proportioned throughout, eyes dark hazel, ears well placed, body long and deep, and well ribbed, stern well placed and carried low, legs straight and powerful with good bone, excellent feet, coat golden liver colour and perfectly flat and correct texture, is moderately feathered as a Sussex should be. A splendid mover and full of Sussex character.

One of the best Bridford studs was Bibelot, owned by a Mrs Kyffin, and Mr Newington was swift to take advantage of the fact, mating Rosehill Rhonda 7706 to him and producing a most successful litter which included the bitches Ch. Rosehill Rag, Celbridge Sorcerer (sold to Claude Cane who by then was a Lieutenant-Colonel) and Rosehill Rock. It is the painting of Rock and Rag that still hangs at Oakover. Rhonda must presumably have come from good stock as she proved a most useful brood and bred several litters containing winners. Many of the Rosehill dogs have similar names; Rhonda must not be confused with Rhoda 1242J, sister of Regalia, these two being whelped by Rosehill Ranji and out of the other unregistered bitch Rummie, whelped in 1903.

Although Mr Newington bred many top-class Sussex, Rock seems to have been the favourite if the pictures in the family album here reproduced are to be believed.

Rock was said to stand 15 in. at the shoulder, weigh 50 lb and be of the correct golden liver colour. Mr Newington wrote thus of his favourite:

Eyes, large, round and hazel in colour. Ears set low, tail rather low and never carried above the level of his back, coat straight and flat, dense and not silky, legs strong and bony with plenty of feather except on hind legs below hocks, hair on ears straight, no curl, coat of correct colour. From an exhibition point of view Rosehill Rock might be considered by some judges an inch too high on the leg, but from a working point of view I think this is an advantage. This dog is a good retriever and worker and won a Certificate of Merit at the last Field Trial.

Rock was a marvellous laster. Having been born in 1901, he appears first in the KCSB for 1903 by virtue of winning at Romford in 1902 under Mr H. Haylock, a well-known Field Spaniel breeder, and winning a second and third at the Crystal Palace under the most noted of all gun-dog men, Mr William Arkwright. Mr Arkwright, apart from his

Pointers, kept and bred a variety of gundogs, including many spaniels, Sussex among them. Rock remained in the Stud Books until 1912, winning over a period of eleven years all the honours of both bench and field. He was truly a most durable and, no doubt, endearing dog.

There were, in truth, few Sussex around in the period 1898 to 1905, the lion's share being at either Bridford or Rosehill, and those in other hands being bred from the same stock. In 1898 Mr Woolland was still exhibiting, with the 10-year-old Ch. Bridford Giddie; Ch. Bridford Queenie, about whose immobility in the ring much was written; the brothers Count and Prince, sons of Bredaboy and Rosehill Rita; and with Bredaboy himself. In 1900 he brought out Bridford Mocky who soon had his title. Mr Campbell Newington came back into the showing world at the turn of the century with Rosehill Rupert, Ranji, Rue, Rhoda, Regalia, Rally, Rashleigh and Reda, all in the KCSB, as well as the redoubtable Rock.

Mr H. Grey of Merthyr Tydfil, who had a large kennel of all types of spaniel and owned some big names in Fields, had bred Sussex for some years. In 1901 he showed Coriolanus, a home-bred dog by Rosehill Rebel out of Carntyne Jessie, with great success; and two sisters of this dog, Chrishill Madge (owner F. Williams), and Glenwood Jess (owned by Mr Standsfeld) were also in the prize-lists. Mr Standsfeld had a small foothold in Sussex, and was also winning with Beechgrove Jessica by the unregistered Bob out of Missenden Rose 716A (Ch. Bridford Giddie x Bridford Minnie). He also showed Prince Minnie (Bridford Prince x Bridford Minnie) and Glenwood Queenie, bred by Robert Chapman in Scotland and by Heather Glen ex Woodside Lass.

Col. Cane was still bringing out the occasional Sussex from his Irish-based kennel. There were Celbridge Stella, by Bridford Prince ex Bridford Minnie, bred by Mr Woolland, and Celbridge Eldorado, who took his title; and he had also acquired Rosehill Rhonda from Mr Newington: when he mated her to Bridford Bibelot she bred him a good dog in Celbridge Sorcerer.

At the end of the last century spaniel Field Trials were introduced and became popular, but to enter these a dog had to be Kennel Club registered. There was then no section for Springers, so Cocker, Sussex and Field registered in the KCSB were boosted for some years by an influx of dogs of unknown breeding, who, it was said, were registered according to the variety they most resembled. Their wins at trials got them in the stud book. Among them is a dog owned and/or bred by William Arkwright, Carry On 748D, a bitch who is said to have been 'by the Sussex dog Forest Guess 31455 out of Dot unregistered'. However, Forest Guess, although a Sussex, according to the KCSB was a bitch!

Carry On was highly successful at the 1899 Sporting Spaniel Club

Working Trials, winning a third in the all-aged stake and also the special prizes for the best-looking spaniel belonging to a member and the best looking over all. Mr F. Winton Smith, whose main claims to fame came in Clumbers, but who also had Sussex and Cockers as well as the odd Field, ran a dog called Beechgrove Burnish 855G, whose name had formerly been Bobs of Penwith. He was said to be by Bob and Belle, both of Penwith, both unregistered and, up to then, both unheard of. Nitro Powder 12205, owned by C.C. Eversfield and bred by B.D. Thomson out of the unregistered Bizzy and Nell, also found his way into the KCSB by virtue of wins in the trials. Once, however, sections in the Stud Book were allotted to Springers of both kinds, these working dogs were quickly moved over or their offspring were entered under either English or Welsh.

7

New Century . . . New Names

In 1905 the whole of the Bridford Kennel went under the hammer. It is said that many of the spaniels were sold overseas, thus still denying breeders the chance to get in on the Bridford act. It was around 1911 that Col. Cane sold his kennel, most of the spaniels going to Mr J.E. Kerr of Dollar in Scotland. Col. Cane, writing in the *Kennel Gazette* of the time, states that Mr Kerr not only bought his kennel, 'but the Bridford kennel as well'. This is just another piece of misinformation given by this writer, whose offerings over the years had contained some questionable statements and who had been mainly responsible for the Relf myth in the Fuller story. Mr Kerr certainly bought some Bridford-bred dogs, but he actually acquired them from Mrs F. Woolland, who had been breeding for quite a few years and used the Newbarn prefix. Mr Kerr does not appear to have made much use of the Celbridge Sussex, but the Newbarn dogs and bitches were to form a solid base for his breeding operations.

Mr J. Ernest Kerr lived in the historic Harviestoun Castle, which lies halfway between Dollar and Tillicoulry in Clackmannanshire. He was another very wealthy man, and had perfect facilities for the keeping, breeding and breaking of spaniels. Not only did he own a large estate, which surrounded the Castle, but also a considerable portion of the Ochil Hills, where grouse and wild duck as well as other game were plentiful. All the spaniels under the Harviestoun banner were trained to the gun as well as being show dogs, and it was said that Mr Kerr required all his spaniels to be dual purpose and would not keep a dog who could not earn his living. Not only was a first-class kennel of spaniels maintained at Harviestoun Castle, but Mr Kerr also owned a model farm kept on the most up-to-date principles of the time. His Clydesdale horses, hackneys, ponies, Aberdeen Angus cattle and Border Leicester sheep were said to 'play havoc in the prize lists at the leading agricultural shows including the Highland Agricultural Show [now the Royal Highland] where one year he won the championship in three breeds'. The kennels were constructed very much in the manner of those at Oakover, and were models for the time, with concrete yards and iron fences and strong, clean and adequate kennelling. Mr Kerr added retrievers to his kennel once the spaniels were established and, like all rich men of his day, kept a very

Mr J.E. Kerr CBE of Harviestoun, Dollar
Reproduced by kind permission of the Royal Highland Show Society.

large number of dogs. For these he required a top-class manager, and at Harviestoun this duty fell to James Macdougal, who was said to have the Harviestoun dogs always in the pink of condition.

Mr Kerr's purchases from Mrs Woolland included Newbarn Billy, whom his former owner had bred, who speedily gained his title. Her two brood bitches, Sultana 1068N and Newbarn Momie 1193M, are two of the most important matrons of the time. Sultana was by Bridford Bobs 1193K and her dam was Rosehill Regalia, a daughter of Ch. Rosehill Ranji whose grandmother had been the Field Spaniel Rolyat Rose. Sultana's mother was an unregistered bitch called Brownie, who, after she had been purchased by Mr Campbell Newington, was renamed Rosehill Rummie. Momie was by the much acclaimed Ch. Bridford

Harviestoun Castle, home of Mr J.E. Kerr and the Harviestoun Sussex Spaniels

Mocky and out of Rolyat Rose. Rose had been bred by Mr Woolland from two of his most outstanding black Field Spaniels, Ch. Bridford Tommy and Ch. Bridford Gipsy in 1889, and had been acquired, possibly as a puppy, by a Mr Taylor who registered her as Rolyat, which is Taylor spelt backwards. Rose was liver and tan, and although she appears in the breeding programme of several dogs, sometimes as just Rose and sometimes as Rolyat Rose, she was not in fact registered at the Kennel Club until 1905, when she was 16 years old! How much credence one can place in claims for her is therefore doubtful.

However, either she, or her name, play a large part in Sussex affairs of the time and she appears several times in the extended pedigree. Momie was mated by Mrs Woolland to Bridford Bobs to produce Ch. Newbarn Billy, and Sultana was mated to Ch. Rosehill Rock to produce Sunny Jane 876P. These two, Billy and Jane, mated together produced Mr Kerr's first Sussex litter, a highly successful one that contained five in the Stud Book, Harviestoun Pedro 854Q, H. Duke 852P, H. Mocky

853P, H. Daisy 851P and H. Marquis 900P. This was a repeat mating of one done previously by Mrs Woolland which had resulted in Ch. Rosehill Rye and Newbarn Queenie 855Q. As well as purchasing Momie, Jane and Billy from Mrs Woolland. Mr Kerr also acquired the dog Newbarn Bronze Dore, a bitch called Belle – later Harviestoun Belle 1010M – by Bridford Jimmy out of the unregistered Racket, and Maggie – later Harviestoun Maggie, bred by Mrs Woolland by Mocky out of Momie.

Mr Kerr set about his breeding operations in earnest. His next litter was a mating between brother and sister, Pedro and Daisy, and this resulted in a most successful winner and sire, Harviestoun Sam 668W. It was Sam, mated to Daisy McMeechin, who sired Harviestoun Marshall 857BB who was himself the sire of Mrs Freer's foundation bitch for the Fourclovers Kennel, Primax Judy. As well as having a number of Sussex Spaniels, Mr Kerr had also a big hand in black Field Spaniels and had purchased one of the great sires in the breed, Ch. Magellan. The black Fields had been established at Harviestoun for some years before the Sussex came, and in 1908 Mr Kerr had bred the black bitch Harviestoun Polly 847P from Ch. Magellan and Hollinbank Flo, both of whom trace back to Bachelor through several generations of black Field breeding. Finding, no doubt, that his Sussex lines were somewhat constricted, Mr Kerr mated Harviestoun Pedro, the Sussex dog, to Harviestoun Bell. Bell does not appear in the Stud Books but crops up in the extended pedigree as the dam, when mated to her sire, Pedro, of Harviestoun Bruno. This bitch, Bruno, was mated to the unregistered Harviestoun Jimmy whose sire was Harviestoun Sam but whose dam was another black Field Spaniel, Rona of Wilts; she was herself a daughter of Carnfield Marquis and Mr H. Grey's great champion from the Welsh valleys, Ch. Ynysowen Iris. The union of Jimmy and Bruno resulted in Harviestoun Beau 753AA. Bell's daughter May was also mated to Rufus and bred the influential Harviestoun Malloch 134Z, sire of Primax Beauty. So it is easy to see that the Harviestoun Sussex breeding was heavily impregnated with black Field Spaniel blood through the bitches Harviestoun Polly, Rona of Wilts and liver and tan brought in by Rolyat Rose.

The breeding programme at Harviestoun was extensive, and several bitches of unknown breeding were used to widen the very constricted Sussex lines. One bitch bought in who appears as the dam of Harviestoun Marshall is Daisy MacMeekin, also down as Daisy Meacham. First said to be unregistered with no breeding, she later acquires a pedigree and is seen to be a sister of Harviestoun Malloch, being by Harviestoun Rufus out of Harviestoun May and so also carrying Field blood.

The period up to the First World War, following the departure of Mr Woolland, is a bleak one for the Sussex breed. At first Mr Campbell

Harviestoun Dirk. KCSB 754AA. Wh: 1919. By Harviestoun Sam 668W ex Daisy McMeekin

Harviestoun Dolly. KCSB 755AA. Wh: 1917. By Harviestoun Sam ex Rona of Wilts 956S (Black Field Spaniel). Dolly was registered and shown as a Sussex Spaniel, and won Challenge Certificates at SKC and Crystal Palace 1920.

Note the straight, strong, slightly longer dogs and muscular bodies of the Harviestoun spaniels who were all trained for work, any spaniel that would not or could not work, being discarded.

Newington was firmly in the driving-seat, but gradually the Harviestoun stars began to emerge, and the KCSB records that these two names only, Newington and Kerr, accounted for the major prizes. In 1908, apart from his new acquisition, Harviestoun Bell, Mr Kerr does not appear and it is left to the maestro of Rosehill to make the rest of the entries. His were the dogs Ch. Rosehill Rock and Rashleigh; two dogs acquired for trials, Rover and Rhyl; and the bitches, Gipsy, Rags, Reda and Rye (the latter bred by Mr Woolland and out of Rolyat Rose). In 1909 it is the mixture as before with the addition of Rosehill Radium 1066N, a son of Ch. Rashleigh and Reda; and a bitch, Ringlet, by Ranji out of an unregistered Bibelot daughter. Sultana makes her bow here in the owner-ship of Mr Kerr, as does Newbarn Bronze Dore, who was the result of the Ch. Bridford Mocky x Newbarn Momie mating in 1906. Mocky had a long career at stud, having been born in 1897. Celbridge Chrysolite also appears in Mr Kerr's ownership. 1910 shows yet another Rosehill, Raspberry, a brother to Radium, while a Rev. W. Shields entered the lists with Sol o' the Border by two unregistered dogs. He could have been a relation of the Rev. Shields who was involved with spaniels in the nine-teenth century.

For the next few years Harviestoun and Rosehill are the only names in the Stud Book, although Mr Kerr did sell Harviestoun Duke to a Miss Epps of Norwood, near London, and she appears to have enjoyed some success as an exhibitor. From Rosehill came the new names of Rattler 901R, Reason 8R and Rocca 903R, all out of a litter by Radium and Rossa, the latter being by Ranji and from Rolyat Rose. It seems likely that the two big names were having difficulty in interesting others in the Sussex breed as both were showing and winning with several males from one litter; obviously it was becoming difficult to dispose of surplus puppies.,

In 1913 two new names do appear in the book. One was Mr C.G. Talbot Ponsonby, whose allegiance to the Sussex breed was to last for the next twenty years. His original address is given as Crown Office Row, Temple, but he had a house at Lindfield in Sussex after the First World War. Mr Talbot Ponsonby won a third at Crufts with a dog called Oldship Bilekin, bred by Mrs Bayley and born in 1910. He was by Ch. Rosehill Rock out of Oldship Rubyskins, who was by Rosehill Radium and out of Rosehill Rona. Bilekin's breeder, Mrs Bayley, was the wife of Admiral Bayley and lived at Horndean in Hampshire. Although she bred a few Sussex from Rosehill stock, she does not appear to have been active in the ring, and the only other Oldship in the KCSB appears in 1914. This was Peterbob, a brother to Bilekin, who was owned by a Mr Bingham (who, strangely enough, lived at a house called Rosehill in Cheltenham). The second name in the 1913 Stud Book is a Monsieur P.

Megnin of Vinciennes, France, who bought Rosehill Luck 307S, a son of Rattler and Rollick, and presumably took him back home. Rosehill Rye had now achieved the title of champion and Rosehill Rough 963S was a new name; he was a son of Rashleigh and Rag. Mr Kerr was winning with Pedro, Daisy and Jane. Harviestoun Sandy 1136T, a son of the brother and sister Pedro and Daisy, and Rosehill Rip 1138T (Radium x Rossa) are the only other Sussex entered in 1914.

The war years (1914 – 18) saw a further decline in the breed. There are only five names in the 1915 Stud Book, and only one new one, Rosehill Randolph 875U by Rough out of Rip. Registrations plummeted; there were only three in 1915, four in 1916, one in 1917 and none at all in 1918. In the 1916 Stud Book all the entries came from Rosehill: Randy 6R, Rough 963S and two new dogs, Robber 577V by Rattler out of Rice, and Ruce 578V by Ch. Rosehill Rock out of a bitch with no papers, Peggie. In 1916 the LKA held its show as usual and Miss Epps took a second in the Open Dog class with Harviestoun Duke, beating Mr Kerr with Harviestoun Sam. 1917 sees the appearance of the interesting Rosehill Ripton, the product of a union between Rosehill Ruce and the black Field Spaniel Rona of Wilts. Ripton gained a third in Sussex classes at the National Gundog Society Show in 1916; the exhibitions were held at Westminster. That year marks the end of the domination of the breed by Mr Campbell Newington. He was by then spending more and more time with his pedigree Sussex cattle and losing interest in the spaniels. Although a few litters were bred at Oakover around this time, unfortunately not all were registered so we are left with several from the line whose breeding is uncertain. The only entry in the 1918 KCSB is, however, one of the most important; it shows a brother to Ripton, Rosehill Rector, by the Sussex Rosehill Ruce and out of the Field Rona of Wilts. This dog was to prove a key factor in the revival of the breed following the cessation of hostilities.

Interest in the breed had dwindled to nothing during the war. Only the lone Harviestoun flag appeared to be flying by 1920. There are no entries in the Stud Book for 1919, and 1920 records only Harviestoun Malloch. However, in 1921 there are six Harviestoun entries, all with a great deal of Field blood in them. Dirk, Rita and Rubra were all from a litter bred in 1919 by Harviestoun Sam and out of Rona of Wilts. Thus all Sussex stock available for breeding had three strong lines to black Fields, who all went back to the ubiquitous Bebb 2101 through Bachelor.

71

8

Broadhurst Sets the Pattern

With the end of the First World War, interest in Sussex Spaniels was rekindled. The breed had been fortunate to have attracted over the years men of wealth to keep it going, and in 1920 yet another was at hand for the much needed revival. Mr J. Stevenson Clarke lived at Borde Hill near Cuckfield in Sussex. Born in 1897, he took up Sussex purely for their working qualities as he was a keen sportsman and first-class shot. His showing activities were conducted with a modicum of enthusiasm but with a good deal of success. In April 1923 he married Kathleen St George of Horsham, a lady who shared his love of dogs and country life, and in 1926 they moved to Broadhurst Manor at Horstead Keynes. There Mr Clarke farmed some 1,200 acres; and he also farmed a further 2,000 acres on the Isle of Wight. He had, among other good livestock, a herd of pedigree Ayrshire cattle. His keeper was Mr S.J. Ling, who often handled the dogs for his master both in the field and the ring. Later Mr Ling was to breed, run and exhibit spaniels under the Beeding affix, and was to become a well-known judge.

Mr Stevenson Clarke had business interests in London, and with these and the running of the farm led a full and varied life, with his sporting interests very much to the fore. I am indebted to his son, Mr Charles Clarke, who allowed me access to the game books and albums kept by his father. In one, for 1920, there is a drawing of a Sussex captioned 'Dollar', so perhaps Mr Clarke's first purchase in the breed was from Mr Kerr, the dog being called after its place of birth. However, there is no other mention of this dog, and Mr Clarke, who used the Broadhurst prefix, bred his first litter from a bitch called Bee in 1921. Three bitches from the litter, Broadhurst Bexie 93BB, B. Beira 92BB and B. Bokra 91BB, are all in the 1922 KCSB – Bexie and Beira by virtue of their wins at field trials. The sire is down as Rosehill Rector (unregistered) and the dam as being from Bang and Buzz. However, Rector was most certainly registered and was Rosehill Rector 30X, bred by Mr Campbell Newington and whelped on 10 September 1915. He was by Rosehill Ruce 578V out of the black Field Spaniel bitch Rona of Wilts 956S. A golden liver, he appears in the 1918 KCSB as owned by the Rev. W Boyce, a gentleman whose name only appears this once, while his dog's

Broadhurst Manor, Horstead Keynes, Sussex, the home of Mr & Mrs Stevenson Clarke and the Broadhurst Sussex Spaniels

Mr Stevenson Clarke ready for a day's shooting

Mr Stevenson Clarke's dual purpose bitches, Broadhurst Bexie 93BB and Bokra 91BB. This is the type of Sussex bred just after the Great War, the lines containing Field Spaniel blood which accounted for the longer legs and forefaces.

name was to become a linchpin in the pedigrees of the future. Rector's sire Ruce was a son of Ch. Rosehill Rock out of the unregistered Peggie. Rector was a brother to Ripton, retained and shown by his breeder. As far as is known, Rector appeared neither in ring nor field, and so one imagines that Mr Boyce must have lived in the same area as Mr Clarke, who tracked the dog down and used him to found his Sussex kennel. Bee (who later became Broadhurst Bee), although at first said to be just by Bang and Buzz, later acquired more particulars. Bang and Buzz were from Mr Talbot Ponsonby's kennel, and in later pedigrees they are shown as Langrish Bang and Langrish Buzz. Although Bang was never credited with any breeding, Buzz was said to be by Ch. Rosehill Rattler and out of Langrish Bud, again with no papers.

Almost at once the Broadhurst bitches attracted favourable comment in the sporting press for their performance at trials. In 1922 Mackay Sanderson wrote:

> Field and Sussex Spaniels are in a somewhat obscure position in the Trials sense at the moment, although at the last provincial meeting of the season a brace from Mr. J. Stevenson Clarke sprung a surprise by proving their ability to more than hold their own with other more popular varieties in open competition. This noteworthy incident only goes to prove that the low position occupied by Sussex at the moment in Trial records, is more due to waning population than inefficiency at work.

Bexie and Bokra at a Field Trial near Horsham in 1922 when they won Certificates of Merit

In *The Country Gentleman* of 1923, a report is given of the Brighton Championship Show, in which is written: 'Sussex Spaniels as one would expect, were catered for at this Sussex show, and a very good one, the property of Mr. Stevenson Clarke, Broadhurst Dolly won Open Dog or Bitch, and the same owner's Broadhurst Barbara, was 1st in Puppy.' Later in the write-up we read:

> Lovers of the beautiful old Sussex Spaniels will be pleased to note that Mr. Stevenson Clarke's wholehearted support for the breed, both in the field and on the bench, his representatives running conspicuously well against Springers in the Spaniel trials. Here the Broadhurst team captured the red in both classes, Dolly standing out well, her expression and character being particularly good, while puppy Barbara should mature into one of the best.'

W. Nichols, writing in *Our Dogs* of 13 January 1922 on the spaniel trials held at Horsham on 5 January 1922, commented:

> Broadhurst Bexie, handler S.J. Ling, a small but wonderfully fast Sussex Spaniel, and she works her ground in a pleasing manner.

After a few moments down, up got a sitter, but she stood staunch. Bexie was also most particularly smart in retrieving, losing no time either going or coming. She marked her rabbit splendidly, and always keeps pace. She found in the bracken, put up, remained steady and without hesitation brought right to hand.

Certainly Bexie and her sister Bokra, also placed at these trials had come to hand well as at that time they were just under a year old.

It is unclear if Mr Stevenson Clarke was aware that the sire of his first and highly successful litter was half-Field Spaniel. There is no mention of the fact in the Broadhurst pedigrees, and even Mr Boyce who owned the dog may have been unaware of it. He possibly did not even have Rector's papers – just his name, Rosehill Rector. It is possible that Mr Clarke, whose keenest interest was in the working qualities of his dogs,

Mrs Stevenson Clarke and her son Charles when a child, with the two Broadhurst Sussex and a Springer

Broadhurst Dolly. KCSB 1119CC. Wh: 1921. Br. J. Kerr. By Harviestoun Sam ex Harviestoun Gem. Purchased from Harviestoun. One of Mr Stevenson Clarke's winners in the show ring.

had not bothered to delve into the Kennel Club Stud Books of the past. If this is the case he would not have known that his puppies had a black grandmother. Rector was liver, and liver to liver can only beget liver, so there would be no black puppies turning up to make anyone suspicious. Mr Campbell Newington by this time had severed his connection with the rings and the trials. He had his farming interests and in the last few years of his life he suffered from poor health, so presumably he was not around to produce Rector's pedigree. Another Rosehill of the time who was used by several breeders was Rosehill Reaper, said to be by Rosehill Raper out of Nell, a bitch with no history. Raper (unregistered) was said to be by Rosehill Ruce, a Ch. Rosehill Rock son out of Rosehill Ruth. Reaper appears in several pedigrees of the time and he and Rector are two of the factors in laying the foundations for the modern Sussex Spaniel. Mr Clarke used Reaper on Broadhurst Bokra in 1922 and her litter was born on 22 June when Bokra was 16 months old. It contained a most important dog, Broadhurst Brush 1395DD. He came out at the Kennel Club Show at a year old and was second in Open Dog. As a stud dog Brush was to prove invaluable. Mr Clarke purchased a bitch from Mr Kerr and called her Broadhurst Dolly 1119CC; she was by Harviestoun Beau out of the unregistered Harviestoun Gem. Mr Kerr was still active in the breed, and in the years after the war won with Harviestoun Daphne and Dolly, and with the dogs Derek, Dirk and Marshall. In 1923 he had two new bitches out in Harviestoun Carina by Beau and Milena by Dirk.

Broadhurst Brush. KCSB 1395DD. Wh: June 1922. By Rosehill Reaper ex Broadhurst Bokra 91BB. A very important stud, he was the sire of Miss Scholefield's first champion, Brosse, who was bred by Mr Stevenson Clarke.

Mrs Stevenson Clarke with some of the Broadhurst Sussex Spaniels. Early 1920s.

Note the Field Spaniel-type heads and length of foreface from the stock descended from the Fields used to keep the breed going

The last litter registered by Mr Kerr under the Harviestoun prefix was born on 3 April 1924. They were by Harviestoun Marshall and out of Harviestoun Pheobe and consisted of four dogs, Commander, Commodore, Captain and Cadet. Mr Kerr has, however, one bitch registered in 1929, Harviestoun Devotee, by Harviestoun Destroyer ex Harviestoun Brietta, of whom no more is known.

The Harviestoun domination of the rings appears to have come to an end in 1924, and the Scottish Kennel Club (SKC) Show, which had always drawn a large number of Harviestoun entries, had only two Sussex entered, both belonging to Mr Menzies: Kenmore and Nona of Leetside. Mr Kerr made a brief reappearance in the rings in 1928, when Harviestoun Destroyer 1438JJ was shown for a couple of years at the SKC only, never achieving a higher placing that third. The bitch Harviestoun Brietta accompanied him and did rather better, gaining a first in both 1928 and 1929. But this was to be the end of the powerful Harviestoun Kennel which for a decade had, almost single handed, kept the breed alive.

The Scottish interest in Sussex Spaniels was maintained for around fifty or so years. It was continued at this point by Mr R. McDougal, who bred some important dogs under the Leetside prefix. He lived at Coldstream in the Borders, and drew his foundation stock from Harviestoun. His first Sussex in the KCSB was Queen Sheba of Leetside, who was bred by Mr Kerr and was by Harviestoun Beau out of an unregistered bitch, Harviestoun Jumper. Mr Menzies, from Uphall in Scotland, bought a bitch puppy called Nona of Leetside 145EE from Mr McDougal. She was by Harviestoun Malloch 134Z and out of Restless of Leetside by Beau out of Harviestoun Sadie, who was another unregistered bitch. Nona was to play quite a part in future events.

Yet another kennel founded on Harviestoun stock was that of Mr S. Mitchell of Chipping Warden, who was engaged in building up a kennel under the Primax label. His bitches, Primax Judy, Beauty and Sally, are three of the most important in the modern pedigrees. Beauty was by Malloch out of the unregistered Delphine, Judy was her daughter by Harviestoun Marshall, and Sally was the result of Beauty's mating to Langrish Bruno.

A very wealthy lady from Earlswood in Surrey took up the breed in 1920; this was Mrs Youell, who for nearly twenty years was to breed and exhibit under the Earlswood prefix. Her lines were founded on several dogs and bitches with no known breeding, Napoleon and Cleopatra among them. However, quite soon in her career she bought in a number of Sussex from other kennels. The Earlswood breeding plan is not clear to those who study the pedigrees of the time, and it appears that Mrs Youell bought in any successful dog, or litters from successful lines, and then muddled them all up to produce a rather mixed result. Photographs of the Earlswood dogs show that they were of all makes and shapes, some with very uncharacteristic heads and others extremely long on the leg. Probably much of the unregistered stock she bred from came from Field or Springer stock, which would account for the mixture of types.

From the point of view of today's Sussex owners, the 1926 KCSB must be the most important and interesting. It brings into the limelight a name which was to endure in the breed for sixty years, that of Miss Joy Scholefield of Poulton Hey, Bromborough in Cheshire. In later years she became Mrs Freer. Miss Scholefield bought her first Sussex from Mr Stevenson Clarke with the sole purpose of having a good spaniel for the gun as she was a keen sportswoman, and it was only on Mr Clarke's insistence that the dog was so good looking that it should be exhibited that she yielded to pressure and made her first appearance in the ring. Brosse, as the dog was called never bore the Broadhurst prefix although he had two registered sisters; they both won but never achieved KCSB numbers. Brosse was by Broadhurst Brush 1395DD and out of Broadhurst Brora, a daughter of the unregistered Punch of Heaton, and Rattle. Punch was by two unknowns, Shot and Ruby, while Rattle was a daughter of the unknown Dandy and out of one of Col. Talbot Ponsonby's bitches, Langrish Buzz, who was by Ch. Rosehill Rattler out of yet another unregistered bitch, Langrish Bud.

Miss Scholefield with the two-year old Brosse picked up the Challenge Certificates at her only three outings, Crufts, Ranelagh and Chester. There were the two other shows in 1926: at the Kennel Club Show Stokecourt Drake 78FF (Harviestoun Derek x a Reaper bitch) won the Dogs Class for a Mr S. Bacheller, and Earlswood Princess 662FF (Harviestoun Marshall x Nona of Leetside) won for Mrs Youell; and the SKC only attracted two dogs, Kenmore and Nona.

Mr Stevenson Clarke continued with the Sussex breed for several years. His entries in the *Kennel Gazette* mainly involve litters bred from Broadhurst Dolly, whom he purchased from Mr Kerr. Broadhurst Bob and Bryn, a dog and bitch, were born in 1924 from Dolly by Brush. In 1925 the mating was repeated and resulted in Broadhurst Beatrice and her brother Brandy. Broadhurst Biddy and Broom were again the same combination and arrived in 1928. Mr Stevenson Clarke's son, Mr Charles Clarke, told me of Biddy whom he had until after the Second World War and supplied me with her photograph. Unfortunately she was never bred from and so a potential brood was lost.

Mr Charles Clarke said that his father gave up breeding Sussex in the early 1930s as he had a great deal of trouble with them suffering from hysteria, and he took up Welsh Springers for his sporting commitments. Although Mr Clarke did not keep or breed a large number of Sussex

Mrs Youell and a group of her Earlswood Sussex Spaniels

Langrish Bruno 83GG. Wh: 1926. Br. J. Stevenson Clarke. By Paxhill Buckle ex Broadhurst Bexie. Sold to Col Talbot Ponsonby who registered him and later sold him to Mrs Youell. A big winner in his day and a noted sire.

Spaniels, his contribution to the breed is great, not only because he insisted that his Sussex should be workers first and show dogs second and so kept the working characteristics in the breed, but also because he was the breeder of Brosse, without whom it is difficult to see where the breed would have ended.

Mrs Youell's Earlswood Kennel went quickly into its stride. Mrs Freer, in a letter to me only a few months before she died, in 1984, referred to 'the mysterious Napoleon and Cleopatra' belonging to Mrs Youell, and said, 'I always thought they were related to French Poodles as both grew topknots!' However, I imagine that both Napoleon and Cleopatra were descended from the Field Spaniel, which had Irish Water Spaniel blood back in its lines. Many Fields of the time were said to grow topknots and, indeed, some still do today. The first litter Mrs Youell bred was registered in 1922 and was by a dog called Peter of Earlswood, who was from the mysterious Napoleon and Cleopatra; the offspring made no mark. In 1923 Mrs Youell repeated the mating, but again the offspring were unremarkable and did not bear the Earlswood prefix. The next litter, in October 1923, is more interesting. By Peter of Earlswood out of Cleopatra, the litter included Peggy of Earlswood and Treyford Jessica. The latter bitch was sold to a Mrs Sampson, but then passed into the hands of Miss Scholefield. In 1924 Mrs Youell purchased three puppies from Mr Menzies by Harviestoun Marshall and out of Nona of Leetside; she registered them as Earlswood Mafalda 80FF, sold on to a Miss Warren; Earlswood Nona 79FF; and Earlswood Princess. Mrs Youell also acquired the dog Langrish Bruno 83GG, who had been bred by Mr Stevenson Clarke by Paxhill Buckle out of his trials bitch Bexie. Bruno had gone from Mr Clarke to Col. Talbot Ponsonby (hence the prefix), who had sold him to Mrs Youell. This dog was greatly used at stud and a look at his pedigree might be of interest.

Miss Warren used Paxhill Buckle on Mafalda and bred a litter using the Ladbroke prefix. Only one, Ladbroke Beau 1296GG, makes a mark, but although she had some success with Mafalda, Miss Warren's interest in the breed appears short lived, and in 1928 Ladbroke Beau was sold to Mr Blagg.

Although Mrs Youell and Miss Scholefield started in Sussex at roughly the same period, Mrs Youell perhaps a year or so sooner than Miss Scholefield, there seems to have been no meeting of minds, nor indeed, any exchange of stock, even though both ladies became highly successful in the breed and met in the rings over a period of fifteen years. Mrs Youell's breeding programme had not the same careful thought and planning behind it as did Miss Scholefield's, and although the latter remarked at one time 'that because of its history one was apt to get a bit of a mixture in a litter', it seems that this was more true of the Earlswoods than of the Fourclovers, judging by photographs of the time. Earlswood proceeded on one track, breeding from stock of unknown pedigree and mingling the offspring with dogs and bitches bought in from a number of different kennels; whereas Miss Scholefield always had a plan, starting with two brood bitches and mating them carefully. If you study the breeding of the Fourclovers for the pre-Second World War period, it is easy to see what she intended and, indeed, how carefully she planned every mating.

Mrs Youell's purchase of three bitches from Mr Menzies was followed by her purchase of Restless of Leetside in 1924 from a Mr J.T. Jones and of Langrish Bruno from Col. Talbot Ponsonby in the same year. She kept the latter dog for three years before selling him on to a Mr T. Strachan. Mrs Youell's first Sussex in the Stud Book is a bitch called Bunty of Earlswood 1296EE, bred by Major C.H. Wild in October 1923. Bunty was said to be by Buster out of Rattle, but whether this is the same Rattle who, when mated to Punch of Heaton, produced Broadhurst Brora is unclear; taking the dates into consideration, it could have been. Bunty's dam is down as Southash Zara who was by Rosehill Reaper out of the unknown Nell. A strange anomaly is that Mrs Youell's first champion, Earlswood Pete, born in May 1926, is said to be out of Earlswood Bunty and beside her name is the word 'unregistered'. Would Mrs Youell really have had a Bunty of Earlswood and an Earlswood Bunty at one and the same time, or was there an error in the Stud Book? No correction is shown in any of the following volumes, so we shall never know for certain if Earlswood Bunty was in fact Bunty of Earlswood.

Another successful Earlswood dog was Earlswood Sam by Harviestoun Derek 589CC out of Alton Sally (who had been bred by Mrs Youell in the litter containing Treyford Jessica and so was out of the doubtful Cleopatra). Mrs Youell further strengthened her kennel by the purchase of two of Mr Menzies's best bitches, Restless and Nona of Leetside. Apart from Cleopatra, who had no fewer than six litters that were registered, the next most used bitch was Earlswood Pixie 1555KK, a daughter of Langrish Bruno and the unregistered Earlswood Min. Pixie whelped in April of 1930 to Ch. Earlswood Pete and this union produced Earlswood Bridget 1526NN. In October of the same year Pixie whelped again, this time to Ch. Dash of Ianmohr; Earlswood Goldie Girl 1937NN, who later became a champion, was one of this litter. In the following year this mating was repeated, resulting in Earlswood Golden Lady 673NN. Mrs Youell purchased several well-known dogs and bitches during the 1920s and 1930s, including Langrish Bruno, Nona of Leetside, Ch. Dash of Ianmohr, Westmark Winonah, Langrish Bangle and a dog who was registered Earlswood Simba 1020QQ from Col. Talbot Ponsonby. Mrs Youell bred Westmark Winonah to Dash, and Mr

Earlswood Nona 79FF. Wh: 1924. Br. Robert Menzies. By Harviestoun Marshall KCSB 857BB ex Nona of Leetside 1452EE.

Ch. Earlswood Pete KCSB 1618HH. Wh: 1926. By Langrish Bruno ex Earlswood Bunty.

Note that Mrs Youell's Sussex were larger than others of the period. Good straight, well boned legs, bodies of a reasonable length. However, there was a wide variation of head types in the Earlswood, some, such as Earlswood Rex being very Clumber like, while others, such as Pete, still show the almost Field Spaniel foreface.

Blagg had a dog puppy back which he registered Westmark Don 533SS and which gained his KCSB number at LKA in 1936. Mr Blagg's interest in Sussex continued and Winonah's sister Minnihaha was by then a champion. Mrs Youell continued with her Sussex until the outbreak of the the Second World War, Earlswood Dash 750TT being one of the last of the prefix in the Stud Book. By then Earlswood Goldie Girl had passed into Mrs Bower's hands, and the dog, Earlswood Terrie 977PP, to Miss Broad, while Mr J.C. Chambers of Marlow had acquired Earlswood Rambler 76SS. The Earlswood Sussex did not appear after the war, and it is strange that a kennel that bred and sold so many puppies had so little lasting effect on the breed.

9

The Fourclovers Influence

Miss Scholefield, after her successful debut with Brosse in 1925 when he won three Challenge Certificates in a row, qualified him in 1927 at the West Midland Field Trial Society. At the time of the debut of Brosse, Miss Scholefield had purchased another Sussex, registered as Red Jacket and born in April 1923; however, the particulars of the dog are unknown and after he was second of two on his first outing no more is heard of him. It was in her selection of foundation bitches that Miss Scholefield was so careful, although she had very little choice as numbers were small and many Sussex had unknown or doubtful pedigrees.

In the spring of 1925 she purchased Primax Judy from Mr Menzies and in July Treyford Jessica from Mrs Sampson. In 1927 Primax Sally came from Mr Menzies, and became, with a change of name, Tehana of Fourclovers. Miss Scholefield did not keep this bitch but passed her on to her friend Mrs Bower, who used her to found the highly successful

Miss Joy Scholefield (later Mrs Freer) with her second champion, The Sagamore of Fourclovers, 1616HH. Wh: 1926. By Ch. Brosse ex Primax Judy 975FF. Pictured with his daughter Huitzel of Fourclovers.

Miss Scholefield's first champion Ch. Brosse KCSB 77FF. Wh: 1923. Br: J. Stevenson Clarke. By Broadhurst Brush 1395DD ex Broadhurst Brora.

Agrivista Kennel. Primax Judy was mated to Ch. Brosse in 1925 and produced another champion, The Sagamore of Fourclovers, as well as Cornplanter and the bitches Maya 79HH and Tyee 259HH. Miss Scholefield loved a dog to work, and to help her with this side of her kennel she had one of the great trainers of the period, Mr T.J. Greatorex. He gave her much help and advice and qualified all the Fourclovers champions in the field. Also in 1925 Treyford Jessica was mated to Brosse, and this union resulted in three bitches, Bebrhos, Jessica Pride and Sandra, the last of whom was to become a key figure in the pedigrees. Although she had had such success with Brosse, Miss Scholefield fared less well with the bitches she had purchased and which she showed at the same time. When Mr W. Humphrey judged at Chester he withheld the CC and first prize in Open Bitch, and awarded Primax Judy only a second and Treyford Jessica a third!

Mr F. Blagg, who lived in Petersfield, came into Sussex, registering the Westmark prefix in 1927. His first Sussex in the Stud Book was Westmark Gleaner 326HH, a daughter of Harviestoun Derek and Westmark Ruth. Gleaner was from a litter that also contained the bitch Steep Nell, who was sold to a Mr F.W. Clarke (not to be confused with Mr. Stevenson Clarke); this bitch proved a useful brood. In 1928 Steep Nell was put to The Sagamore of Fourclovers and bred a litter that was sold to three influential people in Sussex, Col. Talbot Ponsonby having a dog called Langrish Boodle, Miss Scholefield buying a bitch she registered as Keeko of Fourclovers, and Mr Blagg taking three. Whether because the sire had a Red Indian name or whether to emulate Miss Scholefield (who used Red Indian names for all her dogs), Mr Blagg called his three Westmark Chibiabos, Minnihaha and Winonah; as the latter bitch came out at the same time as Winonah of Fourclovers there must have been some confusion.

Mr Blagg purchased Broadhurst Broom 1556KK (Broadhurst Brush x Broadhurst Dolly) from Mr Stevenson Clarke and used him on Gleaner but the litter left no mark. Broom was next used on Minnehaha and this pair produced Westmark Billy 1874MM and Westmark Broom 1446MM. Of all of the Westmark Sussex , the most interesting must surely be Westmark Belle 1317MM, a daughter of Ladbroke Beau and out of Steep Nell.

Belle was sold as a puppy to Major and Mrs Bishop who lived in Gloucestershire. They were keen shooting people and liked to breed their own dogs for their own use. They had at the time their own line of Field Spaniels, and when she was an adult Belle was mated to their original Field dog Benjamin of Bawnoge. This mating produced an influential brace registered as Field Spaniels: Capt. Tredinnick's Newburie Kala 1807LL, who won at Field Trials, and the Bishop's own dog Joseph of Bawnoge, who features prominently in the extended pedigree of today's Field Spaniels. Belle herself, who was born in 1927, had her litter by Benjamin on 27 November 1929. She next appears in the hands of Mrs Bower, who brought her out in the ring and won some useful awards with her at championship shows. Belle was then mated to Agrivista Beta in 1931 and whelped a litter of five including Miss Scholefield's important matron, Pocahontas of Fourclovers, and Agrivista Eugenia 674NN and Agrivista Euphemia 281PP, the latter being sold later to Miss Wigg to found her Hornshill Kennels. Belle was then passed into Col. Talbot Ponsonby's ownership and in March 1932 bred a litter by Earlswood Reaper 1448MM (Ch. Dash of Ianmohr x Earlswood Pixie); this contained Langrish Elizabeth 922QQ and Marshbarn Patsie 1035, owned by a Mrs Knott of Redhill. Belle returned to Mrs Bower, who mated her once again to Beta who was by now a champion. Only one bitch from this litter, born in 1933 made the Stud Book. Col. Talbot Ponsonby bred from Belle's daughter Elizabeth and one of the puppies went to Mrs Bower and became Agrivista Psyche 161UU; the sire was said to be 'unknown'. There is no mention of Belle from then on, but she plays a most important part in the background of both the Sussex and the Field Spaniels of today.

In the years following the Second World War, I had a great deal of correspondence with the Bishops, who were still living in Gloucestershire and still had their original line of spaniels. We were able to use Roshe of Bawnoge, a grandson of Belle, on my foundation bitch Keepsake of Westwind in 1947.

Mr Menzies of Coldstream remained in the Sussex breed for some years. He purchased Broadhurst Bob 1296FF from Mr Stevenson Clarke and the dog proved a highly successful sire. Mated to Nona of Leetside he sired two brothers, Soutar Johnny 1791HH and Dash of Ianmohr 1972HH. Mr Menzies retained Johnny but sold Dash to Mr E.A. Dann of Linlithgow. Both dogs came out at the SKC in 1927 at around 15 months old, and under Mr Grierson, Johnny won the Open Dog and the CC and his mother, Nona, won the bitch CC. Dash was third in Open Dog behind the other Menzies-owned dog, Kenmore. Mr Menzies's Soutar Johnny achieved his qualifying certificates in the field in 1928, whereas Mr Dann only appeared with Dash at the SKC Show, where he was second. Dash won two CCs in 1929 and shortly after was sold to Mrs Youell, who picked up two more CCs in 1930 and got his qualifying certificate with him in 1933 at the Utility Gundog Society's Kent and Sussex Branch Field Trials. Johnny went on winning up to 1932 and then vanished from the Stud Books; Dash also went on winning and appears up to 1935. No doubt it was because Dash was sold to the south of England and was therefore more accessible to breeders than his brother that he was used the most; he appears in many pedigrees of the time. One breeder, however, who did go north to use Soutar Johnny was Mrs Bower, who mated Agrivista Asteria to him and bred her great show and stud dog Ch. Agrivista Beta.

Having tied up the loose ends of the Sussex story at this time, it is now necessary to devote much of this chapter to the lady and her dogs who were to dominate the Sussex scene for the next six decades: Miss Scholefield and the formidable Fourclovers.

Miss Scholefield was truly a breeder of the old school. She did not clutter herself up with a lot of stock but kept only the best in her kennel, selling off the rest. Many were obviously sold with provisos that a puppy should be returned as part of the price. By this means she built up a line of strong, typical and workmanlike Sussex Spaniels that were to be the envy of all and the despair of those who met her in the rings! The only contact Miss Scholefield's Fourclovers had with Mrs Youell's Earlswoods was when Miss Scholefield bought Treyford Jessica from Mrs Sampson, who had bought her originally from her breeder, Mrs Youell.

It is on Primax Judy and Treyford Jessica, and their respective matings to Ch. Brosse, that the fortunes of Fourclovers were founded. Miss Scholefield's first two litters produced dogs and bitches that were to have a long-lasting effect on Sussex Spaniels. Ch. The Sagamore of

Fourclovers was a handsome dog, perhaps even an improvement on Ch. Brosse, his sire. Herbert Hignett wrote of him in 1928, 'Sagamore, one of the best of his breed that has been benched for years, a glance at this head will delight the older fanciers, there is nothing of the Field type about his expression.' This reference speaks volumes for, with their close relationship to the Field breed of that time, many Sussex, judging by their photographs, show strong Field Spaniel characteristics.

Mrs Bower and Miss Scholefield were friends of many years, and Agrivista and Fourclovers stock were constantly changing hands to the benefit of both ladies and their breeding programmes.

In 1929 Miss Scholefield had a dog puppy by The Sagamore back from Mr A. Roper, who had bought Sandra from the Brosse x Treyford Jessica litter, and mated her to The Sagamore. This dog was called Sihoun of Fourclovers and became a noted stud. A sister to Sandra, Bebros, had also been sold as a puppy, but later Miss Scholefield repurchased her and mated her to a dog called Bruan (Ch. Brosse x Nan, unregistered). This union bred Kisha in 1928, and in 1929 Kisha was mated to Ch. Dash of Ianmohr and bred a litter of seven under the Fourclovers name: Trig, Tarhe, Wingenund, Snooks, Mna, Winonah and Kanawha. Wingenund became a well-known sire and both Winonah and Kanawha became

Ch. Okimat of Fourclovers KCSB 1316. Wh: 1930. By Sihoun of Fourclovers 2002KK ex Kanawha of Fourclovers. One of the most dominant Sussex stud dogs in the history of the breed.

Obro of the Indes 63RR. Full brother to Okimat. Owned by H.T. Radford. Winner of one Challenge Certificate.

From these pictures one can see how quickly Miss Scholefield managed to get a recognisable type of Sussex, but also how different types could be born in one litter by comparing the pictures of Okimat and Obro.

renowned broods. In 1930 Kanawha was bred to Sihoun and produced Okimat of Fourclovers, later spoken of by all the spaniel experts of the time as 'the best Sussex ever bred'.

A look at Okimat's pedigree will show with what thought his coming had been planned. Although in her chapter on the breed in *Gundogs of Britain*, 1974, Mrs Freer said she felt she was 'lucky to have bred such a good dog so early in my career', most of her success must go down to her study of the breed, her own well-planned breeding programme and her methods of keeping and rearing her dogs. Okimat had a brother, sold unregistered to Mr H.T. Radford in Devon, who named his acquisition Obro of the Indes. At 5 years of age he appeared at Crufts and won the CC under Major Harding Cox, beating a number of well-known winners. The Major was not a lover of the minority spaniel breeds and said so forcefully on several occasions. He particularly abhorred any spaniel with any length to its back or any tendency to short legs.

Okimat's career in the rings was touched with success from his first emergence into the limelight. At 15 months old he won the CC at the

Mrs Bower's foundation bitch Tehana of Fourclovers KCSB 80HH (formerly Primax Sally). Wh: 1924. Br. S.C. Mitchell. By Langrish Bruno ex Primax Beauty.

Mrs Bower's great winner between the wars, Ch. Agrivista Beta KCSB 1940LD. Wh: 1929. By Soutar Johnny 1791HH ex Agrivista Asteria (a daughter of Ch. Brosse).

SKC, the Metropolitan and Essex, and Birmingham, and topped off the year by running for and attaining his qualifying certificate at the Spaniel Club's Field Trials. Okimat won five more CCs, the last in 1937 under Lt.-Col. Downes Powell. This well-known spaniel man bought Montezuma of Fourclovers from Miss Scholefield, who was winning well in the ring with this dog. Montezuma was a grandson of Okimat, and he trained so well that he was successful for Col. Downes Powell at a number of Trials. Much was hoped of him, but the Second World War came along and upset all the plans. Montezuma was by Osseo out of Okimat's mother, and even without his promise in the field he must have been a great stud prospect.

Among Okimat's sons and daughters who appear in the KCSB are Osseo 1609PP and Wabasso 271QQ, born in 1932 and out of Pocahontas; Sachem 2033QQ, born in 1934 and out of Talula; Agrivista Iota 497TT, born in 1936 and out of Agrivista Asteria (Ch. Brosse x Wendy of Oakerland); Aimsa of Fourclovers and Kwasind of Fourclovers from a repeat mating with Talula, 1935; Plush of Oakerland 807TT, bred by Miss Reed in 1936 and out of Goldilocks of Oakerland; and Mike of Easingwold 81UU out of Westmark Jane. It is notable that all the well-known Sussex breeders of the time used Okimat, with the notable exception of Mrs Youell of Earlswood. Miss Scholefield in later years wrote, 'oddly enough Okimat never produced his equal, and his son Tamenund was the dog who made the most impression at stud'. However, recourse to the KCSB gives Tamenund as being not a son but a grandson of Okimat, Tamenund's breeding being Sachem 2033QQ out of Lilluar of Fourclovers; possibly an error had crept into Mrs Freer's text and it should have read 'grandson'.

Mrs Bower's name has appeared a number of times already, and it now seems an appropriate time to appraise the Agrivista Kennels. Mrs Bower's foundation bitch was Primax Sally which she purchased from Miss Scholefield, who had bought her from her breeder, Mr Menzies, and renamed her Tehana of Fourclovers. She was mated to Ch. Brosse in 1928 and produced Agrivista Apollo and Asteria. Asteria, who was born on 25 September 1928, whelped her first litter, by Soutar Johnny, on 10 September 1929 and this produced one of Mrs Bower's most successful winners – and a great sire – Ch. Agrivista Beta 1940LL as well as Miss Reed's Beta of Oakerland 1362LL. The purchase of Westmark Belle from the Bishops proved fortuitous. Her mating to Beta bred Miss Scholefield's great matron Pocahontas of Fourclovers, and also Agrivista Eugenia 674NN and Euphemia 281PP, sold to Miss Wigg as a foundation for the Hornshill Sussex.

In June 1930 Asteria whelped to Soutar Johnny's brother, Ch. Dash of Ianmohr, but the union was not nearly so successful, Agrivista Gamma

272QQ sold on to Mr I. Ferguson being the only one of this litter in the Stud Book. Asteria whelped to Okimat in 1936 to produce Agrivista Iota 497TT. Agrivista Ceres 76TT was bred by Miss Reed and was by Beta out of Wendy of Oakerland; she was mated to Ch. Rummy of Oakerland who was also out of Wendy and they bred Agrivista Silica 358UU. Kappa 1545TT was born a year later out of Ceres and by Okimat, while Psyche 1615UU was bred by Col. Talbot Ponsonby and was from Langrish Elizabeth and by an unknown sire.

Ch. Agrivista Beta won a considerable amount, his first CC coming in 1930 at Birmingham under the well-known spaniel man Mr R.R. Kelland. In 1931, when he was still very young, he found himself up against Ch. Okimat of Fourclovers and Ch. Dash of Ianmohr and had to play second or third fiddle to these two at his six championship shows. The same thing happened the following year, with Earlswood Rex joining in the hunt. In 1933 Beta started the year off well by winning, at Crufts, his second CC under the Matford maestro Ernest Trimble, but for the rest of the shows it was the mixture as before, with Okimat, Rex and Dash taking most of the spoils. However, Beta, who had spent some time in training, collected his qualifying certificate in the field at the Southern Counties Gundog League Trials at Horndean; won his third CC at Birmingham under the well-known all-rounder George Wallwork in November 1934; and in the following run up to the war years collected several more. His sons and daughters who found fame in the ring, apart from those already mentioned, were Rex of Oakerland 1677RR, Hornshill Marigold 1923RR and Betty of Trinity Chest 1477SS.

Mrs Youell's Earlswood Rex 1525NN. Wh: 1931. By Ch. Dash of Ianmohr 1792HH ex Earlswood Bridget 1526NN.

Miss Reed's Ch. Rummy of Oakerland KCSB 1370NN. Br: A.E. Clapperton. Wh: 1931. By Ch. Brosse ex Wendy of Oakerland 622MM (daughter of Kenmore 1443FF and an unregistered bitch).

These two pictures show the change in type of the Earlswoods and Oakerlands from the Fourclovers, the dogs pictured having an almost Clumber cast of head

Another lady whose Sussex breeding programme had a bearing on the lines was Miss M.F. Reed, who lived at Corbridge in Northumberland. She was a country gentlewoman of the old school. Tall and spare and always clad in a severe brown 'costume' with calf-length straight skirt and long jacket, flat-crowned wide-brimmed felt hat and well-polished brogues, she was a rather austere figure and appeared very reserved at shows. A great sportswoman, she rode to hounds into her 90s, was a good shot and was immensely keen on training her spaniels for the gun.

She registered her Oakerland prefix in 1921 when she started a kennel of Clumbers, and she added Sussex around 1927. Her first Sussex in the KCSB was Beta of Oakerland 1362LL, bought from Mrs Bower, born in 1924 and by Soutar Johnny out of Agrivista Asteria. Wendy of Oakerland was purchased from her breeder, Mr A.E. Clapperton, and was by Mr Menzies's dog Kenmore 1443FF (Harviestoun Marshall x Nona of Leetside) and out of an unregistered bitch called Betsy. Wendy produced several litters in her lifetime: firstly, mated to Ch. Dash of Ianmohr, she bred Dalehill Boy; then mated to Ch. Brosse in 1931 she bred three successful Sussex, Lizzie 1407PP, Rummy 1370NN and Rex 1677RR, all of Oakerland. Although Lizzie and Rex did well, it was Rummy of Oakerland who was to become Miss Reed's most successful Sussex.

Rummy ran up a large tally of CCs, starting in 1933 with the SKC and Kennel Club Shows. He won three more in 1934 and qualified in the field at the Spaniel Club Field Trials in November at East Harling in Norfolk. Many more CCs, Field Trial placings and Certificates of Merit came his way in the years just prior to the Second World War. Mated to his mother, Wendy, Rummy sired Nora of Oakerland who also won on the bench and qualified in the field, taking her title and often accompanying her father to shows and Trials with success. Wendy was next mated to Ch. Agrivista Beta and bred Tawny of Oakerland 77SS, Goldilocks of Oakerland 1544TT and Agrivista Ceres 76TT. Goldilocks was put to Okimat and bred Plush of Oakerland 807TT. All Miss Reed's spaniels worked and most ran Trials. That Miss Reed liked her Sussex to have Clumber outlook is evidenced by photographs of some of her dogs, Rummy himself being a case in point. In fact Miss Reed made several crosses of the two breeds, registering them in the Interbred Spaniel register of the time. Although Miss Reed was active in Clumbers after the war, she only briefly renewed her association with Sussex.

In the 1930s an interest in Sussex on the Continent manifested itself in the purchase by Mrs t'Hoen of Wassenaar in Holland of some well-known dogs from this country. These included Miss Scholefield's Ch. Winonah of Fourclovers, who had won nine CCs; Ch. Agrivista Buzz and Agrivista Zeta from Mrs Bower; Westmark Jane and her son Jumbo (by Okimat) from Mr Blagg; Marigold of Oakerland from Miss Reed and Fairway Leo from Miss Broad.

Miss L.N. Wigg of Hawkhurst in Kent – just a few miles over the boundary with Sussex and near to Ticehurst and all the Newington and Rosehill connections – registered her Hornshill prefix when she came into Sussex in 1934. Her first purchases were some well-bred bitches and on these she founded her kennel. Agrivista Euphemia 281PP was bought from Mrs Bower, Wabasso of Fourclovers 271QQ (Brosse x Pocahontas) from Miss Scholefield, and from Miss Reed there was a sister to Rex of Oakerland, Mary Jane of Oakerland, whom Miss Wigg speedily renamed Hornshill Marigold 1923RR. The first Hornshills are from a litter bred in May 1934 by Earlswood Brian 675NN (Ch. Dash of Ianmohr x Earlswood Bridget) and out of Wabasso (Okimat x Pocahontas); and as well as Hornshill Robin there were three dogs from the litter in the KCSB all shown by their breeder: Hornshill Bellamy 383RR, Benson 1036RR and Buckle 1676RR, all successful in 1935. Miss Wigg also bred from Marigold in 1935, her mating to Bellamy producing three useful bitches, Mirabel, Miranda 1648SS and Meriel 80UU. Quickly back to form after maternal duties, Marigold appeared at both the Metropolitan and Essex and the Birmingham Shows that autumn, winning the CC both times. Wabasso whelped to Brian again in 1936, the bitches Hornshill Rowena 1703TT and Russett being among the litter. Hornshill George 1527UU was the result of Robin x Mirabel, in 1937; and the same year he was mated to her sister Meriel and produced Dandy, Dickon and Dolly. Miss Wigg bought in a bitch from a litter by Dalehill Boy out of Ticehurst Floss — bred by Mr H.R. Ward in 1937 — and registered her Hornshill Elizabeth. She was sold to a Mr J.R.F. Smith at the same time as Robin passed into the ownership of Mr C. Ingrams. Other Hornshill stock of the time are of little interest. With so many males in her kennel Miss Wigg no doubt deemed it prudent to place some in other hands. She sold Robin's brother Bellamy to Mrs C.M. Sewell of Connecticut, USA, and sent with him Hornshill Marigold. Mrs Sewell also purchased Rex of Oakerland from Miss Reed, and a little later Hornshill Rowena and Russett crossed the ocean. Miss Wigg's early association with the breed ends at the outbreak of war. Many years later she returned to it, and one of her most successful bitches again bore the name Hornshill Elizabeth, just twenty years after the first with that name.

Although there was a fair amount of activity in the Sussex breed during the 1930s and a number of people engaged in breeding, showing and

A group of Miss Wigg's pre-war Hornshill Sussex Spaniels. Hornshill Dickon, H. Meriel 80UU, H. Miranda 1648SS, H. Buckle 1676RR & H. George 1527UU. All born in the mid and late 1930s.

Miss Wigg revived her kennel of Sussex Spaniels in the 1950s, with Hornshill Celendine KCSB 582AM. Br: Mrs Freer. By Wendigo of Fourclovers ex Neenemoosha of Fourclovers. Wh: 1946.

Hornshill Duke KCSB 167AN. Wh: 1953. By Kenau of Fourclovers 95AH ex Hornshill Celendine 582AM.

Miss Wigg bred a very distinctive type of Sussex keeping very much to the standard. Duke has a very typical head, good proportions and bone, and is well coated.

exporting, almost none of these dogs or their descendants survived the 1939 – 45 war years. Only the Fourclovers remained to fly the flag. The dogs bred, owned and shown by Miss Scholefield in the 1930s are of supreme importance to those who breed Sussex Spaniels today. Though Okimat had quickly come to notice, his success did not take away from others in the kennel. Miss Scholefield was in the winner's enclosures with Winonah, who won three CCs in 1931; she also won with Winonah's sister, Wingenund. Huitzel of Fourclovers 1780KK, a daughter of The Sagamore and Langrish Bess who had been bred by Col. Talbot Ponsonby, won in 1932 and Winonah took the CCs at Crufts and Manchester. Osseo 1690PP, a son of Okimat and Pocahontas, won CCs at Manchester, Richmond and the SKC in 1934. He also qualified in the field at Northern and Midlands Spaniels Club's Trials, at the same time as Mr Blagg's Ch. Westmark Minnihaha. Osseo's sister, Ahmeek 64RR, who was to prove such a dominant brood, came out a year later accompanied by Sachem 2033QQ, a dog by Okimat and Talulah (Brosse x Primax Judy). This mating was repeated and accounted for Aisma 808TT and the dog Kwasind 359UU, both of whom were very successful in the rings. The dog Kago 2079UU and the bitch Megissogwon 357UU were respectively by Kwasind and Sachem and out of two sisters, Chicamin and Lilluar, who were by Okimat out of Langrish Bangle. All these accounted for a large share of the prizes at the time, and they are the dogs and bitches on which the modern pedigrees are based.

It is sad that after so much effort, so much breeding, and so much interest, only Miss Scholefield managed to keep the Sussex Spaniel lamp burning over the war years. Somewhere there were Sussex – Broadhurst Biddy is a case in point – but like her, no doubt, they were just kept as pets and died of old age.

10

Problems of Another Revival

The Second World War dealt harshly with the minority spaniel breeds, whose star had been on the wane even before hostilities broke out. Sussex, whose numbers and support had fluctuated ever since their revival in the 1870s, would no doubt have died out had it not been for the efforts of Joy Scholefield to keep the breed from extinction. After 1946 there were to be no rich country gentlemen with money, premises, interest and time to take over the breed, as had happened in the past, now it was up to the ordinary man to take an interest in the old breeds and get them back on the road. Strangely enough, although other breeds quickly collected a circle of admirers, the minority spaniels had an uphill struggle. At one time it was difficult to give away puppies, let alone sell them. At the beginning of the Second World War only Miss Wigg, apart from Miss Scholefield, kept up an interest in Sussex. Her last litter before she left the breed was born in 1940, but only one puppy was registered.

With Miss Scholefield (later Mrs Freer) the only person left who bothered about the breed during the war, it is well to take a look at her stock, which forms the base of all today's Sussex Spaniels. Only two Fourclovers litters were registered in 1938. One born on 25 March by Okimat out of Montana consisted of the dogs Adjidaumo, Chiviabos and Keego, and the bitches Oga, Onassia, Shaugodata and Uli. Some time later a transfer appears for Shaugodaya to a Miss J. Pruddah, but there is no further record of any of this litter. On 23 December 1938 a litter, also out of Montana and sired by Tamenund, consisted of the dogs Abenaki, Cheroke, Chipawyn and Shaubomin, and the bitches Sehis and Sequoia. Only the dog Chipawyn has any relevance, although Abenaki was transferred to a Mrs Harvey in April 1940.

Montana was bred by Miss Reed and by Earlswood Pete out of Goldilocks of Oakerland and was one of a litter whelped on 12 January 1937. Two of the litter went to Mrs Youell, the owner of the sire, and became Earlswood Dash and Dragoon; one was registered Oakerland Judy by her breeder; another, bought unregistered, was Fairway Joan, owned by Miss Brook.

Montana is not heard of again until 1943, when she is down as the dam of Kemsdale Brownie, a bitch by Tamenund. Brownie was born on 2 February 1943; there is no record of any other puppies in the litter. Kemsdale was the prefix of a Miss D.M. Neve; her name does not appear anywhere else in Sussex history except for Brownie and her daughter Kemsdale Silk, the latter in Mrs Freer's ownership. In the same year a litter of interbred spaniels were born that contained a dog called Sunny South. He was by Ch. Osseo of Fourclovers and out of the English Springer bitch Brownie. Sunny South was mated to the Sussex bitch Mildred of Oakerland, and produced Timothy of Oakerland who won considerably in trials for his breeder. A sister to Sunny South, an unregistered bitch called Jane owned by a Mr H. John, was mated to Kenau of Fourclovers 95AH and whelped a litter on 16 February 1954; one dog from this litter was registered by Miss Reed as Shon and was successful in trials.

In 1946 Neenemoosha, a bitch by Chipawyn out of Ahmeek, was put to Wendigo (Tamenund x Kago) and bred Mahngotay of Fourclovers; South Lopham Sammy, who went to Mrs Johnson of Diss who had been in the breed before the war; and two bitches, who went to form the base of Miss Wigg's new line and were registered Hornshill Celendine and Primrose. In February 1946 the bitch Hatorask was born to Wabun and

Mrs Joy Freer's important stud dog Pontiac of Fourclovers KCSB 94AH. Wh: 1948. By Wabun of Fourclovers ex Mahotgonay of Fourclovers.

101

Mrs Joy Freer in the garden of her Norfolk home with two of her famous Fourclovers Sussex Spaniels

Kago. Hatorask was a remarkable Sussex who whelped her first litter on 1 December 1946 when she was just 10 months old. This litter was by her sire Wabun, so presumably it was a stolen mating. It contained a dog, sold to Mrs Bower and registered Agrivista Helios, and a bitch, Menominee of Fourclovers. Hatorask whelped again in October 1947, this time to Wendigo. Wahana and Wawanaissa were born, the former joining Helios at Mrs Bower's kennels. In November 1948 Hatorask whelped her third litter, also by Wendigo. It contained the important Kenau 95AH. Hatorask had a further litter in 1949.

I first met Mrs Freer and Mrs Bower before the war, and after global hostilities ceased we renewed our friendship. As all three of us were showing minority spaniels, we were always benched together. I was fortunate in being able to see not only Helios, who won so well for Mrs Bower, but also the debut of the new Fourclovers star Pontiac 94AH, a son of Wabun and Mahngotay, who was whelped in May 1948. Mrs Freer was also showing Wabun, who had survived the war years and was then 10 years old, and the versatile Hatorask.

There was at this time no championship status for the Sussex Spaniels, the allocation of Challenge Certificates being linked to the registration figures. However the breed did get back CCs in 1950, four sets, but then lost them again until 1954. It has managed to hold on to an allocation ever since. In those days a system of registering 'paper puppies' was practised by most in minority breeds. This consisted of registering more puppies in a litter than were actually born, or registering a non-existent litter. With litter registrations at only £1 for the whole litter, this was financially possible for those anxious to raise the registration figures and get CCs back in a breed. There are to my knowledge many Field Spaniels as well as Sussex who appear as registered who in fact never saw the light of day! If one studies the large Sussex litters registered at certain times and then looks at the transfers, one will find that only a minority ever figure in the records again.

Mrs Freer produced a number of litters during the 1950s, and dogs and bitches from these form the base of today's Sussex. Montour arrived in May 1956 in a litter of four; the other three registered do not appear again. Mrs Freer wrote of Montour:

Montour I have always considered to be the best Sussex dog I have had since Okimat. It was he who brought back to the breed the long neck which up to then had virtually disappeared. In fact our supporters in America went so far as to say the Sussex had a shorter neck than other varieties, I hasten to point out that this is not so. The old scale of points insisted that the 'neck should be, long, strong and slightly arched', and this has never been altered. Montour had a wonderful neck, which has, I am glad to say, been handed down. He would probably have been used more if he had not had the misfortune of being undershot. His only other fault was that his coat was not as good being of a harsh texture. He was an excellent retriever and could be relied to pick up anything you asked him on land or water.

Although only used a few times at stud, Montour, because of the small number of Sussex around at the time, appears many times over in the pedigrees of today's dogs. That undoubtedly accounts for the many bad mouths in the breed over the last twenty years. The fault is very difficult to eradicate, and the problem is bravely tackled by today's breeders.

In June 1956 Mrs Freer bred a litter from Kemsdale Silk, the daughter of Kemsdale Brownie. Silk was mated to Pontiac, and only one from the litter of four is remembered; this is the bitch Muskoka. Two litters registered in 1957 did not produce anything known, nor did one in 1959. During the 1950s Mrs Freer was exhibiting a powerful string: Pontiac (who won a number of CCs), Kenabeek 1121AN (Pontiac x Kemsdale Silk), Menominee, Oolak 681AQ, Montour 158AR, Muskoka 159AR

Common ancestor to all the present day Sussex Spaniels, Mrs J. Freer's Montour of Fourclovers KCSB 158AR. Wh: 1956. By Sh.Ch. Kenabeek of Fourclovers ex Keeko of Fourclovers (by Pontiac of Fourclovers). Mrs Freer commented 'it was Montour who brought the long neck back to the breed.'

and Sonoma 595AR. Most of these won a proportion of CCs. One of the most important of the 1950s Fourclovers litters was that bred in 1958 of Montour to Cadillac (Nooneeds x Ungana), which produced the dog Hiawatha of Fourclovers, sold in 1961 to Miss Daphne Dodson and Miss B.J. Dyson of the Weiden prefix. Another of the litter was Framsden Rusty, who went to Mrs Johnson, owner of South Lopham Sammy. Rusty did rather better for Mrs Johnson that Sammy did, winning three CCs.

In the late 1950s and early 1960s Mrs Freer struck a bad breeding patch, being unable for several years to get any bitches in whelp. The Fourclovers, however, got going again with the purchase of a bitch bred by Mesdames Dobson and Dyson. They had the Fourclovers pair Hiawatha and Muskoka, bred them together, and from the union came Minnihaha of Fourclovers, who went to Mrs Freer – back to the source, as it were, as her parents were all-Fourclovers breeding. Minnihaha proved a valuable brood and her various matings produced, among others, Saba, Tanosay, Tinamou, Chesara Golden Glem and Uncas, all of whom appear in modern pedigrees, Uncas being particularly potent. During the 1970s Mrs Freer's breeding programme included a litter by Uncas and out of Petulama (Caribou x Tansay) and this produced

Sahoni, a double granddaughter to Minnihaha. She not only won her CCs in the ring but also qualified in the field, making her the first and, so far, only full champion bitch since the war. Another winning bitch was Okechobe 774BE, who gained her Stud Book number in 1970. In 1974 Okechobe was shown again and, winning at a championship show, was given yet another KCSB number, 2654BI, under a name spelt as Orchibe! No doubt the North American Indian name bemused the registration department of the Kennel Club as much as it will the historians of the breed. Huron 190BG (Mattawin x Paleface, an Uncas daughter) came out in 1971 and Tibeash 2982BG in 1972. Tibeash later became the property of Mr and Mrs Muirhead. There was also the bitch Sahoni, who was last campaigned by the Fourclovers expert.

After 1976 Mrs Freer continued her interest in the breed, but mainly as an elder statesman. She was always on hand to give help and advice, and to entertain with her wonderful tales of Sussex in past years. In 1984 she celebrated her sixty years in the breed, and it was planned to mark this milestone at the Sussex Spaniel Association's Diamond Jubilee celebrations that summer. Sadly Joy Freer died in the spring of that year, and with her died sixty years' knowledge of her breed. She was often urged to write a book, but in a letter to me, written just before she died, she said how pleased she was that I was contemplating writing a book on Sussex. She wrote, 'I was approached once to collaborate on a book but felt that the co-author and I would never agree, so I declined.' If only, we say now, she had committed all her knowledge to tape.

Mrs Bower, who had been such a successful breeder and exhibitor before the 1939 war, came back into the breed with the purchase of a dog puppy from Mrs Freer's 1946 litter from Wabun and Hatorask, and registered him Agrivista Helios. A little later she acquired Wanaha (Wendigo x Hatorask). When the first CCs were on offer in 1950, Mrs Bower won all four sets with these two, and also the reserve CC at Chester with Claxton Careless, a bitch bred by Mrs Freer and sister, later litter, to Pontiac. Helios was a consistent winner for some years, and notched up a good tally of CCs besides being a useful sire. Helios and Wanaha were mated together and in 1952 bred Agrivista Persephone 154AP. Mrs Bower purchased Bridget of Tarbay 293AM and mated her to Helios, breeding Agrivista Cassandra 134AQ; both of these bitches were successful in the rings. Mrs Bower also bought in and won with the dog Agrivista Havalldan, bred by P. Wicks and by Sh.Ch. Kenabeek of Fourclovers and out of Agrivista Aspasia, a sister to Cassandra. During the 1950s Helios had been used on Intruder Isobel, a bitch from an inter-bred litter going back to a Springer Spaniel through Agrivista Irene. This litter was registered under the Buxton prefix belonging to their breeders, Mrs Merridew and Miss E.C. Gregory, from Buxton in Derbyshire.

Buxton Trigger 596AR, Buxton Bounce 1064AQ and a sister, Buxton Belle, all feature in the KCSB; the dogs because of their wins at championship shows. Belle, mated to Kenabeek of Fourclovers, was the dam of Silkie of Oakerlands 2589AS who won for Miss Reed in Field Trials and was shown a couple of times; she was Miss Reed's only essay back into Sussex competition after the war. Mrs Freer used one of the Buxton dogs, but there is no record of any modern dog going back to this line.

Miss Wigg's Hornshill Kennels were revived in 1946 by the purchase of two bitch puppies from Mrs Freer's Wendigo x Neenemoosha litter, registered as Hornshill Celendine and Primrose. Later Miss Wigg acquired the dog Kenau of Fourclovers, a brother to Menominee, and this dog and Celendine won consistently through the early 1950s and even managed a few CCs when they were at last returned to the breed. Miss Wigg did not stay long in the breed, but her contribution to its continuance is considerable. She bred Celendine to Kenau in February 1951 and produced Hornshill Bandit, Bangle and Bracken, starting off two new owners in the breed when she sold Bracken and Bangle to Dr Rickards and Bandit to Mrs Manley Cooper. The mating was repeated in

Mrs Manley Cooper's Cissbury Storr of Mountgarvey. She bred one litter but died at 3 years from Hard Pad.

106

Mrs D.K.F. Peck's Penruddock Edita 166AN. Wh: 1950. Br. Miss M. Gardener. By Piah of Fourclovers ex Seneca of Fourclovers. Both Piah & Seneca were out of Hatorask. Note how Edita had thrown back in type to the early 1920s.

1953 and this time resulted in Hornshill Duke, who won three CCs for his breeder, and Hornshill Elizabeth, who won two CCs and also went to Dr Rickards.

Mrs Manley Cooper, who lived in Worthing, Sussex, soon established the Mountgarvey Sussex Spaniels; as she and I were both enthusiastic show-goers in the same area, many a needle match resulted between her Sussex and my Fields! As well as Hornshill Bandit, she acquired a puppy from Miss Gardener. Miss Gardener had purchased Seneca of Fourclovers (Wabun x Hatorask) and mated her to Piah of Fourclovers (Wendigo x Hatorask), the result being Cissbury Storr of Mountgarvey who became a show champion for Mrs Manley Cooper and mated to Hornshill Bandit produced Sh.Ch. Patchem of Mountgarvey and also Winston 22305NN, who was sold to Mrs Dixon. Mrs Manley Cooper acquired Kenabeek of Fourclovers and mated Patchem to him in 1958; the result was Sh.Ch. Bury of Mountgarvey. Mrs Manley Cooper served the Sussex Spaniel Association for fifteen years as treasurer, and was then invited to take the presidency. Although she had a number of well-known Sussex none survives in today's pedigrees.

Sh.Ch. Patchem of Mountgarvey KCSB 1350AM. Wh: 1953. By Hornshill Bandit 1008AM ex Cissbury Storr of Mountgarvey.

Sh.Ch. Patchem of Mountgarvey with Kenabeek of Fourclovers 1121AN. Wh: 1953. Br. Mrs Freer. By Pontiac of Fourclovers 94AH ex Kemsdale Silk.

Perhaps the most remarkable person to enter the breed was Dr Esther Rickards, who lived near Windsor. She had owned Cocker Spaniels since the late 1930s under the Tarbay prefix. Highly respected in the medical profession, she was attached to one of the London hospitals. She was also deeply interested in music and was an expert on the works of Mozart. As an organiser she knew no peer. She was the first chairman of the Mid Wessex Gundog Society, later the Windsor Gundog Society, and the instigator, organiser and first secretary of the Windsor Championship Show, an event which was very much her own creation and in which she played a leading role up to her death. I first met Dr Rickards when we were both living in London prior to the war and showing our first Cockers. She lived in a flat in Paddington and we lived in Maida Vale, so she in her little Austin Seven would call round and collect me and my dogs and off we would go to the many evening sanction shows held around London in those days. It did not surprise me to hear that Dr Rickards had decided to take up the Sussex cause; she loved a challenge and the breed at that time must have posed an enormous one. Mrs Freer, writing some years later, said, 'While I was stagnating due to infertile bitches Dr. Rickards came into the breed and really did get the registrations up.' Dr Rickards remained in the breed for twelve years, breeding something in the region of ten litters and registering around sixty puppies.

The Tarbay Sussex start with the purchase of Hornshill Bangle, Bracken, Meg and Elizabeth. The first litter, Bangle to Agrivista Helios, bred the dog Byrony of Tarbay; the next litter, Bangle to Pontiac, was responsible for Rosalind, who, after breeding a litter for her owner, went to Margaret Scarr and Mary Harris as a foundation bitch. Pontiac to Meg produced Maggie of Tarbay. Hornshill Elizabeth to Byrony was responsible for Sh.Ch. Bobbie of Tarbay 135AQ, who won his title before he was 2 years old, and when mated with Maggie bred Lorna. Bobbie to Rosalind failed to produce much, although a dog, Skipper, went to the Marquis de Moustier in France. Bobbie mated to Meg bred Gayle, an important bitch in our modern pedigrees. In 1958 Elizabeth, by now a show champion, went to Kenabeek of Fourclovers and bred the large 'K' litter: Kate was sold to Miss Patterson but was returned in 1961, Kitty went to Miss Wigg but also came back to her breeder, and Kingfisher was retained. Of this litter of twelve registered, only four have any history.

Dr Rickards's last litter, Meg to Kingfisher, arrived in March 1961. Wanda and Wise One were the only ones kept, and were later sold to the USA. In 1961 Dr Rickards purchased the important stud dog Penruddock Evelyn and quickly won his title; he too was shipped to America. Dr Rickards had carried out what she had set her mind on. She

CRUFTS 1956
Judge Frank Warner Hill with his Challenge Certificate winners, Mrs Manley Cooper with Sh.Ch. Patchem of Mountgarvey and Miss Wigg with Sh.Ch. Hornshill Duke.

had raised the level of registrations, and she had persuaded a number of people to take Sussex bitches and breed from them, thus widening interest and ensuring larger entries of better quality and enough registrations to keep Challenge Certificates. When Dr Rickards disbanded the Sussex Spaniels of Tarbay, Kate went to Miss Adams to found what was to become the very successful Sedora Kennels; Gayle went to Mr and Mrs Larry Elsden, who were already engaged in other breeds but had become interested in the Sussex breed and its survival; Lorna went to Miss Collings and Mrs Eysemount, and ultimately to Creswelshaw; and Sh.Ch. Kingfisher set off for the home of Mr A. Gaudream in America. The whole operation, concluded in just over a decade, had been highly successful and did much to ensure the continuance of the Sussex breed. Dr Rickards then turned her attention to the flagging fortunes of the Irish Water Spaniels; one of her first dogs became a show champion. Truly, she was a remarkable lady!

Mr & Mrs Elsden's Chesara Pride KCSB 452AX. Wh: 1963. By Sh.Ch. Penruddock Evelyn 1063AQ ex Gayle of Tarbay (Sh.Ch. Bobbie of Tarbay ex Hornshill Meg).

Mr & Mrs Elsden's Chesara Pride 252AX and Chesara Joy 251AX. Litter brother and sister whose mating forms the basis of today's lines.

Miss Daphne Dodson and Miss Dyson had been fortunate in being able to acquire Hiawatha 2535AU (Montour x Cadillac) and Muskoka 159AR from Mrs Freer. This partnership used the Weiden prefix, and their first two purchases were followed in 1962 by the bitch Janshi of Patmyn 922AV, who had been bred the previous year by Miss Collings and Mrs Eysemount who had mated Lorna of Tarbay to Hiawatha. Hiawatha was a tremendous success in the ring, and won his title in 1963 with three CCs on the trot under Joe Braddon, Mrs K. Doxford and Frank Warner Hill. Hiawatha x Muskoka produced Weiden Son of Hiawatha 1330AX and Weiden Dawn 2170AY. This partnership will be best remembered for undertaking the cross to the Clumber Spaniel which had long been a subject of discussion in the breed. Although Mrs Freer was against it, the decision to go ahead was taken on a majority vote, and the puppies born in 1964 were by a Clumber dog. These were five in number, and a dog from this litter, Weiden Bronze, was next mated to the Sussex bitch Weiden Dawn, producing a second generation. From this litter a bitch Weiden Daisy May was selected, and she was put to Weiden Alexander of Creswelshaw and bred the third generation, which included the dog Shataukok Spandax and his sister Looby Loo. The cross in the end did not appear to appeal to Sussex breeders, as only one availed themselves of its use, and the line looked likely to die out. However, later the line from Looby Loo was again picked up and it survives today through Mrs Gardner's Novacrofts.

Mrs Freer, returning to exhibiting and breeding about this time with Minnihaha – which she had acquired from the Dodson/Dyson partnership wrote, 'During my bad period I found the breed had shrunk in size and developed far too much coat. However now, [writing in 1974] we have five generations from Minnihaha and size has thankfully increased, and thank goodness we have more of the real sealskin coat. This is a great joy to me as I was always afraid we would lose it.'

Meanwhile Mr and Mrs Elsden, who had taken on Gayle of Tarbay, a bitch originally sold to a Mr Wildman and later returned to her breeder, mated her in 1963. Sh.Ch. Penruddock Evelyn was bred by Mrs Peck, who entered the breed with a sister of Sh.Ch. Cissbury Storr of Mountgarvey, which she registered as Penruddock Edita. Edita did her share of winning and won CCs under Miss Reed, Gwen Broadley, Pop Saunders and Mr A.A. Winfield of Fieldwin fame. She was mated to Kenau of Fourclovers, and Evelyn is the only one of note of this litter. After winning a small amount for his breeder he went to Dr Rickards who had no trouble in making him up. This was the dog chosen by the Elsdens for Gayle, and she bred them Chesara Pride 452AX and Chesara Joy 451AX. One year later in August 1969 the brother and sister produced a litter, Chesara Chervil 1579AY and Chesara Carroway 272AZ sold to Miss

Adams of Sedora, Chesara Joyful 868BD who went to Mrs Munday of the Sharland Gundogs in Sussex, Chesara Triumphant 1580AY, and several more.

Miss Adams came into Sussex with the acquisition of Kate of Tarbay 1578AY (Kenabeek x Hornshill Elizabeth), mating her purchase to Hiawatha. The puppies arrived on Christmas Day 1963 and were appropriately named Christmas Rose, Christmas Carol and Noel. With Chesara Chervil as her stud dog Miss Adams set about building a line. Carol was mated to Chervil in 1966; the result was very satisfactory, Sedora Comfrey 2910AZ, Chicory 2649AY and Chive. In August 1965 two Sedora litters were born. The first was on 10 August and contained amongst the seven registered Aniseed, sold to Mrs Munday and Althea, who went to the Elsdens; this bitch was from a brother to sister mating of Christmas Rose and Noel. The second litter, by Noel and out of Kate of Tarbay, was also seven; Broom going to Mr and Mrs Muirhead of Shipden. Chervil had by this time gained his title, while a litter by him born in 1966 accounted for Sedora Comfrey and Costmary 1736BA; both took their title. Sedora Chive mated to Weiden Alexander of Creswelshaw accounted for Sh.Ch. Sedora Dill 867BD, born in 1968. Miss Adams bought in Chesara Golden Gleam, who had been bred by Mrs Freer from the Chesara Pride x Minnihaha mating; a mating to Comfrey bred Sedora Evron, one of three Sedoras winning Challenge Certificates for the kennels in 1972. Chervil and Dill bred Galingale 985BG and Gherkin, and Evon and Chive produced Hyssop 771BH. The last litter in the KCSB from Sedora were Indian Maize 2252BJ, Indian Corn 347BJ and Ixia 350BJ, born of Evron and Dill in 1974.

The next influential kennel to be looked at are the Sunreefs, owned by Margaret Scarr and Mary Harris, already highly successful in the Cocker Spaniel rings. In the mid-1950s the partnership purchased the 3½-year-old bitch Rosalind of Tarbay from Dr Rickards. Unshown until then, Rosalind was soon brought into the rings in the sparkling condition for which the Sunreef Cockers were noted. She clocked up the remarkable tally of fifteen CCs at a time when only four sets were available in any one year. In those days the groups at Birmingham were judged in two parts, the sexes being separated, and Rosalind won the bitch section of the Gundog Group at the Centenary Show. Rosalind's litter to Sh.Ch. Bobbie of Tarbay produced the partnership's best and most successful Sussex, the bitch Sh.Ch. Sunreef Harvest Glow. Harvest Glow rejected the show ring utterly for the first two years of her life and then suddenly took to the idea in a big way, becoming a most extrovert show-woman and winning sixteen CCs, most of them with Best of Breed. She was placed fifth in the Gundog Group at Crufts at 9½ years of age and is one of the illustrious few of any breed who have won five consecutive BOBs

Foundation bitch for the Sunreef Sussex Spaniels owned by Miss M. Scarr and Miss M. Harris. Rosalind of Tarbay KCSB 1258AR. Wh: 1954. Br. Dr E. Rickards. By Pontiac of Fourclovers 94AH ex Hornshill Bangle 292AM.

Misses Scarr and Harris' Sh.Ch. Sunreef Harvest Glow KCSB 2454A. Wh: 1958. By Sh.Ch. Bobbie of Tarbay 135AQ ex Sh.Ch. Rosalind of Tarbay. Photographed on her 12th birthday.

at Crufts. Harvest Glow had the honour of being awarded a special trophy by the Sussex Spaniel Association for her services in publicising the breed and for achievements in variety classes where she was frequently best Not-Classified Gundog in Show, many times Best Gundog and a prodigious winner of veteran classes. Sadly, she left no issue; after an undiagnosed viral infection at the age of 9 months she was left with a heart condition and on veterinary advice was never bred from. She lived a long happy, healthy life, only needing the occasional heart pill, and died aged 13 years.

In 1967 the partnership bought in two bitches from Mrs Freer, Tinamou of Fourclovers 1735BA (Montour x Minnihaha) and Twigtree (Chesara Pride x Minnihaha). Tinamou proved a useful brood but was never shown much as she dropped her coat at awkward times and the ladies were sticklers for good presentation for the show ring. At 7 years of age and in full coat, Tinamou won the CC at Windsor and came good at 10 years to win a reserve CC under Violet Yates. Twigtree was not such a good-looking bitch as Tinamou, being rather higher in the leg; but she proved to be an excellent brood and mated to Sedora Noel produced Sunreef Rich Harvest, a dog of character who did his share as a stud to keep the Sussex lines going. He was only shown twice, at 9 months and 6 years, winning the reserve CC each time. He had the habit of talking under his breath and judges were apt to think he was growling and to

Mr & Mrs Elsden's litter from the brother and sister mating of Chesara Pride and Joy

Miss E.M. Adams' Sh.Ch. Chesara Chervil of Sedora 1579AY. Wh: 1964. Br. Mr J. Elsden. From the brother and sister mating of Chesara Pride and Chesara Joy.

penalise him accordingly. Much talk was bandied about his 'temperament' but Mary Harris describes him as 'a lovely boy, who loved everyone who came to the house, especially if they brought him a wife!' He lived to the grand old age of 14 years, and his descendants carry his outstanding quality and type. Unfortunately there is no photograph of this fine dog. Tinamou was mated to Rich Harvest and in February 1971 bred the litter which contained the brother and sister Sunreef Harvest Honey and Harvest Brew. They were both sold to Rosemary Paull, the first wife of Air Commodore Chris Paull of Alresford in Hampshire; Mrs Paull had great success with them and made each a show champion. It was sad that in the 1970s Margaret Scarr suffered two minor strokes and a bad heart attack, which necessitated the ladies giving up their kennel and reducing the number of their dogs to a few house pets. Miss Harris regrets that during this traumatic period many valuable Sussex papers and references were destroyed. Both ladies have continued with their interest in the breed, attending any functions possible. Miss Harris has judged the breed over the years while Margaret Scarr is the president of the Sussex Spaniel Association.

11

Taking the Breed Forward

The continuance of any breed, particularly a minority breed, is only ensured by people becoming interested in it as a breed and not just for what they can win with whatever specimen they have purchased. All breeds are beset with those who take them up, take what they can get (or alternatively fail to get anything), give nothing and leave. Breeds also attract people with a genuine interest and the right ideas; but who come in too late in life, have monetary or family problems, illness or other misfortunes, or the wrong environment for the breed, and have to leave before their full potential for the breed's good has been realised. The Sussex have been fortunate that in every decade there have been one or two who have stayed the course for ten or more years and left their mark; notably there was Mrs Freer, who provided a link over six decades and devoted her life to breeding the Sussex Spaniel for posterity.

Early Creswelshaws. Mrs Mavis Lancaster & Mrs Brookes' Lorna of Tarbay 2843AW, Tamsin Tess 1516BA, Briar of Creswelshaw 308BA.

118

Teal of Creswelshaw. By Uncas of Fourclovers ex Weiden Alexandra of Creswelshaw.

Continuity of interest is the greatest gift anyone can bestow on their breed. Perhaps in 1963 when Mavis Clarke and her sister Mrs Brooks acquired their first Sussex Spaniel, a 6-year-old bitch, Lorna of Tarbay, they had no idea how this interest and the continued survival of the breed would take them over! A quarter of a century later, Mavis Lancaster (as she became), is still working hard for Sussex Spaniels, not only as a breeder and exhibitor (she cannot be persuaded to judge), but also as secretary of the Sussex Spaniel Association and never-tiring public relations officer. Lorna of Tarbay was bred by Dr Rickards, who sold her to Mrs Eysemount and Miss Collings from whom she was acquired. She was a granddaughter of Pontiac on her mother's side and a great-granddaughter of Helios on her sire's side. The breeding could not be more right for a foundation bitch, so it must have been disappointing that her mating to Sh.Ch. Hiawatha of Fourclovers produced only one puppy, a bitch, who was registered Tasmin Tess; however, she went on to found a dynasty.

The partners made their debut in the rings in 1963 and Lorna acquired her Stud Book number 2843AW. In July 1965 Tess whelped a litter to Sedora Noel, the first under the Creswelshaw prefix; these were Annette, Anthea, Alexandra, Alexander, Adrian and Alexis, the last named being sold in the USA. In Stud Books of later years, it should be noted, Alexandra is credited with a Stud Book number which is in fact her brother's; Alexandra herself did not gain a number. This mating was repeated the following year and produced the 'B' litter, of which Briar went into the Stud Book. Alexandra, from the first litter, was then bred to Uncas of Fourclovers – a Montour son – and this accounted for one of the most dominant dogs in today's pedigrees, Teal of Creswelshaw. He is behind all the modern lines and his pedigree reveals that every line bar one goes back to the source through Pontiac of Fourclovers; the exception traces to Pontiac's sire, Wabun of Fourclovers. This salutory thought will perhaps make newcomers to the breeding of Sussex Spaniels pause and remember what frail material they are dealing with. Before commencing breeding operations they should take especial care to find out which combinations of the blood lines are producing the soundest and most typical stock.

Sh.Ch. Discreet of Creswelshaw KCSB 2129BE. Wh: 1968. By Sh.Ch. Sedora Comfrey 2910AZ ex Tamsin Tess 1516BA.

Mr George Lancaster's Sh.Ch. Oakmoss Ruff 434BK. Wh: 1974. By Teal of Creswelshaw ex Oakmoss Meg.

In 1968 Tess was mated to Sh.Ch. Sedora Comfrey 2910AZ and this resulted in the sisters' first show champion, Discreet of Creswelshaw. Discreet was mated to a dog descended from the Clumber cross, Shatautok Spandax. It was an interesting experiment, but the line ends with the bitch Echo of Creswelshaw, his daughter, who was mated to Sunreef Rich Harvest. Their dog puppy, Florin, was the first in the breed at Mrs Dorothy Gardner's Novacroft Kennels, already well established in Labradors. Florin won a bit for his new owner, but as his mouth was not his fortune he was given away as a pet and spent a long life as a country companion.

Mavis Clarke had by now become Mrs George Lancaster. Her husband was also interested in dogs, but mainly in the working side, being a keen shot and trainer. George joined his wife in her interest in the Sussex breed, and was encouraged to start his own line under the Oakmoss prefix when Mrs Freer gave him the bitch Saba of Fourclovers. Saba was a wonderful present for anyone seeking to start in Sussex. By Montour and out of Minnihaha, she was mated to Teal of Creswelshaw and bred Oakmoss Spice 1478BG and Oakmoss Meg. The latter, when mated to her sire, produced one of the most successful studs of the period, Sh.Ch. Oakmoss Ruff, as well as Avocet 3158BJ, Lapwing 1004BJ and Curlew 1593BH. Discreet attained her title and was also mated to Teal; this union produced the second show champion for the sisters in Creswelshaw Gemini Girl. In 1976 Discreet was mated to Ruff and this produced the important brood bitch Hannah, and also one of the truly great dogs in the breed, Creswelshaw Hannibal, whose show career was one long, triumphal progress. He was made up by 18 months of age, and went on to hold the breed record for the number of CCs won by a male Sussex. Old-timers in gundogs likened him to Okimat, and indeed he does greatly resemble this legendary dog. Hannibal, for some reason unknown, was not as sought after by breeders as one would have expected. The excellent stock he left from the bitches who visited him point to the inability of those connected with the breed at the time to appreciate that here was a dog who could improve the breed, in looks, coat colour and texture, size and temperament. Unfortunately Hannibal did not live long enough to have a vogue in old age, as some studs in minority breeds do once the tardy ones connected with the breed realise what they are missing.

Hannah was mated in 1977 to Sh.Ch. Elmbury Pevensey Hero, a dog bred from the only litter out of Oakmoss Meg's sister, Oakmoss Spice, when she was mated by her owner, Mr R. Hall Jones of Malvern, to Sunreef Rich Harvest. As one would expect from such breeding, the litter were very successful and included two title-holders. The Hero x Hannah mating accounted for three notable Creswelshaws: Idris, Isobelle and Isadora. Idris went to Mr Chris Bexon, who took the Oldfield prefix. Always shown in excellent order, Idris became a consistent winner, gained his title and was a useful stud. Isobelle went to Mr and Mrs Ifor Williams to found their Bryntonian Stud, and had the distinction of producing Sh.Ch. Bryntonian Aelwyn who made breed history when he won the Gundog Group at Crufts in 1984 under Mary Roslin Williams. Isadora went to Mr and Miss Fox, for whom she became a title-holder. She bred a litter to Sh.Ch. Quintic Joby; two of the puppies returned to Isadora's first home, for Nordahl Sea Otter of Oakmoss went to George Lancaster and Sh.Ch. Lorna of Creswelshaw went to his wife and her sister, Mrs Brooks. Hannah bred one more litter before going to Mr and Mrs Dalebo, and then mated to Sea Otter. Mrs Lancaster put Lorna to Aelwyn and bred Melanie, dam of the current big winner in the breed, Mrs Bailey's Sh.Ch. Creswelshaw Oriel of Daleyb, as well as of Sh.Ch. Creswelshaw Olwen and Orator.

It was in the mid-1960s that Mrs Joyce Munday became interested in Sussex Spaniels. Living in the county of Sussex, she decided to add its native breed to the gundogs with which she had been successful. Although only a few litters were produced over the next twelve years

Sh.Ch. Oakmoss Ruff, Sh.Ch. Discreet of Creswelshaw, Creswelshaw Hannah 2002BM, Sh.Ch. Creswelshaw Gemini Girl 1003BJ and Sh.Ch. Creswelshaw Hannibal

Sh.Ch. Creswelshaw Hannibal 1140BL. Wh: 1976. By Sh.Ch. Oakmoss Ruff ex Sh.Ch. Discreet of Creswelshaw. Thought by many to be the best Sussex Spaniel since Okimat.

Sh.Ch. Nordahl Sea Otter of Oakmoss KCSB 1503BQ. Wh: 1980. Brs. Mr & Mrs Dalebo. By Sh.Ch. Quintic Joby ex Creswelshaw Hannah 2002BM. (Sh.Ch. Oakmoss Ruff x Sh.Ch. Discreet of Creswelshaw.)

It can be seen that by selective breeding and choice of stock to breed from and show, how the Creswelshaws and Oakmoss have standardised a good type over several generations.

bearing her Sharland prefix, they had been most carefully thought out and stock from these lines figure very prominently in the modern lines. Mrs Munday bought in Chesara Joyful 868BD (Chesara Pride x Joy) and Sedora Aniseed (Sedora Noel and Christmas Rose); both bitches were the products of brother to sister matings. Later Mrs Munday purchased the dog Kilcoram Andross and his sister Adelma from their breeder, Mr G.P. Avis, who owned Golden Gleam of Sedora and had mated her to Sedora Chervil. Sharland Sussex Keg 1316BD, Sussex Mild 111BE and Sussex Mead were from a litter bred in October 1967 by Chesara Chervil and out of Aniseed; all three won CCs and Keg was made up by the time he was 2 years of age. Sussex Mead was sold to Miss J. Harvey, who added the prefix Treherne. She later sold Mead to Mrs Ann Findlay of Oldholbans. Sharland Sussex Mayqueen 721BH, who did a great deal of top winning for her breeder, was born in 1970 by Mattawin of Fourclovers 449BD out of Kilcoram Adelma, while her brother Sharland Sussex Mayday became an important sire. It was the litter born on 2 September 1972 that was to have the most far-reaching effect. Sussex Mead was mated to Sh.Ch. Sunreef Harvest Brew and bred the bitch Sharland Sussex Wine who was sold as a puppy to Mrs Eileen Moore of Dorset as a foundation bitch. Perhaps this bitch more than any other in the last twenty years has had the most effect on the breed. I have personal memories of Sussex Wine's show ring debut at the age of 6 months. I was judging at an open show in Romsey when into the ring came this Sussex pup, tail wagging and looking immensely pleased with herself. I thought 'here's a promising babe', and so she was; unfortunately, she knew it and as soon as anyone spoke to her she immediately rolled on her back and waved her legs in the air! This stance she adopted for the judge, which

Mrs Moore's Sh.Ch. Sharland Sussex Wine appeared on the BBC Children's Tele-vision programme Blue Peter. Seen here with her litter of seven bitches with the sire Sharland Sussex Mayday in background. Shown with presenters Peter Purves and John Noakes. 1975.

Mrs Moore's Sh.Ch. Sharland Sussex Wine 3087BH. Wh: 1972. Br. Mrs J. Munday. By Sh.Ch. Sunreef Harvest Brew 453BG ex Treherne Sharland Sussex Mead 48BF.

Typical Sunreef Sussex litter, good heads, well grown with good bones. Centre: Sunreef Harvest Brew.

126

caused great merriment, and I think everyone round the ring fell in love with her. I well remember telling the embarrassed Eileen not to worry; once she had got her puppy to remain upright she would do well. Sussex Wine certainly learned how to stand on her feet as the months went by. She did a great deal of winning and gained her title, but it was as a brood bitch that she was to be so successful.

No doubt much thought was given about her first mate, and eventually Sharland Sussex Mayday, the son of Mattawin of Fourclovers and Kilcoram Adelma, was chosen. It is interesting how throughout Sussex history a dog or a bitch from a litter bred by someone with just one Sussex, who probably takes little interest in the breed for any length of time, proves dominant. This possibly comes about because the few breeders of the time were so anxious to bring more people into the breed that they sold useful puppies from well-thought-out breeding plans as foundation bitches. Although in many cases these bitches did found kennels, all too many bred the one litter and then both dog and owner faded from the Sussex scene. Such was the case of Golden Gleam of Chesara, a valuable Minnihaha daughter who went to Mr G.P. Avis. Mated to Sh.Ch. Chesara Chervil of Sedora she bred the pair Kilcoram Andross, a dog, and Kilcoram Adelma, a bitch. Both were purchased by Mrs Munday and therefore were saved to serve the breed, Andross proving a useful stud. Adelma, as the dam of Mayday, more than proved her worth, and her daughters were also successful. This Sharland Sussex Mayday x Sharland Sussex Wine litter was born on 2 September 1975 and contained seven bitches, all of whom survived. The breeding record of Sussex since the Second World War had not been easy: too many lost litters, too many bitches failed to breed, there were too many male offspring – these were just some of the bugbears that had beset the faithful.

The seven bitches caused quite a stir, and news of their arrival reached the media. Sussex Wine and her daughters were featured on the children's television programme *Blue Peter* as one of Britain's rarer breeds. The family looked enchanting and must have won a lot of hearts. Media exposure has caused vast problems of over-breeding to supply instant demand in some breeds, but this could not happen in Sussex Spaniels as there have never been enough to go round. The nine days' wonder was soon over, and the Sussex folk settled back to await developments. The best of these puppies were wisely settled, and their impact on the breed has been far reaching. An inspection of their pedigree is interesting. The closeness of the breeding cannot be denied with Chesara Chervil, from the brother/sister mating of Pride and Joy, featuring as a grandfather on one side and a great-grandfather on the other; and Sedora Aniseed, from another brother/sister mating, is grandmother of the dam's side. In five generations you therefore have

Hiawatha appearing five times and Penruddock Evelyn six times, not leaving a great deal of room for any other males! However, the mixture worked admirably. The bitches, under Mrs Moore's Penygader prefix, went to their new homes: Penygader Esther to Ifor Williams, Penygader Hannah to Faith Gilham, Penygader Psalm 693BL to Mrs D.M. Norman; and Penygader Naomi to Mr and Mrs Bishop. Mr and Mrs Bishop mated her to Tibeash of Fourclovers and bred the dog Senator of Shipden; and when mated to Shipden Impressario she bred Comely Humphrey, a good dual-purpose dog of the 1980s. On 6 July 1976, Sussex Wine gave birth to her second litter, this time to Sh.Ch. Oakmoss Ruff, which resulted in Penygader Song of Solomon 691BL and Penygader Dorcas, who went as a foundation bitch to Mr and Mrs Perkins – already well known for their Quintic Bulldogs. In the litter there was also the dog Penygader Exodus, who sired Corraline Pippin 0075BR and Oldholbans Flash Again. Penygader Priscilla was another of the litter; bought by Mr and Mrs Learmouth, she bred the CC winner Troilvea Golden Magus when mated to Invermay Atholl Brose. Sussex Wine was next mated to Sh.Ch. Creswelshaw Hannibal, and her daughter Jehosheba went to Faith Gilham.

Mrs Gilham's choice of foundation bitches when she decided to add Sussex to her already successful Clumber Kennels was wise. Penygader Hannah of Topjoys was quickly off the mark in the show ring and won considerably, including her title. Bred to Sh.Ch. Oakmoss Ruff in 1977 she produced one of the big winners and great characters in the breed, Sh.Ch. Topjoys Sussex Harvester, and also Topjoys Sara Sussex. In 1978 Hannah went to Sh.Ch. Creswelshaw Hannibal and this alliance produced one of the all-time big winners in Sussex, the bitch Sh.Ch. Topjoys Sussex Nutmeg, who holds the record for a bitch of the breed, nineteen CCs. Nutmeg has also won Best in Show at open shows, been pulled out in the group at championship shows, and endeared herself to everyone who has met her by her charming personality. In 1981 Hannah visited Sh.Ch. Quintic Joby and this resulted in Mrs D. Bailey's Sh.Ch. Topjoys Bisto Brown and Sh.Ch. Topjoys Hovis Brown, winning in Sweden. Mrs Gilham's purchase of Jehosheba was successful both in the rings and in the breeding kennel. Once her title was secured, Jehosheba was mated to Shipden Fleche, a Tibeash son owned by Mr Chris Wakefield, and possibly the unluckiest dog as he never got his title; the resulting litter accounted for Sh.Ch. Topjoys Charlie Brown of Thixendale and Topjoys Brazen Raisin. Jehosheba's mating to Joby produced Topjoys Harvest Moon and Topjoys Sussex Enchancia; the latter was the dam of Topjoys Last Chance, who was exported to New Zealand where she has won twenty-two certificates. Sh.Ch. Topjoys Sussex Nutmeg 0880BP has found time amongst her many show engagements to

Mrs Ann Findlay's Oldholbans Sussex Spaniels situated a mile from the original Rosehill of Mr A.E. Fuller. Fourclovers Shiki, Oldholbans Flashlight 2809BK, Sh.Ch. Oldholbans Flashpoint, Oldholbans Rowena.

Sh.Ch. Oldholbans Flashpoint 2900BK. Wh: 1975. By Fourclovers Shiki 1478BJ ex Oldholbans Rowena.

breed two litters. In 1982, to Aelwyn, she produced Topjoys Sweet Chestnut. The next litter to Joby resulted in Frank Bacon's very typical and good-looking Sh.Ch. Topjoys Sussex Passtime, a dog of great character and style, who, given time and a bit of luck, may become a cornerstone of future generations. Mr Bacon also owns Passtime's sister, Topjoys Paws For Thought, while Mr J. Goodwin purchased Topjoys Sussex Mist, from whom he bred his show champion dog Serendel Crusader.

Mr and Mrs Perkins confess that Penygader Dorcas grew up with the Bulldogs, and although they had had working spaniels in the past Dorcas was not trained for work. She was shown briefly and won a reserve CC, and was then mated to Ann Findlay's Oldholbans Flashlight and produced a litter of nine. From the start, Mrs Perkins says, one dog stood out. He was registered Quintic Joby and was kept by his breeders, together with his sister Clover for company. Joby's debut in the rings was highly successful: he won his first CC at WELKS at the age of 18 months and was made up the same year. In spite of coming out when Creswelshaw Hannibal was at the peak of his career, the precocious young man from Quintic gave a good account of himself, strolling round the ring in his own inimitable fashion and determined to do things his way. He won six CCs and was BOB at Crufts in 1980, but it is as a sire that he has had most success. To date he has sired fourteen British CC winners and several overseas champions. His sister Clover mated to Creswelshaw Jupiter bred Sh.Ch. Quintic Fern, while another purchase, Corraline Pippin, mated to Joby bred the CC winner Quintic Cowslip. Cowslip was bred to Serendel D'arcy and bred Pedlarmans Bill Bosham of Quintic which to date has two CCs. Fern's first litter produced Mr and Mrs Wakefield's successful Quintic Hartley of Norriss, and also Hascall, who won at the World Show in Tel Aviv. Today's pedigrees are already showing the influence of Joby on the present-day Sussex, and no doubt he has to thank his dam for much of that influence.

Mrs Ann Findlay, who lives at Dallington in Sussex − hardly a stone's throw from the historic Rose Hill residence of Mr A.E. Fuller, now bearing its former name of Brightling Park − came into the breed with the purchase of Treharne Sussex Mead, who gained her title and in January 1972 whelped four bitches to Sharland Kilcoram Andress. One of these bitches made a little piece of history when she went to Mrs Rosemary Grizzell, the present owner of Brightling Park. Another of this litter, Brunnehilde, was sold to Sweden, while another went to Mrs Frances Stanely who exported her to the USA. Mrs Findlay purchased Treherne Taffamai from her breeder, Mrs Harvey; she was a daughter of Uncas of Fourclovers and was mated to her father. She died whelping after a Caesarian section when eleven live puppies were brought out. Mrs

Mrs Ann Findlay's Sh.Ch. Lesannlea Paperchase 4301BU. Wh: 1984. By Oldholbans Walnut 2204BT ex Oldholbans Saintly Sorrel at Adurni.

Oldholbans Sussex in their natural setting
Photo: Robert Smith

Findlay acquired the dog Fourclovers Shiki from Mrs Freer; Rowena was put to him and their union produced Flashlight (two CCs) and Flashpoint 2900BK. Although mated a second time, Rowena unfortunately died in whelp after eating infected sheep. Flashpoint was mated to Penygader Exodus and bred Oldholbans Fashion, who went as a foundation bitch to Mrs Betty Purkis. Mated to Joby she produced the beautifully coated and coloured bitch Sh.Ch. Chisham Touch of Gold. A number of useful winners have emerged from Oldholbans over the years, the latest being Sh.Ch. Oldholbans Lessanlea Paper Chase, a son of Oldholbans Walnut.

Mr & Mrs Colin Muirhead's Ch. Shipden Ambassador KCSB 1813BG. Wh: 1971 by Uncas of Fourclovers ex Sedora Broom. The only full male champion Sussex since 1938. Mr & Mrs Muirhead specialise in the dual purpose spaniel.

Mr & Mrs Bishop's Comely Humphrey KCSB 1498BV. Wh: 1981. By Shipden Impresario (a son of Ch. Shipden Ambassador) ex Penygader Naomi. A new generation of dual purpose Sussex. A winner on the bench and at Working tests. A steady worker on land and in water, and a tender retriever.

Mr and Mrs Colin Muirhead were drawn into the breed in the late 1960s by an article written by Frank Warner Hill in which he appealed for people to become interested in the Sussex Spaniel and to take an active part in breeding to secure its continuance. Their purchase of Sedora Broom from Miss Adams in 1965 was a direct result of reading the article and talking to the few then interested in the breed. Sussex bitches have had breeding problems over the years, and Broom was no exception. It was not until she was 5½ years old that she finally whelped a litter, and then five of the eight puppies died. The only bitch saved died at 4 months of obstructive jaundice; and one dog was sold and tragically killed when a car ran out of control and crashed into the field where he was playing. This left Shipden Ambasssador as the sole survivor, but he more than made up for the tragic end of his litter mates by becoming the first full champion dog since the Second World War, and one of only two

Mr & Miss S. Leslie's Sh.Ch. Shipden Finial KCSB 0732BQ. Wh: 1977. By Sh.Ch. Tibeash of Fourclovers 2982 BG ex Shipden Countess 372BM.

Mr & Mrs C. Wakefield's 'Norris' Sussex Spaniels. Foreground: Shipden Fleche 2072BM, full brother to Finial. Next to him: Topjoys Sara Sussex 5385BR. By Sh.Ch. Oakmoss Ruff ex Sh.Ch. Pengader Hannah of Topjoys. With their offspring: Norris Bo Duke, Norris Boogie Baby and Norris Boss Hogg.

134

full champions for the breed in that period. Needing a bitch to mate to Ambassador, the Muirheads purchased Elmbury Pevensey Belle, a sister to Hero, and the pair bred Shipden Conquistador 692BL. Belle, mated to Tibeash of Fourclovers who with Maco had been acquired from Mrs Freer, produced Shipden Ella the dam of Shipden Fleche. Tibeash was the result of a misalliance between Sahoni and her sire Uncas; he was 4½ when he went to Shipden for which he won four CCs and started a stud career quite late in life, siring two show champions and several CC winners. Maco was the product of two champions, Ambassador and Sahoni of Fourclovers, and his daughter Shipden Harnser went to Mrs and Miss Leslie of the Risdene spaniels who already had had great success with the Tibeash son, Sh.Ch. Shipden Finial. Harnser was mated to Tibeash and bred Sh.Ch. Risden Albatross of Shipden, who accompanied the Muirhead's daughter Kate to Australia after her marriage. Albatross created a great deal of interest in his new home, won his Australian title and is a group winner. He has recently been joined by a Maco granddaughter, Shipden Minnie the Moocher. Senator of Shipden has done well; he is also by Tibeash and was acquired from his breeders by Mr and Mrs Bishop. All the Muirhead family are dedicated to training their dogs for work with the gun, so here the Sussex have a fine chance of fulfilling their early destiny.

Mrs D. Gardner's Novacroft Thyme. Wh: 1986. By Sh.Ch. Topjoys Sussex Passtime ex Novacroft Herself.

Mrs D. Gardner's Sh.Ch. Novacroft Hello Holly 2001BM. Wh: 1977. By Sh.Ch. Creswelshaw Hannibal ex Novacroft Wisteria of Whitegrounds and Sh.Ch. Novacroft Esther 882BP. Wh: 1978. By Sh.Ch. Elmbury Pevensey Hero 34BI ex Novacroft Wisteria of Whitegrounds.
Mrs Gardner's Novacroft line is the only direct line to the Clumber cross of the 1950s through Wisteria. Careful breeding and selection of puppies has eliminated any trace of Clumber characteristics.

Dorothy Gardner became interested in Sussex Spaniels when she met the Lancasters at a show. She took possession of Creswelshaw Florin who was shown briefly, attaining his Stud Book number, and then retired to a nice country home as his mouth was not his fortune. A bitch, Creswelshaw Pochard, was the next purchase, but misfortune struck when she died suddenly of a heart attack after being mated. It was in 1976 that Mrs Gardner received a telephone call from Mrs June Moxon about a Sussex bitch whose owner had died. Mrs Moxon, in an endeavour to place the bitch at short notice so that she should not be put down, contacted Mrs Gardner. However, before she could be collected, a telephone call to Mrs Moxon advised her that a Will had been found, and that the bitch had been left to the deceased owner's son. Twelve months later, the son, who was a gamekeeper, rang Mrs Gardner and said the bitch was 'too lazy for him' and if she liked she could have her. It seemed as if fate had stepped in to ensure that the Novacroft Kennels came into Sussex! Sherry arrived in a shorn condition, but a glance at her good shape and perfect mouth raised her new owner's spirits. Novacroft Wisteria of the Whitegrounds, to give her her correct title, proved to be a daughter of the third generation from the outcross to the Clumber, Shataukok Looby Loo, and it is this Novacroft line that goes back to the much discussed outcross of the 1950s. Sherry was mated to Sh.Ch. Creswelshaw Hannibal, being his first bitch, when she was turned 5 years of age. She produced eleven puppies, of which four dogs and one bitch were reared successfully, the bitch becoming Sh.Ch. Novacroft Hello Holly. Sherry bred two further litters, one to Sh.Ch. Elmbury Pevensey Hero (Sunreef Rich Harvest x Oakmoss Spice) which resulted in Sh.Ch. Novacroft Esther, while the litter by Fourclovers Maco (Ch. Shipden Ambassador x Ch. Sahoni of Fourclovers) bred Novacroft Major. Hello Holly mated to Sh.Ch. Quintic Joby produced two show champions, Novacroft Jason and Novacroft June from Upend. A second mating, this time to Major, bred Novacroft Herself who went to Shipden Fleche to produce Sh.Ch. Novacroft Fleck, the current star of the kennel. Holly was bred to Sh.Ch. Topjoys Sussex Harvester and accounted for another big winner for the kennel, Novacroft Thyme. The Novacrofts have been bred with care, along lines well thought out by someone who for many years has been breeding a good line of Labradors. Each generation of the Novacroft Sussex produces specimens just that bit better than the succeeding generation, which is what breeding is all about. For those who condemned outright the Clumber cross the success of the Novacrofts is a salutory lesson. However, it must be said, if Wisteria had ended up in less experienced hands her descendants might not have turned out the way they have.

Some small attempt has been made to illuminate the lines up to the present-day dogs, and the author has endeavoured to show how the breeding of certain lines together produces the established type. One of the most interesting bitches out today is Mr Bexon's Sh.Ch. Harvest Glow of Oldfield, who was bred by Mr and Miss Fox from their bitch Scotshill Felicity Brown when mated to her uncle Sh.Ch. Creswelshaw Idris. Close breeding has always taken place in the breed, mostly owing to the fact that there just are no outcross lines, and Harvest Glow is a case where this has proved highly successful in producing a bitch of very high standard. Harvest Glow came out as a puppy and from that moment has not stopped winning, taking the eye of specialist and all-rounder alike for her overall balance, breed type, coat, colour and good movement. Add to this the fact that she is always put down in the immaculate condition seen

Mr & Mrs Perkin's Sh.Ch. Quintic Joby 672BN. Wh: 1977. By Oldholbans Flashlight 2899BK, exPenygader Dorcas 1592BL. A very dominant sire.

Mr & Mrs Ifor Williams' Sh.Ch. Bryntonian Aelwyn 0074BR. Wh: 1980. By Sh.Ch. Oakmoss Ruff ex Creswelshaw Isobelle 0575BP. Winner of the Gundog Group at Crufts 1984.

some years ago in the Sunreefs and you have a combination hard to beat. It will be of great interest to see what she produces. Harvest Glow is an interesting mix of the best of the Oakmoss, Creswelshaw and Sharland lines.

Mrs Bailey's Creswelshaw Oriel of Daleyb is another lovely bitch whose career has also been meteoric and whose breeding should ensure that she produces true to type. But there is no full assurance in Sussex Spaniels. Mr and Mrs Perkins made a wise choice when they acquired Penygader Dorcas 1592BL as their foundation bitch. They decided on a different combination of the lines, using Ann Findlay's Oldholbans Flashlight, a Shiki son, on their first bitch. The experiment paid off handsomely and Sh.Ch. Quintic Joby is more than proving his worth as a sire. He quickly made his mark in the ring, and won so well that he was up in senior classes while still a youngster. He had to wait in line behind the great Hannibal before stepping into the spotlight. Another dog who has proved useful is Inveray Atholl Brose 673BN. He was bred by Mr and Mrs Gilmour, and was by Sh.Ch. Oakmoss Ruff out of Sh.Ch. Pitchill Pansy of Inveray, a very well-bred bitch, being by Sharland Sussex Mayday and out of Sharland Sussex Cyder 1977BI – a bitch from

Mrs D. Bailey's Quintic Cloverleaf of Daelyb 1243BU, Sh.Ch. Creswelshaw Oriel of Daelyb, Sh.Ch. Topjoys Bisto Brown and Topjoys the Brazen Raisin.

Mrs D. Bailey's Sh.Ch. Creswelshaw Oriel of Daelyb. Wh: 1984. Br. Mrs Lancaster & Mrs Brooks. By Sh.Ch. Nordahl Sea Otter of Oakmoss 1503BQ ex Creswelshaw Melanie 0214BT and Sh.Ch. Topjoys Bisto Brown.

the first mating of Sunreef Harvest Brew and Sussex Mead and so a sister (earlier litter) to Sussex Wine. Pansy was bred by Mrs C. Spooner and sold to the Gilmours, who campaigned her to Mrs Spooner before breeding a litter.

Although a clearer pattern seems to be emerging when one studies pedigrees as to the type of Sussex one will get when certain combinations of lines are put together there is no guarantee that any litter will turn out as expected. Mrs Freer wrote in a letter to me in the early 1980s that, 'the breed was still very mixed in type, and still various shapes were being produced with some too tall on the leg and some too short, but with their history one must continue to expect that, and only bring the good specimens forward.' There are, fortunately, in the mid-1980s a small core of people dedicated to the Sussex Spaniel, and the breed is lucky to have such as George and Mavis Lancaster and Mrs Brookes with their long association with it and with its ups and downs. There are also Colin and Carolyn Muirhead, who had close contact with Mrs Freer and therefore were able to learn much of the breed from her; they have the working qualities of the breed at heart. Others who serve the breed well are Faith Gilham, with her good grasp of blood lines and determination to produce the very best in the breed; Dot Gardner, whose line improves with every generation; and Ann Findlay, with several generations of winners to her credit. It is heartening to see the enthusiasm amongst those who are only a few years in Sussex for the breed and its future, and it seems that the Sussex Spaniel, given average chance, will still be around for future generations of fanciers.

12

Deductions

That the Sussex Spaniel is mainly a creation of the 1870s cannot be denied if the reader truly studies the pedigrees of the time. Little, if any, of the blood of Mr A.E. Fuller's spaniels bred at Rose Hill in Sussex was left, and even if some were used, what sort of spaniels were there? Apart from the drawing of George and Romp in Stonehenge's book of 1859, there are few other illustrations of the breed. That artist's impressions can hardly be taken as fact; all artists at that time relied on the patronage of the wealthy, and they depicted the animals as the owners desired them to look and not as they actually were. To make this point clear, take the Tredegar painting, said to be of Sussex Spaniels, which hangs in one of the hallways of Tredegar House outside Newport. This depicts a gamekeeper surrounded by fourteen liver spaniels. By kind permission of the administrator, I obtained a private viewing of this painting, so that I could spend an uninterrupted half-hour studying it. It is clear that nowhere as many spaniels as the fourteen pictured were involved – several spaniels have been painted two or three times – and also the spaniels in the group bear no resemblance to Sussex Spaniels of that period. The administrator was puzzled about why the gamekeeper featured in the painting; he explained that the aristocracy of the time did not, as a rule, have their servants painted with the dogs or horses they owned, but rather with themselves or their families. This painting is by John Chalmers and dated 1904, it depicts 'Mr. Hazell', a stout game-keeper, in the Tredegar livery of green coat and waistcoat, fawn breeches, brown gaiters, black boots and bowler, standing under a beech tree in the park, with deer in the background. Five of the spaniels depicted have white flashes on their chests. None is leashed, and it is plain to the meanest intelligence that even Mr Hazell was not going to keep fourteen unleashed spaniels down for any length of time with deer grazing so close! One concludes that the artist painted the tree and the deer and then put in Mr Hazell and a couple of spaniels, others being added to compose the picture. The spaniels are all fairly long in the muzzle, and are Field-like in size and head properties. However, as Lord Tredegar did not show dogs (there is no mention of any dogs in his name in any variety of spaniel in Stud Books of the period), my guess is that the family had their own strain of working spaniel possibly bred from the Welsh Cocker – many of whom were liver – and the Fields of the day, all of whom contained some Sussex blood. Perhaps four or five actual dogs are depicted, the rest being copies of those.

I have dwelt on the Tredegar painting at length as it has been mentioned on and off over the years, gradually acquiring its own mythology. If anyone doubts my findings, I advise them to go to Tredegar House – which is open to the public – and really study the painting, forgetting all that has been written about it. The administrator told me that there was no reference to spaniels or to the reason for the portrait in any of the Tredegar papers so far studied. The early Sussex Spaniel depicted in this book seems to me to be a much more possible likeness of the spaniels used in Sussex in the days before the Kennel Club and dog shows existed. It is nobody's dog in particular, so the artist would not have any proud owner's axe to grind and could therefore draw the spaniel as it was or as it was described. It is not exactly a pretty dog, and it bears little resemblance to the breed after Messrs Jacobs and Woolland got their hands on it. The original illustration of this dog appears in Gen. W. Hutchinson's *Dog Breaking*, published in the 1850s and republished by his son in 1908. The illustration is entitled 'Short legged, strong limbed Sussex Spaniel', and it fronts page 136. As can be seen in the reproduction in this book, the dog portrayed was one of some substance, long in rib cage, strongly loined and with wide thighs. The skull is not dissimilar to that of today's dogs, although the length and construction of the muzzle are a little different, and the ears appear longer. The legs are straight and not overdone in bone, and the feet are large but well shaped and appear to have been trimmed! The dog has what is obviously a dense and weatherproof coat. The tail has been docked, but has been left a little longer than is the fashion today. Whether this artist drew an actual dog or drew one from the description of a dog we shall never know. It was this type of Sussex Spaniel that the revivalists sought to breed. No doubt they would have done so without any trouble but for the intervention of Mr Jacobs with his craze for long, low spaniels. Mr Jacobs preference became the popular image of the time for both Field and Sussex, with the inevitable consequences. It was only the arrival of Mr Campbell Newington and his insistence that Sussex should work for their living that got the dog up off the ground and made it a viable proposition again, ensuring that the breed survived.

The material with which the revivalists of the 1870s had to work was mixed in the extreme. That the breed had to lean heavily on Bebb, who, although registered and shown as a Sussex, had no Sussex blood in him was just one of the anomalies. The number of black, liver and tan, black and tan and even coloured puppies born in litters from which liver

Mr C. Bexon's Sh.Ch. Creswelshaw Idris 671BN. Wh: 1977. Brs. Mrs M. Lancaster & Mrs Brooks. By Sh.Ch. Elmbury Pevensey Hero ex Creswelshaw Hannah.

Mrs Betty Purkis' Sh.Ch. Chilsham Touch of Cold 0457BQ. Wh: 1979. By Sh.Ch. Quintic Joby ex Oldholbans Fashion of Chilsham. (Penygader Exodus ex Oldholbans Flashpoint 2900BK.)

144

Mr C. Bexon's Sh.Ch. Harvest Glow of Oldfield 1094BU. Wh: 1983. Brs. Mr &
Mrs Bexon & Mr & Miss Fox. By Sh.Ch. Creswelshaw Idris ex Scotshill Felicity
Brown 1189BU. (Sh.Ch. Topjoys Sussex Harvester ex Sh.Ch. Creswelshaw Isadora
2278BM.) Combining some of the best of the lines this typical bitch has been a consis-
tent winner since puppyhood.

puppies were registered, shown and bred from as Sussex, is many. The
base of the breed was founded on the tenuous strands left from the
pre-1857 days of Mr Fuller, none of which can be proved, and on the
hotch-potch of working spaniels owned by the gentlemen of the time. All
the well-known breakers owned specimens of most of the other spaniel
varieties, developing to fit the new show scene Sussex, Field, Cocker,
Clumber and various working spaniels of no particular breed, variously
described as Norfolk, English Water or just land spaniels. Add to this the
old Irish Water Spaniel, and the breeders of the time, who were nothing

if not adventurous, had all the material to hand to breed long or short legs, long or chunky bodies, short and fat bodies, long and thin bodies, short or long heads and every colour under the sun in their efforts to establish a strain of distinguishable spaniels which would not only catch the judges' eye but which would also sell well. Those connected with dogs were very much 'in the market', and adult dogs which were big winners frequently changed hands five or six times in their lifetime, winning prodigiously for every owner and thereby bringing them a little bit of limelight and establishing them in the world of dogs. One cannot look at the early pedigrees with any degree of sanguineness. Undoubtedly many are not what they purport to be: not everything that was done was written down, and not every record of sire and dam stated can be taken as gospel truth! And what about all the dogs and bitches, mostly the latter, used in the manufacture of the Sussex breed? What were they? Right up to the 1930s it was possible to use an animal whose pedigree and origin were quite unknown – indeed, you will find many such at the time.

Sussex Spaniels have never been numerous, not even when their revival had got underway around the 1880s and they were enjoying some small popularity. Then with the ridiculing of the long, low, heavy, stumped legged dogs, quite useless for work, came a decided slump in the Sussex popularity stakes, and only a very few gentlemen carried on with the breed. From the 1890s on, it was noticeable how few names figure in the entries in the Stud Book. By this time, Mr Newington had found it necessary to use bitches with no history (such as Rosehill Rhonda) to keep the lines going, and to fall back on Field Spaniels (such as Rolyat Rose) to carry on a line. Into the 1900s Mr Kerr had to use two black Field Spaniel bitches (Harviestoun Polly and Rona of Wilts), in order to continue breeding Sussex, so decimated and inbred had the stock become. By the end of the First World War there was only a dilute line to the 'original' Rosehill stock, if any at all. When Mr Stevenson Clarke formed his kennel, he did so on the bitches Broadhurst Bexie – who was out of the black Field Spaniel Rona of Wilts – and Broadhurst Bokra – who was a granddaughter of the half-Field dog Rosehill Rector. One of the dominant matrons in the erly 1920s Nona of Leetside, goes back four generations to the black Field Harviestoun Polly, and few, if any, can escape the line back to the Field, Rolyat Rose. Colour in this instance would supply no clue as to the forebears of the stock being used by the new breeders of Sussex after 1918: all the dogs and bitches used were liver, and as liver to liver can only beget liver, there would be no little black puppies turning up to cause consternation! So only the best of the Field blood – for, make no mistake about it, Rolyat Rose, Harviestoun Polly and Rona of Wilts were all top-class Field Spaniel bitches of their day and the dams of many winning Fields as well – was used to make sure

Mrs Joy Freer, sixty years in Sussex Spaniels at her famous Fourclovers Kennel, seen at home with her husband Jack, and left Mrs Faith Gilham of the Topjoys Sussex. Mrs Freer giving her valued opinion on a Sussex Spaniel.

of the continuance of the Sussex lines. As all Field and Sussex lines went back to the same source, no doubt the breeders of those days said, 'So what does it matter?'.

Then we come to the spaniels used to increase Sussex numbers in the 1920s, 'the doubtful Napoleon and Cleopatra' as Mrs Freer dubbed them. They are the sire and dam of Treyford Jessica, one of the rocks on which the Fourclovers empire stands; another is Ch. Brosse, whose great-great-grandmother was a black Field Spaniel; the third is Primax Beauty, who went back to Rona of Wilts. There are numerous Sussex bitches at this time of no known breeding, many with 'breeder, date of birth or pedigree unknown' beside their names when reference to them occurs. Who was Nan, the grandmother of Kiska of Fourclovers? Or Betsy, the mother of Wendy of Oakerland? Or Bogie, the sire of Earlswood Bunty? Or Nell, the dam of Southash Zara – was she the same Nell down as the dam of Rosehill Reaper, and if so, what were her parents Dash and Floss? And where did Marie and Mildred come from? Alas, we shall never know.

Then there is the question of the breeding we do know. How much of

147

it can we trust? In many cases the evidence is extremely intriguing, like the case already cited of two bitches who are eight years older than their dam! In a number of instances dogs entered the Stud Book as having no breeding, but by the time they have appeared in three or four issues they have miraculously acquired a pedigree. This is evident in all the spaniel varieties if one cares to make a detailed study of the KCSB. There is the case of Pax and Buckle, who appear as the sire and dam of Miss Brown, the dam of Langrish Bess 85GG who was bred by Gen. The Hon. W. Schlater in 1924 and owned by Col. C.G. Talbot Ponsonby in 1926. A little later on, Bang and Buzz acquire the Langrish prefix of Col. Talbot Ponsonby. Were they originally from his considerable spaniel kennel? This is probable as Col. Talbot Ponsonby acquired the two grand-children; no doubt the Langrish prefix was added to give Bess an air of respectability once she had attained Stud Book status after winning second in Open Bitch at Crufts in 1926. When Earlswood Pete went into the KCSB in 1928, his dam was listed as Earlswood Bunty (unregistered) with no further particulars; but Pete later became a champion, and Bunty acquired breeding. Although her sire Bogie has no particulars, her dam Southash Zara is credited on her sire's side with going back to the Camp-bell Newington Rosehills.

All these little inconsistencies appear to have become a thing of the past by the 1930s. The Interbred section of the Stud Book was available. This was to accommodate crosses within a variety, such as Cockers x Springer, or Sussex x Clumber. Up to then the cross had simply been noted in the registration of the dog and was quite acceptable. After the introduction of the Interbred section, it became ncessary, should a breed wish to encompass another to enlarge the gene pool or for any other reason, for three generations from the original cross to take place before the dogs could go back into their section of the Stud Book; thus, say, Bloggs (Sussex) mated Brim (Cocker), the offspring mated back to Sussex, their offspring also mated to a Sussex, and their offspring again mated to a Sussex could then be registered as Sussex without the stigma of 'inter-bred' being given against their name.

Offspring from these matings between spaniel varieties do not turn up in the KCSB unless winning at field trials, so we have to wait until 1954 to find Timothy of Oakerland in the book. He was by a dog called Sunny South, the son of the Sussex Spaniel, Ch. Osseo of Fourclovers 160PP and a Springer called Brownie. Timothy's dam was the Sussex Spaniel Mildred of Oakerland, a daughter of Tamenund of Fourclovers and Goldilocks of Oakerland. Goldilocks, who produced a number of litters in her lifetime (bitches in those days being expected to earn their keep), was also the mother of a litter born in January 1937 by Ch. Earlswood Pete. This litter included Fairway Joan, owned by a Miss M. Broad;

Earlswood Dragoon and Dash, owned by Mrs Youell; and Montana of Fourclovers, owned by Mrs Freer, who did not register her until early in 1938 when she bred from her.

The Springer Brownie was around in the early days of the war. Jane, an unregistered sister of Timothy of Oakerland, was mated to Kenau of Fourclovers 95AH and whelped a litter on 16 February 1954; Miss Reed had a dog from this litter and registered him as Shon. In casting about to discover quite why so many long legs are found in the modern Sussex, one is led to wonder if the Springer Brownie played some part in the scheme of things as one would hardly expect this trait to hark back as far as the doubtfuls of the 1920s. But who knows? Heredity is a strange and complex thing.

Mrs Bower also accounted for an interbred line. Agrivista Irene (half-Springer), was mated to Kenau whom Mrs Bower owned, and bred Intruder Isobel, one of a largish litter although only Isobel features in the scheme of things, becoming the mother of the 'Buxton' litter. Two sons of this litter won, and one bitch, Belle, was used for breeding. Mrs Freer used one of these interbred Buxton dogs on one of her Sussex bitches.

The only officially recorded interbreeding since the war was that to the Clumber Thornville Snowstorm, three generations from this cross being bred and then absorbed into Sussex lines. In the past thirty-five years the continuance of the Sussex Spaniel has only been assured by inbreeding: the brother to sister matings of Chesara Pride and Chesara Joy and of Sedora Noel and Christmas Rose feature in most, if not all, of today's pedigrees. The Fourclovers line was consistently inbred and line-bred. All of this poses an intriguing question. If only Sussex have been bred to Sussex, and so much inbreeding has taken place, where have the long legs and untypical heads still seen on some specimens come from?

Perhaps just because the Sussex is so in-bred, he is carrying the genes of those far-off Field Spaniel ancestors; as each succeeding generation is bred, more lines to these old lines are introduced. With inbreeding, good and bad points are both doubled up, and if something sneaky got into the lines then, twenty, thirty or forty years ago, it is liable to pop up today. Once something has been introduced into the breed it can never to totally eliminated; it can be diluted by careful breeding but never quite bred out. It is a case of 'the sins of the fathers' or, in the case of the Sussex Spaniel, more probably the mothers! Mrs Freer's letter to me in early 1984 says, 'puppies arriving in litters are still very mixed in size and type', but she gave no explanation of why this should be so.

13

Standards and Their Implications

The Standard of the Sussex Spaniel, 1879

In general appearance the Sussex Spaniel is lighter in build and higher on the leg than the Clumber:

> *Head.* Should be of good length but broad as well so should not appear long.
>
> *Ears.* Should not be large and should be set on in front, rather above the level of the eyes, the feather on the ears should be straight and silky.
>
> *Nostrils.* Should be very large and the lower jaw rather recede.
>
> *Eyes.* Of a dark hazel colour, should be deep set; and the expression should be one of extreme intelligence.
>
> *Neck.* Strong and slightly arched.
>
> *Body.* Long and deep, the ribs well sprung, the shoulders oblique and the loins very broad.
>
> *Legs.* Rather longer than a Clumber's, bony and muscular, the front ones as straight as possible, the hind ones very much curved at the stifles and hocks, the latter placed close to the ground like a cat's.
>
> *Feet.* Large and round and well furnished with short hair.
>
> *Tail.* Should never, except under peculiar excitement, be carried above the level of the back. The correct carriage of the stern indicates purity of breed both in the spaniel and the setter sooner than any other point.
>
> *Coat.* Of a golden liver colour should be smooth and very dense, the feather should not be very long anywhere, and should on no account hang from the stern like a flag (as a Clumber's does) nor should it extend beyond the hocks.
>
> Vero Shaw, *Classic Encyclopaedia of the Dog*, 1879-81

(Mr Lort, a noted spaniel breeder and judge of this era, describes the Sussex as having 'large head, yet not too narrow or long, yet not chumpy, in measurement I should for a dog say eight and a half inches, a bitch half an inch less'. Of forelegs he remarks 'Forelegs in many of the dogs I have been shown as pure bred, are bowed, but why this should be I do not know. It will have the effect of making them slower in their work, and possibly that is desirable, but for appearance give me straight limbs.' Mr Lort puts a Sussex at 40 lb. in weight, a bitch at 35 lb. He decribes the tail as being about 10 in. long, and the make and shape of the dog to be long, low and heavy.)

The Standard of the Sussex Spaniel, 1890 approx.

Head. The skull should be moderately long and also wide, with an indentation in the middle and a full stop, brows fairly heavy; occiput full, but not pointed, the whole giving an appearance of heaviness without dullness.

Eyes. Hazel colour, fairly large, soft and languishing, not showing the haw overmuch.

Nose. The muzzle should be about three inches long, square and the lips somewhat pendulous. The nostrils well developed and liver colour.

Ears. Thick, fairly large and lobe shaped; set moderately low, but relatively not so low as in the black Field Spaniel; carried close to the head and furnished with soft, wavy hair.

Neck. Is rather short, strong and slightly arched, but not carrying the head much above the level of the back. There should not be much throatiness in the skin, but a well marked frill under the coat.

Chest and shoulders. The chest is round, especially behind the shoulders, deep and wide, giving a good girth. The shoulders should be oblique.

Back and ribs. The back and loin is strong, and should be muscular, both in width and depth, for this development the back ribs must be deep. The whole body is characterised as long, low, level and strong.

Legs and feet. The arms and thighs must be bony, as well as muscular, knees and hocks large and round, and with short hair between the toes. The legs should be very short and strong, with great bone, and may show a slight bend in the forearm, and be moderately well feathered. The hind legs should not be apparently shorter than the forelegs, or be too much bent at the hocks so as to give a settery appearance which is so objectionable. The hind legs should be well feathered above the hocks, but should not have much hair below this point. The hocks should he short and wide apart.

Tail. Should be docked from five to seven inches, set low and not carried above the level of the back, thickly clothed with moderately long feather.

Coat. Body coat abundant, flat or slightly waved with no tendency to curl, moderately well feathered on legs and stern, but clean below the hocks.

Colour. Rich golden liver; this is a certain sign of the purity of the breed, dark liver or puce denoting unmistakably a recent cross with the black or other variety Field Spaniel.

General appearance. Rather massive, and muscular, but with free movements and nice tail action, denoting a tractable and cheerful disposition. Weight from 35 to 45 lbs.

Footnote
It will be seen from the above Club standard (Spaniel Club) that a somewhat lighter weight is allowed than that alluded to in my description. However I must say that I have not yet, as far as I am aware, seen a good specimen of a pure Sussex Spaniel so small as 35 lbs. and, on the contrary, some of the most perfect specimen dogs I have met must have closely approached 50 lbs.

Rawdon Lee, *Modern Dogs*, Sporting Division, Vol. 2.

The Standard of the Sussex Spaniel, 1920s

General appearance. Massive and strongly built. An active, energetic strong dog, whose characteristic movement is a decided roll, and unlike that of any other spaniel.

Head and skull. The skull should be wide and show a moderate curve from ear to ear, neither flat nor apple headed, with a centre indentation and a well pronounced stop. Brows frowning, occiput decided but not pointed. Nostrils well developed and a liver colour. A well balanced head.

Eyes. Hazel colour, fairly large, not too full, but soft expression and not showing the haw too much.

Ears. Thick, fairly large and lobe shaped, set moderately low but above eye level. Should lie closely, hair soft and wavy, but not too profuse.

Mouth. Strong and level, neither overshot nor undershot, with scissor bite.

Neck. Long, strong and slightly arched, not carrying the head much above the level of the back. Not much throatiness, but well marked frill.

Forequarters. The shoulders should be sloping and free, arms well boned as well as muscular. Knees large and strong, pasterns short and well boned. Legs rather short and strong, moderately feathered.

Body. Chest deep and well developed, not too round and wide. Back and loin well developed and muscular both in width and depth. The back ribs must be deep. Whole body should be strong and level with no sign of waistiness from aitches to hips.

Hindquarters. The thighs must be strongly boned as well as muscular, hocks large and strong, legs short and strong with good bone, moderately feathered. The hind legs should not appear shorter than the forelegs, or be too much bent at the hocks as to give a settery appearance, which is objectionable. The hind legs should be well feathered above the hocks, but not much hair below the hocks.

Feet. Circular and well padded, well feathered between the toes.

Tail. Set low and not carried above the level of the back. Free actioned, thickly clothed with hair but no feather. Docked 5 to 7 inches.

Coat. Abundant and flat with no tendency to curl and ample under-coat for weather resistance.

Colour. Rich golden liver and hair shading to gold at the tips, the gold predominating. Dark liver or puce objectionable.

Weight. Ideal size: Dogs 45 lbs., bitches 40 lbs.

Height. 15 to 16 inches.

The Standard of the Sussex Spaniel, 1987
(Reproduced by permission of the Kennel Club)

General appearance. Massive. Strongly built, Active, energetic dog, whose characteristic movement is a decided roll, and unlike any other spaniel.

Characteristics. Natural working ability, gives tongue at work in thick cover.

Temperament. Kindly disposition, aggression highly undesirable.

Head and skull. Skull wide, showing moderate curve from ear to ear, neither flat nor apple headed, with centre indentation and pronounced stop. Brows frowning, occiput decided but not pointed. Nostrils well developed and liver in colour. Balanced head.

Eyes. Hazel colour, fairly large, not full, but soft expression and not showing much haw.

Ears. Fairly large and lobular, set moderately low, just above eye level, lying close to the skull.

Mouth. Jaws strong with perfect regular and complete scissor bite, i.e. upper teeth closely overlapping lower teeth and set square to the jaws.

Neck. Long, strong and slightly arched, not carrying head much above the level of the back. Slight throatiness, but well marked frill.

153

Forequarters. Shoulders sloping and free, arms well boned and muscular. Knees large and strong, pasterns short and well boned. Legs rather short and strong.

Body. Chest deep and well developed, not too round and wide. Back and loin well developed and muscular both in width and depth. The back ribs must be deep. Whole body strong and level with no sign of waistiness from withers to hips.

Hingquarters. Thighs strongly boned and muscular. Hocks large and strong, legs short and strong and good bone. Hindlegs not appearing shorter than forelegs or over angulated.

Feet. Round, well padded, well feathered between toes.

Tail. Set low and never carried above level of back. Lively actioned. Docked to a length of 5 to 7 inches.

Gait/movement. True fore and aft with a distinct roll.

Coat. Abundant and flat with no tendency to curl and ample undercoat for weather resistance. Ears covered in soft wavy hair but not too profuse. Forequarters and hindquarters moderately well feathered. Tail thickly clothed with hair but not feathered.

Colour. Rich golden liver and hair shading to gold at the tips, gold predominating. Dark liver or puce undesirable.

Size. Ideal height at withers 15 to 16 inches. Weight approx. 50 lbs.

City of Birmingham Ch. Show. 1970. Mrs Mavis Lancaster, Mrs Joy Freer and Mrs Joyce Munday with their exhibits.

Working Test at Metfield. Mary Williams, Mavis Lancaster, Mrs Peacock, Ken Peacock, Mr J. Wylie the judge and Mr Jack Freer, with the Sussex who ran in the Tests.

A study of the standards issued for Sussex Spaniels over the last hundred years can tell us many things: firstly, that each time the standard was altered it was not with an eye to improving the breed, but rather to accommodating the dogs then being shown. The first standard, of 1879, states that the Sussex should be higher on the leg than a Clumber, but by the end of the century – and after the administrations of Messrs Jacobs and Woolland – the legs were 'short and strong with great bone'. The 1879 standard asks for the body to be long and deep; by 1890 this wording had been replaced with 'long, low, level and strong'. In 1879 the forelegs asked for were to be 'as straight as possible'; by 1890 the standard says 'may show a slight bend in the forearm'. The Sussex by this time had become so long, heavy and ungainly, that he was unable to take his weight on his forelegs, and undoubtedly many Sussex had bowed fronts. Not knowing how to correct this fault, the breeders turned it into a virtue and added it to the standard.

Only subtle changes appear in the standard for the head, that of 1879 asking for 'a receding jaw'; this was never repeated in succeeding standards. In this standard the ears, we are told, should 'be set on in front rather above the level of the eyes', which makes one wonder how the poor dogs could see where to go! The skull in every standard is described as 'broad' or 'wide', but not long, and by 1890 'brows fairly heavy, and an indentation in the middle of the skull' had been added. The wording 'not apple headed' was inserted in the 1920s. The neck in both early standards is described as 'short and strong and slightly arched'. It is not until we get to the 1920s verion that a long neck is called for. In none of the standards is there any description of the correct fore-face. Not until after the First World War was the Sussex supposed to have a roll when he moved, 'unlike any other spaniel'.

It is unclear why this rolling gait was added to the standard; one can only surmise that some important dog or dogs of the day had developed this kind of movement and that once again the standard was made over to fit the dog. The long neck is another case in point; never before had the Sussex been required to have a long neck, but as the post-First World War dogs were all closely related to Field Spaniels – who had longer necks – no doubt many of the Sussex of those days also had them. A line was added to the standard, giving the Sussex too long a neck and a very important characteristic of the old Sussex was lost.

There is no mention in the original standards of teeth; maybe the old breeders did not set so much store by a full even mouth as we do today. From the 1920s the standard calls for a scissor bite, but in fact over the past six decades mouth problems have beset the breed. Even today breeders are still running on otherwise promising puppies only to find the mouths go wrong when they cut their second teeth. The fact that the standard over sixty years ago called for a scissor bite has never deterred the breeders of the time from showing and breeding from dogs and bitches with bad mouths, which is why the problem persists. However, one must add, when dealing with a breed of such small numbers any likely stock must be bred from if the breed is not to die out; all things being equal, a bad mouth has often to be accepted if an otherwise good Sussex is not to be discarded, while dilution of the fault should be the aim of all breeders.

The tail of the Sussex Spaniel has been most important in standards down the years. It 'should never, except under peculiar excitement, be carried above the level of the back', says 1879, but this line has been deleted from succeeding standards and 'set low and never carried above the level of the back' inserted. The first standard calls for the feather on the tail not to 'hang from the stern like a flag as a Clumber's does'. The length of the dock is not stated, and although in one book there is a quote from an old breeder of the last century saying that the dock on a Sussex should be 10 in. long and well feathered, the standards through the years agree on from 5 to 7 in. Weight has varied little, with bitches accepted at

35 lb. and up, and dogs at 40 to 50 lb. As for coat, the breeders who altered the standards down the years seem in complete agreement: 'of a golden liver colour, very dense' (1879); 'body coat abundant, rich golden liver' (1890); 'abundant and flat, ample undercoat, rich golden liver, hair shading to gold at the tips, gold predominating' (1920). Liver or puce coloured Sussex were regarded as showing Field blood, and there was a good deal of this in the early part of the 1900s. No doubt colour played a very big part in placings in the last century as exhibitors strove to rid themselves of the 'manufactured breed' label.

Looking at the new standard brought out in 1987 by the Kennel Club, one can question quite a few items in it. The general appearance is said to be 'massive'. Few modern Sussex Spaniels fit this description, and the occasional dog who does has a decided overall Clumber outline. In characteristics it says 'natural working ability', yet only a very tiny proportion of the breed over the past thirty years or so have ever been encouraged to develop this accomplishment. And 'giving tongue in thick cover', which is a new line altogether, has not been recognised since the days when Sussex worked the thick cover in a pack as beaters − in the days before the Kennel Club and the show scene was upon us. I do not think the shooters of today, certainly not the Trials people, would tolerate a dog who made a noise when working; one wonders quite why this line was added and what purpose it seeks to serve. Personally I feel that the line on temperament has been unfortunately worded; it includes 'aggression highly undesirable'. 'Aggression' is a word that has never been used when referring to the breed up till now. Those reading this standard for the first time would naturally assume that Sussex were agressive and that one actually had to look for a non-aggressive dog if one wished to purchase a specimen. I prefer the 1890 description, 'a cheerful tractable disposition'. The description of the neck follows the 1920 edict of a 'long neck', as against former standards that called for a short strong, crested neck'. The line 'there should not be much throatiness of the skin' (1890 and 1920) now reads 'slight throatiness', which is not at all the same thing. The word 'slight' means different things to different people, allowable throatiness to some, and it paves the way for Sussex to finish up with a dewlap if breeders are not very careful!

Nothing is said in the description of the forelegs about whether they are preferred straight or crooked. As earlier standards came down on one side or the other, perhaps mention should have been made of them, if only for the sake of the inexperienced judge. Another unfortunate line is 'no waistiness from withers to hips'. A dog's waist is its loin; it cannot be waisty from the withers, which are atop the rib cage − the waistiness, or lack of it, is apparent in the loin.

Those who compile the standards are apt to go off course when it

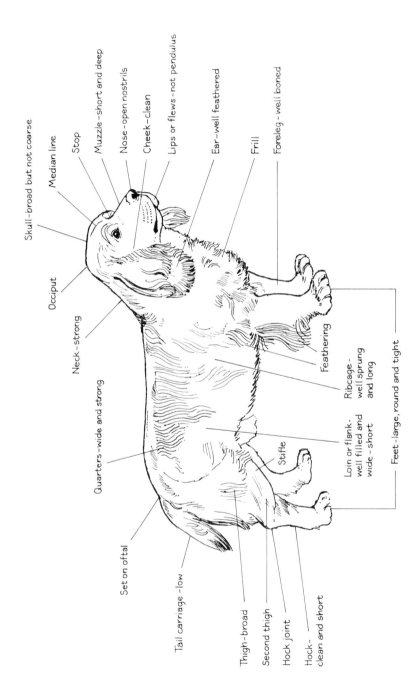

Skull - broad but not coarse

Median line

Stop

Muzzle - short and deep

Nose - open nostrils

Cheek - clean

Lips or flews - not pendulus

Ear - well feathered

Frill

Foreleg - well boned

Occiput

Neck - strong

Feathering

Ribcage - well sprung and long

Quarters - wide and strong

Loin or flank - well filled and wide - short

Stifle

Feet - large, round and tight

Set on oftal

Tail carriage - low

Thigh - broad

Second thigh

Hock joint

Hock - clean and short

Points of the Sussex Spaniel

comes to hips. The 1920 one calls for no sign of waistiness from 'aitches to hips', a most odd statement as the aitch or haunch bone is the hip bone, so the actual wording does not make sense. I was pleased to see that the new description of the feet says 'round', not 'circular' as in the 1920s, as the latter description makes one expect to find feet shaped rather like dustbin lids!

Now, with the latest standard encompassing a section on gait/movement, the 1920 wording regarding the need for the Sussex to 'roll' is included. Actually, a few Sussex do roll nowadays, and I have noticed that the roll is more likely to be present if the front legs are not straight. This is a personal observation, but Sussex whose forelegs are strong and straight do not seem to have the roll. If you watch a bandy-legged human walk down a road, he or she will roll from side to side. This makes one wonder if fronts were so bad in the 1920s that the majority of Sussex developed this mode of locomotion, and the movement was then added to the standard as a virtue. The roll in Clumber movement is quite different; is an all-over exertion of a bigger dog built on quite dissimilar lines.

The colour of the Sussex as set down has not varied over the years, puce or dark liver still being unacceptable, although dark liver Sussex are still to be found. Mrs Freer made great use of the expression 'the true sealskin coat', although this description has never been used in official standards; however, it is a good description of the type of coat most likely to be the correct colour. Study of the desired type of Sussex over the past decades is very rewarding, and may one add, revealing!

14

Judging the Sussex Spaniel

It is unfortunate that the average show secretary and his or her committee have very little interest in minority breeds; these are usually lumped together and given either to the all-rounder engaged or to someone who is anxious to get on in the judging world and for whom a clutch of minorities is considered something of a coup. The judging of the Sussex Spaniel breed by such people is rarely satisfactory as most have little knowledge of the history or problems of the breed, and therefore cannot weigh up the merits of the individual dogs. The critiques of such judges bear careful study; they usually consist of chunks of the standard, usually applied to dogs who do not have those particular charcteristics! Such reports raise a smile in most quarters, but they also

National Gundog Show 1982. Miss Margaret Scarr judging. Challenge Certificate winners, Mrs Gilham's Sh.Ch. Topjoys Sussex Harvester and Sh.Ch. Penygader Hannah of Topjoys, daughter of Sh.Ch. Sharland Sussex Wine.

Mrs D. Bailey's Sh.Ch. Topjoys Bisto Brown 0345BR. Wh: 1981. Br. Mrs F. Gilham. By Sh.Ch. Quintic Joby 0672BM ex Sh.Ch. Penygader Hannah of Topjoys.

give rise to great irritation with a system that allows such inexperienced people loose on an important old-established breed. What show secretaries never realise is that it is far more difficult to judge a minority breed than it is a popular breed, for the simple reason that there are more of the well-known breed about to be watched and studied at shows and so the aspiring judge has some sort of yardstick to go by.

The evolution of the Sussex breed has been a long and at times hazardous process, and the need to study it before embarking on judging it is very real. The casual and modern approach to judging is 'you are only there to choose the best on the day'. That is a naive and simplistic view and can simply mean that the judge picks out the ones that appeal to him or her, without thought of the needs of the breed in question. The various faults found in a breed (there are indeed faults in all breeds) and the failings, have to be balanced one against the other. Mouths appear to give most difficulty. Anyone who has taken the trouble to study the breed will know there has been an ongoing problem with mouths ever since the advent of Montour into the lines – and undoubtedly before this, as

Montour himself had to inherit the fault from somewhere. Judges have been known to dismiss out of hand any Sussex in the ring with mouth faults, which is, to my mind, very irresponsible.

There are worse faults in the breed than bad mouths: over-long legs, inadequate bone, twisted forelegs, weak hind movement and untypical heads all crop up from time to time, to say nothing of undesirable coat and colour. Bad mouths are undesirable and in breeds of large numbers there is no need to tolerate them when judging; but in a minority breed, whose numbers, or lack of numbers, over the years have given cause for concern, mouths have to be put in perspective. I would rather put up a Sussex who conforms in most other aspects to the standard but has a poor mouth than put up a poor type or unsound dog just because it has a good mouth. Many Sussex handled over a long period have what is termed in some breeds 'a reversed scissor'. In fact, this is the most likely mouth one will meet. It is not a true undershot jaw: that is a structural fault, in which the lower jaw itself projects beyond the upper; this, being a malformation, should be penalised as must the wry mouth. The 'reversed scissor' means that the lower teeth close over the upper teeth. It must be judged against the other faults or failings the dog may have.

So what does one look for when judging the Sussex Spaniel? Firstly, overall balance. If you can find this then it goes without saying that the fore end and hind end match, the middle piece fits neatly into place and the bone is adequate for the size. The height from the ground and the length of body will be right, the head will be of the correct size and properly carried. If the dog looks wrong to you but you cannot fathom why, it is off balance: the head may be too small for the rest of it, the bone inadequate for its size, the feet too small, the rib cage too short – there are any number of permutations. If the dog looks wrong, then it probably is wrong. Coat and colour are most important in this breed, and any tendency to dark liver colour, or to stringy, coarse, thin or houndy-type coverings, must be penalised. Without his soft, deep, golden liver coat, the Sussex is just another liver spaniel.

Head properties are very important. The heavy brows, the median line, the proportion of muzzle to skull, set of ears, and well-shaped clean eye with the correct expression are essential. Any tendency to long fore-faces, domed Cocker-type heads, peaky setter-type occiputs, coarse cheeks or poor set or shape of eye should all be penalised accordingly. The length of leg seems to have bothered numberless judges. One listens with amusement to those who propound the theory that the Sussex should be a small, knobby-legged, go-by-the-ground dog; and also to those who say he should be big and with good leg to work, and so on. Sometimes in the past these theories have been given by people who actually owned dogs like that and were seeking to promote their own type, but more often they are given by judges who have not the remotest idea how a good Sussex should look. The overall outline of a Sussex is quite different from any other spaniel. He does not have the same length as the Field. He should not have the legs of a Springer, although over the years I have seen Sussex with this characteristic, and he should not have the outline of the Clumber, although, again, over the years this has been seen.

To get a true idea of the correct Sussex outline, look at the photographs of the past dogs such as Okimat; of those of the recent past, such as Hannibal; and of today's dogs, like Sussex Passtime and Harvest Glow. A look at old photographs in this book will show what stock your lines hark back to. Study carefully the longer legs and lighter bone of the Broadhursts, and follow on to see how Mr Stevenson Clarke and those who came after improved the outline and type of the Sussex of the day. A careful perusal of the selection of pictures in this book should give the reader an idea of the different types of Sussex which, in their day, have been big winners. Not all have been good Sussex, some were very light boned, some very clumsy headed, some too small or too big – or too tall. Some were quite lacking in type, but all these melted down have evolved into one recognisable type of Sussex, as described in the standards over the years. Perhaps, give or take one or two anomalies, the 1890 standards gives the best picture of the breed's requirements.

When judging the Sussex Spaniel of the 1980s it is necessary to have read about and evaluated the breed over a period to realise just how the breeders are hoping to take the breed forward; and it is essential not to put down in the ring a potentially good Sussex because it has a fault or failing unacceptable in a majority breed. The breeders of today are doing sterling work. Seldom in the breed's history have so many dedicated people all been pulling in the same direction with one aim in view, to improve with each succeeding generation the type and standard of the Sussex, and to dilute those faults, such as mouths, that have been such a stumbling-block in the recent past.

163

15

Breeding Sussex Spaniels

All that has gone before in this book must surely convince readers that breeding Sussex Spaniels, good ones at any rate, is no easy task. When I talked to Mavis Lancaster on contemplating this chapter, she told me, 'you can plan the perfect litter on paper and the result can be an absolute disaster, without a single really good pup in the litter'. Mrs Lancaster believes, for Sussex at least, that the stud dogs should be the best-looking ones with the least faults. They should have masculinity without coarseness, presence and good temperament, and they must complement the bitch in every way possible. Study of photographs of the dog's antecedents is essential, and questions must be asked. Were his sire and dam of similar type? Is this line-breeding in any way true? Are the litters mixed for type, size and length of leg? What is the coat quality and colour like? It is possible to breed an excellent specimen from quite mediocre parents, and conversely to breed very disappointing puppies from very typical parents.

Study of the past history of the breed will tell the potential breeder of the pitfalls to be encountered. There are some cardinal rules to be observed. Do not ever breed from a dog that has a bad temperament, however good it might be in other respects. The breed in the past has not been without its rogues, and it is up to breeders of the present and future to ensure that this trait is bred out, as far as humanly possible. Mouths are a long-term proposition. As has been shown from foregoing chapters, good specimens with poor dentition have had to be used if the lines are to continue producing Sussex of the correct type and size, but it must always be a long-term aim to breed fewer and fewer with bad mouths. This fault is so deeply embedded in the lines that it will be impossible ever to eradicate it, but it can and must be minimised.

The true Sussex head, with the broad short muzzle and with only a moderate curve across the front, tends to contain teeth that incline towards the straight bite, and the better scissor bites are often found in rather untypical heads that verge on the too narrow and have overlong forefaces. It is still necessary to breed from stock that is not totally correct in dentition, but as more litters are bred and the lines become more diffused, the mouth faults should diminish, albeit very slowly.

Sussex Spaniel Association Diamond Jubilee Celebration. Held in Sussex in 1984. Two days included a Match, a working test, an exemption show and a barn dance. The gathering was attended by a large number of Sussex Spaniel owners and members of the SSA.

Length of leg is yet another problem. Long legs crop up very frequently, but the very low-to-ground knobby-legged animals are happily fading out; it will only be the idiosyncracies of some judges that keep this bad trait to the fore. Some Sussex are far too long, while some incline to the shorter rib cage, giving them a foreign appearance.

Coats go in families. It is possible to observe two and perhaps three generations of one particular line nowadays, and to notice whether the coats in this line are breeding the flat, straight, seal-like coat of good depth and with the desired golden sheen; whether the line is producing the coarser, longer, plain liver coat of the Field Spaniel; or whether the line is throwing shorter hound-type coverings. There are some very good correct coat lines today, and breeders have been diligent in trying to breed for this type of covering.

Eyes need to be watched. Be sure that the sire you choose has good clean eyes with no tendency to entropion or ectropion. Most eyes todays appear to be good; the correct thoughtful, slightly quizzical expression of the Sussex is most necessary.

The shape of the stud dog is all important. A long rib cage is required, and a wide loin so that there is no waistiness − a pinched loin is very uncharacteristic − and the quarters should be wide. The hind legs should be very characteristic with wide thick thighs and bone as strong as that found in the front legs. Head type must be good: it is the strongly differing heads that set the spaniel varieties apart. The wider, moderately curved skull with its median line, pronounced stop and well-developed brows, coupled with the deep, wide fore-face, is a must for the Sussex stud. To breed to a male with an uncharacteristic head is, candidly, a waste of time. As a result of one of those quirks that occur in the minority spaniels, you might possibly get one 'sport' in the shape of a top-class head from such a mating, but you are more likely to get a collection of poor headed puppies. If you do get one good-headed 'sport', he is unlikely to pass on his good head; more likely his stock will hark back to his poor headed sire. But there are always exceptions to disprove the rule, especially in the minority spaniel breeds. One cannot say with any certainty what this or that mating will produce. It is only those breeders who have stuck with Sussex and bred several generations who know just what is likely to occur when different combinations of the existing lines are put together.

The gene pool is very small, with all lines going back to the same dogs in that pool. It is fascinating to see how some lines blended together click, and how others do not. It is also fascinating to look back and see what breeders have done. Some have continued on one line in tenacious fashion, although if they were honest with themselves and looked fairly at other breeders' stock they would see − if they would only admit it − that to go to someone else's dogs might be beneficial for their future stock. However, rivalry in breeds has always been present, and many a good chance to improve breeds has been missed because people have thought their way best and that other people and their stock were wrong. This is bad in a minority breed. It is only by all pulling together, pooling knowledge and resources and taking a good honest look at where the breed is heading that a sound future for the breed and an improvement and standardisation can be achieved.

The owner of a Sussex bitch must give very careful thought before deciding on a sire. It is necessary for this owner to study as many pedigrees as possible and to see as much stock as possible. In particular, take a long hard look at the stud dogs that are available, note puppies sired by them and look closely at the pedigree of these puppies. Because a dog has perhaps sired stocked which is too tall or too low to one bitch, it does not mean that he is wrong for your bitch. He will only be wrong if her pedigree or type is the same as that of the puppies' dams. What is wrong for one bitch is not necessarily wrong for another. Breeding a Sussex litter is not to be undertaken lightly, and to my mind it is not to be attempted by the newcomer unless he or she has very good advice from an established breeder.

The Sussex bitch should be as typical as possible and have the desired coat. She may or may not have a good mouth; she will have as good bone as possible; and she will be as near the desired size as possible. Balance in both dog and bitch is most important; breeding from unbalanced parents will only produce unbalanced puppies, i.e. incorrect in length of rib or length of loin, with weak quarters and/or upright shoulders, and with a very small head. The balanced Sussex has the correctly sized head for body size and length; good carry back of rib to strong, well-filled loin; and it stands on four good legs and feet, with well-laid shoulders and strongly developed quarters. Approaching the ideal is not easy, but it is a fact that the better balanced and proportioned the parents are, the more likely they are to produce the desired type of puppy.

Getting the Sussex bitch in whelp has proved a problem in the past, and this is still a difficulty for breeders today. It is a problem encountered in other minority breeds. Perhaps in a way this has its advantages as it prevents the breed becoming over-popular or over-populous, and these traits being great problems to any breed. When to mate the bitch for the first time, given that she may miss, is something to be studied. Many think that to mate a bitch under the age of 2 years is wrong, but a study of the Kennel Club Stud Books of the past shows that most of the big winners of their day came from litters born to bitches of just under or just over 1 year of age. It is also clear these bitches themselves were good winners; they bred on average anything from three to six litters in their lifetime, and they lived to a good age with none of the many problems encountered in modern dog breeding.

A younger bitch is far more likely to carry a litter in comfort and whelp with ease than an older bitch having a litter for the first time. I speak as a breeder of many years' experience who has bred popular breeds, such as the Cocker Spaniel, where bitches were mated at a comparatively young age. I encountered little or no trouble at whelping times, and no trouble at all in getting bitches in whelp. But I have also bred, over a long period, the sister breed to the Sussex, the Field Spaniel. Provided you can get your Field in whelp at a comparatively young age, you will find that those of 14 months to 2 years will carry a litter with greater ease and whelp far easier than the bitch that whelps her first litter at a later age, say over 3½ years. Difficulties are often encountered when the bitch whelps, frequently resulting in Caesarian sections and lost puppies.

Bitches whelping late in life only produce one litter at most, or if there are subsequent litters these are of one or two puppies only.

To those who know anything about the growth and development of the physical as well as the mental structure, it will be obvious that a young and pliable animal, whose muscles and bone structure are still malleable, is better able to adapt to a litter than an older animal, whose muscles and structure are fully developed and set in hard pattern. A young bitch is mentally more ready to accept the responsibilities of puppies and motherhood than an older bitch, particularly one kept as a pet, as many minority breeds are these days. Such a bitch, having channelled her affections to the humans in her life, finds it unacceptable to have to divert here attentions to puppies. She may reject them out of hand and in some cases even seek to kill them because they threaten to come between her and the first claim on her affections, her master and/or mistress.

When the Sussex bitch first comes into season governs when she will be ready to be mated for the first time. Some will have a first season at 7 to 8 months, some at 12 months and some not until 18 or 24 months – there is, I am afraid, no hard and fast rule for the breed. Should your bitch have first season at 8 months of age, provided her cycle is the normal one of six months she should come in again at 14 months. You may decide this is too young to mate her, and if she is a very immature and puppyish bitch you will right. However, she may be a very well-grown bitch and mature for her age. You must decide what is best for her and you, and in all probability you will wait for the third season, at 20 months of age.

Most minority spaniel bitches do not have their first season until they are from 10 to 12 months old, which means that a mating at their second season is a good proposition. Many bitches do not have a six-month cycle at all, some going eight, nine, twelve or even twenty-four months between oestrus, which makes the planning of litters very difficult. The bitch that comes in season for the first time at 18 to 20 months should, in my opinion, be mated. She may be one of those who only come in season every twelve months or so, and if you delay mating until the second season when she is 3 and she misses, you will be left with a middle-aged bitch who may prove to be a difficult whelper or an uninterested mother.

People actually engaged in breeding Sussex know the problems and the following are thoughts from two of today's top breeders and producers of Sussex Spaniels.

Mrs Mavis Lancaster, who has bred and exhibited Sussex for over 25 years says:

"It is important that bitches bred from are in the best possible condition, which means fit not fat. The day when the bitch is ready for mating varies greatly. Novice owners who have been taught to think that the bitch will be ready by the 11th day, as is the case in some breeds, invariably bring their bitches too early. Sussex on the whole are ready much later in their season than many other breeds."

The same can be said for Fields. I find that the bitch tends to ovulate fairly late in the oestrus and fourteen to twenty-one days is the usual time when the bitch is ready to mate successfully. The same is probably true for Sussex. Mrs Lancaster goes on:

"The care of the bitch is unchanged for the first five weeks, but good food and vitamins are essential. I feed on wholemeal biscuit and green tripe. When the bitch begins to get heavy, usually about the seventh week, I divide her meal into three so that she can digest better. I do not increase the amount as this sometimes makes puppies grow too big, resulting in difficulties at whelping. What one has to aim for is the good sized, healthy puppy which can be delivered easily and naturally by the mother. As quite a number of Sussex puppies are born backwards you can see the reason for this thinking."

Backwards births are quite usual and normal; it means that instead of the front legs being presented, the back legs are presented. A breach birth is when the legs are folded under a puppy which is presenting the buttocks or breach first; these births can prove difficult and may necessitate the assistance of a veterinary surgeon. Mrs Lancaster continues:

"At one time I used an outside kennel for whelping and rearing, but I found that this was not ideal as the puppies often found relating to humans difficult. I now whelp the bitches in the house and the puppies remain there for rearing and I find temperaments much improved and puppies very willing to be handled by humans. The problems of socialisation may not be apparent in some breeds, but Sussex need early introduction to modern living, door and phone bells, television and radio noise, washing machines, etc. I find my indoor bred and reared puppies accept all this as a matter of course, and settle easily in their new homes.

While the puppies are tiny the bitch and her family are left in peace until they are stronger and I do not handle them until they are 3 days old; after that I tend to handle frequently as part of the socialising programme. At 2 to 4 days tails must be docked and dew claws removed."

If you are a novice, docking must be done by a veterinary surgeon, and the general rule, says Mrs Lancaster, is leave half the tail and also one joint more. It is necessary to attend the docking and to insist that the right length of tail is left as most vets are so used to docking Cockers that they are apt to remove more of the Sussex tail than they should. It is as well to have a good photograph of an adult Sussex with tail showing that your vet can see before commencing docking.

Mrs Lancaster goes on:

"I do not find Sussex puppies difficult to rear and on the whole the Sussex bitch makes a good mother, and has a good lactation period; there are, of course, exceptions! Sussex puppies are not very active and do not move far from the next feed, sucking until full, falling asleep on the spot and waking to suck again, and not struggling round the box as other breeds do. This causes them to put on weight rather rapidly and with their breed structure leads to a heavy puppy, which causes the chest to become flat, especially in small litters in which the pups get more milk. In some breeds they would be termed 'swimmers', but I can assure you that once the puppy is ready to get up on its feet it will do so, and then the chest will drop and the puppy will be perfectly alright. Some breeders and no doubt veterinarians would I am sure disagree with me, but my own thoughts are that Nature keeps them inactive to a certain extent, to allow the legs to grow strong enough to support the weight for size. The Sussex puppy takes far longer to open its eyes than most breeds, and it is often 14 days before the eyes begin to open. Sussex are slow growing and developing and it is unwise to try and hurry the process.

I don't begin to wean puppies until they start licking, and then I introduce them to a mix of baby foods. Sussex from an early age have very decided views on whether to eat or not, and if they decide not, it is wise not to try and force them; they will come to it in their own good time, even puppies. I do not feed much milk; many Sussex puppies do not care for milk, and anyway, most of the dams have ample supplies and weaning puppies are ready for solid food. I wean them on raw tripe which I squeeze on my finger and let them lick it off; as soon as they are proficient the tripe is finely minced and later mixed with wholemeal puppy biscuit. After six weeks the dam ceases to take interest in them to a great extent, although it is well to remember that any bitch will hop in with the pups after she has had her own meal and may regurgitate for them, so it is as well to feed her on fine mince and biscuit at that time, so as to avoid puppies choking on large lumps mother has provided for them.

By 8 or 9 weeks I have chosen the pups I am going to keep and allow them to toddle along with adult dogs on a short walk, not of course, on a lead. They can go further if carried and put down every now and then for a few more yards. I am fortunate to live in the country where this sort of exercise is possible. For those in urban or semi-rural situations, the puppy should not be allowed to walk on public ground until all inoculations are complete. When taking these pups out I also take the whistle, so from a very early age they learn to obey commands in this medium. I am a great believer in plenty of rest for growing puppies, and find that short walks which stimulate muscles and get the puppy using its senses make for a sleepy puppy that will take his rest deeply and peaceably when he returns home. I feed the pups four times a day at 8 weeks old, and at the eleventh week cut one meal, increasing the size of the other three so they do not miss out on content or amount. It is essential to see that the Sussex puppy is correctly nourished but not allowed to become over-fat. The pup stays on three meals until he is 6 months old, unless he rejects a meal, when I adjust the feeding pattern to his needs. There are difficult feeders in the breed, and these have to be distinguished from those who are just playing you up. Difficult feeders who lose weight have to be encouraged by various means and by trying all types of food until one hits on what attracts that particular dog. I never, however, leave uneaten food down, but always take it up. Food left around goes sour and collects flies, and it can upset the dog if eaten in this state. For those who would breed a Sussex litter with thoughts of breeding a show dog for themselves, I would say this; you must be prepared to keep some of them up to six months or even longer, the breed does have its devotees but it is not a widely known breed and there is not always a ready market for them. It is no use breeding and expecting to sell your surplus to new owners when the puppies are 8 weeks.

Apart from that, if you are really anxious to keep the best for yourself, then to run on as many promising babies as possible means that you have the best chance, as Sussex puppies do alter greatly between birth and maturity and there is always the mouth factor to be taken into consideration. If you have not got the facilities necessary to run on unsold promising puppies, then please do not breed. People who breed puppies and then sell them to the first comer because they have no space, cannot afford the food or have just lost interest can do lasting harm to our breed, as many of these puppies turn up in unsuitable homes and may fetch up in rescue homes.''

Mrs Faith Gilham added Sussex Spaniels to her successful Clumber Kennels in the 1970s. She has bred a number of good winners and her advice runs as follows:

"When contemplating breeding a Sussex litter, the sire and dam should complement one another; they should be sound and as free as possible from hereditary defects, and of compatible breeding lines. The dam should be in good physical condition and free from worms. Age is to be considered, but the third season seems a good time to commence breeding as the bitch has done most of her growing and developing then and is mature enough for motherhood. When my bitches have been mated I treat them as normal up to five weeks, with their usual food and exercise. At five weeks if they show in whelp I divide the food into two meals, instead of the usual one, and supplement the meals with an extra amount of fresh meat."

Mrs Gilham, like Mrs Lancaster, places great emphasis on the fact that the bitch must be fit and not fat. Mrs Gilham continues:

"Many breeders tell me that they feed calcium and vitamins to their bitches in whelp, but I do not do this. All dogs are fed a well-balanced diet with a 21% protein intake, ox cheek, tripe and a freely available supply of goats' milk being the principal food used.

Sussex litters vary in size; I have bred them from three in number to thirteen, but the average is six to eight. Peace and quiet is the order for newly arrived puppies, and the bitch should have as much wholesome food as she demands, and plenty of clean drinking water. I use Calo Carb additive, which is homeopathic; none of my bitches when whelping is given antibiotics or pituitarin, but they do sometimes have the homeopathic equivalent. When the puppies are 3 weeks I introduce them to scraped raw meat, by 4 or 5 weeks they are on four feeds a day, two of mince and puppy meal and two of cereals and milk. I like to socialise my puppies from an early age. I cut nails regularly to ensure well-shaped feet, worm them regularly, and spend a great deal of time actually watching them and trying to assess their potential. However, whatever their potential, or lack of it, all puppies receive the same feeding, care and affection; just because a puppy does not have show potential, it does not mean it must be treated differently from its littermates.

Trying to choose the best from a litter is a difficult matter. With

Sussex one should be looking for the miniature adult. Good mouths, right length of leg for age; both continue to be a problem and must be carefully studied. At 8 weeks one can usually spot those that will be too short on the leg because they do not look balanced, being all head and body and no legs, and they will almost always be the small ones. Those that are going to be too long on the leg tend to shoot up early, so are easily spotted. I tend to go for the medium-sized puppy. Mouths at this age cannot be decided; it is rather a question of 'fingers crossed and pray'! Rearing, exercise and discipline have got to be right, and how you set about getting the correct proportions depends on whether you end up with a nice-looking show dog of the correct temperament or not. On top of all this, the puppy you have chosen which seems to have the most desirable breed characteristics must have as good a mouth as possible when he changes his teeth, so keep looking at the mouth from the time when the baby teeth start to fall out, and have any stubborn first teeth removed, as these, if left in after they should have been shed, can result in second teeth coming up crooked or out of line. There is a distinct knack in bringing on a promising puppy to adulthood; it can only be accomplished with great dedication, correct rearing and education, but if you have the will then you can be rewarded with a beautiful Sussex adult that will do you proud, be good to look at and a joy to live with."

The Sussex Spaniel has always been considered a dual-purpose dog. Up to 1939 a large majority of the breed worked in the field, and many achieved their working certificates and took their titles. Unlike other gundog breeds, the Sussex has remained the same. Working interest declined sharply after the Second World War during to scarcity of numbers, difficulties in breeding, changing circumstances and new comers who had no interest in the working side. Happily, this phase is now past and the Association is doing all it can to promote the working side of the Sussex. A large majority of the members are finding wider pleasure in owning the breed, and are enjoying the training and the tests, where all have an equal chance. It is up to the individual to spend time and trouble on conditioning and training his or her Sussex to shine in what is, after all, their natural sphere.

A working dog must have the build and stamina to do the job; therefore the breed benefits from enthusiasm for working dogs and the show rings are more likely to be filled with sound typical dogs in the pink of condition. Training a Sussex to work is not easy; it requries much patience and, let it be said, a sense of humour! But once they have decided to co-operate the Sussex are excellent at their job, and it is a distinct advantage for the rough shooter to have one. New owners of a Sussex are asked to consider their dog as an all-rounder – a companion, a show dog and a worker – and to strive to help him to excel in all three areas. If he succeeds, which with dedication, time and love he will, they will be rewarded beyond measure.

16

The Sussex Spaniel Association

Extracts from Minutes of Meetings, 1924 to 1985

1924

The Sussex Spaniel Association was formed in 1924, when a group of enthusiasts met on 3 April at White City during the Kensington Canine Society's Show. The following were present: J.P.S. Clarke, C.G. Talbot Ponsonby, S.C. Batchelor, Major C.H. Wilde, S.C. Mitchell, R. Sharp and Mrs Youell. It was decided to create an association 'for the protection of the Sussex Spaniel'. The following were proposed, seconded and duly elected, without dissent, to form the committee: J.P.S. Clarke, C.G. Talbot Ponsoby, J.E. Kerr, S.C. Mitchell, R. Sharp, Major C.H. Wilde and S.C. Batchelor. Talbot Ponsonby was elected chairman of the committee, with S.C. Mitchell being elected as secretary/treasurers.

After the original meeting, the first Annual General Meeting was held, all concerned having been duly notified. At this meeting the following gentlemen were present: C.G. Talbot Ponsoby, chairman; Major C.H. Wilde; S.C. Batchelor; R. Sharp and S.C. Mitchell. Resolutions proposed at this meeting were:

1. That Mr Campbell Newington be approached to be the first president.
2. That the honorary secretary should duly register the association, which shall be known as 'The Sussex Spaniel Association'.
3. That the entrance fee for all members shall be 10s.0d. (50p) and the annual subscription shall be 10s.0d.

1925

The second Annual General Meeting was held at the Agricultural Hall on 11 February 1925. At this meeting secretary/treasurer, Mr S.C. Mitchell, resigned. Mr John Clarke was then elected to this office.

1926

This meeting was held on 11 February at Crufts. Major Wilde tendered his resignation from the committee as he was then residing abroad. Mr J.

Clarke proposed and Mr Batchelor seconded that Miss Scholefield (later Mrs Freer) be elected in Major Wilde's place. At this meeting, Mr J.E. Kerr (Harviestoun), was elected a vice-president and his place on the committee was filed by Mr R.C. Morris. In those days the association had a representative on the Field Trial Council of Representatives, and at this meeting it was decided that the subscriptions of the association to the Field Trial Council should be renewed and that the secretary/treasurer, Mr J. Clarke, was to be the association's representative.

1927

Classes would be guaranteed at the following shows: Crufts, Crystal Palace and Edinburgh. A complaint was lodged by Mr Blagg (who seems to have become a member that year), regarding the stud dog Stonelands(?) Drake (the nature of the complaint is not specified). The secretary was instructed to write to Mr Batchelor 'in a suitable manner'.

1928

It would appear that Mr J.E. Blagg was the secretary, although there is no indication of when this happened. Mr Campbell Newington presented a challenge cup to be competed for annually at Crufts, for the best dog or bitch in the breed. The annual subscription was increased to 1 guinea (£1.05). Classes were to be guaranteed at Birmingham, West Kensington and Edinburgh. At this meeting it was decided that the association should draw up a list of persons acceptable as judges of the breed. The following were provisionally accepted: Major Wilde, Lt Col. Talbot Ponsonby, J. Clarke, R.C. Morris, Mrs Youell, Miss Scholefield, E.I. Long, R. Sharp, J.E. Kerr, R. Menzies, J.W. Nicholls, Col. Claude Cane, Major Harding Cox and Mr Croxton Smith.

At a committee meeting held on 12 April 1928, one of the items discussed was the question of the awards by Mr Hoylake, the judge at Crufts. Correspondence relating to the complaint was read and it was decided to put the matter to the Kennel Club. Major Wilde was to be asked to judge at the Metropolitan Show and Capt. Incleton Webber at Birmingham. It was further decided to apply for classes at Reigate, Miss Blades, Mrs Knott and Mrs Youell guaranteeing a class each.

1929

Capt. Claude Cane was elected vice-president. Amongst members present was Mrs M. Bowers (Agrivista). It was decided that the resolutions of the previous year regarding subscriptions should be rescinded and that a 10s.0d. entrance fee and yearly subscriptions of 10s.0d. should be paid. Shows to be guaranteed were: Metropolitan and Essex, City and Suburban, LKA, Richmond, Brighton, Sheffield,

Windsor, Bournemouth, Birmingham, the KC Show and Edinburgh. Arrangements regarding classification and judges were to be left in the hands of the secretary.

1930

Claude Cane was elected as president in place of the late Campbell Newington. The committee of the previous year were re-elected, Mrs Youell having withdrawn her resignation and agreed to pay her guarantee for Brighton Show. (No detail is given anywhere about this.) Amongst new members elected at this meeting was Miss Reed (Oakerlands). Classes were to be guaranteed at Richmond, the KC Show, Edinburgh and Birmingham and 'any other shows giving KC certificates'. The association's attention was drawn to an article in the *Kennel Encyclopaedia* on Sussex Spaniels. The secretary was instructed to write to the editor. A sub-committee was formed to consider drawing up a fresh standard of points of the breed. Mr Talbot Ponsonby, J. Clarke, Capt. Incleton Webber and the secretary formed the sub-committee.

1931

Mrs Youell's resignation was considered. Correspondence between her and the secretry was read and it was agreed tht Mrs Youell had no cause whatsoever for complaint and that the secretry had done the only thing possible in the circumstances. A letter had been sent to Messrs Virtue and Co. with reference to the article in the *Kennel Encyclopaedia* to which exception had been taken. The printers had replied that the comments had been passed on to the editor so that alterations could be made in the next edition. Regarding the question of the standard of points, it was decided that there was nothing to alter in the present standard, especially the description 'long, low and strong'. It was pointed out that this did not mean that the dog should not be too high, 17 in. being considered the limit. As the accounts had shown a deficit of £5.3s.3d. (about £5.16) it would be impossible to guarantee any shows unless members were prepared to contribute to a prize fund, especially in view of the fact that twelve subscriptions had been paid for the year, which left only eighteen outstanding. In spite of these financial problems, it was unanimously agreed that the classes be guaranteed at LKA, Richmond, Edinburgh, the KC Show, Metropolitan and Essex, and Birmingham, and any other shows at which CC's were on offer. The secretary emphasised that the members would have to be prepared to find the money for the guarantees. Miss Blades said she would not contribute to a guarantee fund but would guarantee a limit class at LKA, Richmond, and Metropolitan and Essex shows.

1932

Col. Claude Cane resigned as president due to ill health. The presidency was filled by Mr J.P. Stevenson Clark and Viscount Eblisham was to be invited to become a vice-president. Mrs Youell presented a silver rose bowl, to be known as the Earlswood Cup, for competition at the KC Show for best dog or bitch not having won a CC, any exhibitor winning it three times to win it outright. The accounts were still showing a deficit and it was agreed that the loss must be provided for. (Apparently the membership still wanted to guarantee classes even though it was stated that it would be impossible to do so because of the financial state.) A great deal of discussion ensued and the following resolution was passed unanimously: 'that at all shows where classes are guaranteed by the association, the classes shall be open to all but that the loss should be made up by the members who win at these shows, out of prize winnings *pro rata* according to the prize money won'. The following shows would be guaranteed: LKA, Richmond, KC, Metropolitan, Birmingham, Edinburgh and Crufts 1933.

On 12 May 1932, an extraordinary general meeting took place at the LKA Show. The topic for discussion was the financial state of the association. The secretary stated that the association was not in a financial position to guarantee classes at any show. Mrs Youell proposed that the resolution passed at the AGM to guarantee classes and also regarding the pooling of prize money be rescinded. This was passed *nem. con.*

1933

Present at this meeting was Miss Wigg (Hornshill), and she was elected on to the committee in place of Mrs Bower, who had resigned. The question of the standard was raised once again and it was eventually arranged that the secretary should send a copy of the standard to Mrs Youell in order that she would suggest revisions and submit them to the chairman (Talbot Ponsonby) for his opinion; they would then be submitted to the committee for final approval. When approved, a copy of the standard points should be supplied to each judge and they would be requested to judge according to them. Once again guarantees were proposed for Richmond, LKA, Metropolitan and Essex, and Crufts 1934, but not Birmingham. The chairman, Mrs Bower, Mrs Youell and Miss Wigg signed a guarantee to provide £5 each to cover losses at shows.

1936

Mr J.S. Blagg resigned as secretary/treasurer and Miss Scholefield was elected in his place.

1937

The death of Lt Col. Talbot Ponsonby was recorded. Miss Wigg proposed that there should be a challenge cup in his memory and that all members should be invited to subscribe, also that the cup should be awarded under the same conditions as the Campbell Newington Cup but to the dog of opposite sex. Capt. Incleton Webber was elected as president.

1939

Capt. Incleton Webber's death was recorded; Col. Downes Pownell was elected president. It was agreed to guarantee classes at Crufts 1940, LKA, and all KC shows at which CCs were offered for the breed. Miss Reed proposed that the Association be carried on; this was seconded by Mrs Maxted and was carried. Miss Reed proposed that all classes guaranteed by the Sussex Spaniel Association be confined to member of the SSA This was seconded by Mrs Bower and carried.

No further meetings were held until after the war. In 1949, Mrs I.B. Johnstone (Framsden) recorded the minutes. At this meeting four members were in attendance: Col. Downes Pownell, Mrs Bower, Mrs Freer and Mrs Johnstone. It was decided not to give a subscription to the AHT until the association's funds were larger. The secretary was advised to state in the breed notes in the dog press that new members were welcome. The breed outcross was discussed and either a Field or Clumber Spaniel was considered. The financial report showed a balance of £9 in hand. Miss Wigg said she wished her silver salver to be awarded at Crufts instead of at LKA.

1951

Mrs T. Manley Cooper (Mountgarvey) and Dr E. Rickards (Tarbay) were present at this meeting and were amongst the new members elected. Miss Wigg's Silver Salver was to be awarded for Best Sussex Spaniel Puppy Dog or Bitch at Crufts; if won three years in succession by the same owner it was to be won outright. Members were urged to register puppies as soon as possible after birth to keep registrations up. Mrs Manley Cooper was elected as treasurer in place of Mr R.H. Johnstone. Outcross was discussed again.

1953

The finances had improved; there was £44 in hand. At this meeting, it was decided that no specials were to be offered from club funds, it being felt that the money could be more usefully spent in other ways, such as helping with the training of a dog for field trials. Mr Curtis, the head keeper at Knapp Castle, Horsham, was to be asked about the cost of training a Sussex and entering it in field trials. The possibility of forming a syndicate to run one was discussed. Mr W. Graham Golding presented the Coronation Bowl for competition at the Brighton Show.

1954

Mrs Woodyatt was elected first honorary member as a token of gratitude from the members for competition at Windsor. The Association wanted to transfer the CCs allocated to Birmingham National to Brighton. The secretary said she had done all she could to persuade Mr Grindy to release them but he had thought it most unlikely that his committee would agree.

1957

The association was still trying to get CCs at Brighton.

1958

Miss M. Scarr and Miss M. Harris were amongst the newly elected members. The death of Col. Downes Pownell was recorded; Mr F. Warner Hill was elected as president. Mrs Johnstone offered a trophy for WELKS.

1959

The president, Mr F. Warner Hill, suggested that an American Cocker be used for the outcross.

1961

Miss D.P. Dodson was amongst the new members elected. Miss Scarr was elected on to the committee. It was agreed that the subscription for a partnership should be 15s.0d. (75p). It was also agreed that in the future no guarantees or specials were to be given to Birmingham as they had refused to release the CCs. Dr Rickards informed the meeting that the CCs were to be taken from Windsor and allocated to the SKC. The Members asked the secretary to do all in her power to get the decision altered and it was suggested that a letter be written for all to sign in protest.

1962

The secretary was instructed to write to the SKC to tell them that the entry at Windsor, without CCs, was twenty dogs, as against five at Glasgow with CCs. The secretary was asked to write to the Royal Veterinary College asking for help and advice in view of so many bitches apparently being infertile, which was causing the association great concern.

1963

It was reported to a committee meeting that the Royal Veterinary College advised that members should consult their own vets. Mrs Manley Cooper's vet's advice was to breed right out, even not including any spaniel breed. It was agreed that members could use any recognised breed if the puppies were registered at the KC. Dr Rickards said that she was taking a bitch and two dogs to be mated under supervision at the RVC to try to determine if the fault was in the dogs or bitches. She also offered to give one or two bitches to anyone willing to breed and also a free stud to Wise One of Tarbay to any one interested. Two letters had been received from Miss Adams (Sedora) saying she had had similar trouble in her Cockers but treatment had restored their stamina. She offered to take a Sussex bitch and have it treated. The Clumber Spaniel Club had written offering a free service from a choice of stud dogs. Another suggestion was that a GSP be used. Miss Dodson was co-opted on to the committee.

1964

Miss Clarke (later Mrs Lancaster), Mrs Brookes (Creswelshaw), Miss Adams and Mr Orton were amongst the new members elected. It was agreed that no specials should be given; the association's money was to be spent when necessary on helping breeders with stud fees, etc. The chairman (Mr W.G. Golding) donated 70 guineas (£73.50) to be used to help with expenses incurred in outcrossing. Miss Dodson reported that she had five Clumber/Sussex puppies out of her Sussex bitch to Mr Ghent's Clumber dog. Miss Wigg resigned from the committee and was replaced by Mrs Oxley.

1965

Miss Clarke was elected on to the committee in place of the late Mrs Bower. Mr Orton suggested that the secretary should ask for a puppy class at WELKS as there seemed to be good prospects that it would be filled. Mrs Freer was to be asked to judge at this show. There was a discussion about travel allowance for the mating of bitches and it was decided, on Mr Elsden's proposition, that, once the donation for that purpose was finished, on no account should an allowance be paid out of club funds. This was unanimously agreed. Dr Richards offered a free service by Penruddocke Evelyn to any member who wished it as she, and others, felt not sufficient use was made of this excellent dog.

1966

At this meeting, the president, Mr F. Warner Hill retired. Mrs Manley Cooper retired from the treasurership and Mrs Johnstone from the secretaryship. All resignations were regretfully accepted. Mrs Manley Cooper was elected president, Mrs Lancaster was elected secretary and Mr Lancaster was elected treasurer.

1967

The financial position shown was a balance of £139.17s.9d. (about £139.88). Mrs Johnstone asked if it was necessary to increase the subscription in view of this excellent report. (Subscriptions had been doubled in 1966.) It was pointed out that from this total an amount had been paid out for the outcrossing, which would show on the next statement. It was agreed that the increase should stand.

The breed standard was discussed. The standard for the skull was to be amended to read, 'brows frowning', as in the 1937 standard.

Mrs Johnstone asked if the less popular breeds of spaniel could jointly organise a show of their own. (As the Kennel Club rules were at that time, no breed other than the one in the club's title could hold a show. The idea was not pursued.)

1968

Mrs B.I. 'Queenie' Johnstone's death was recorded. Air Commodore Paull was one of those applying for membership.

It was decided that the Annual General Meeting should be held at a venue other than a show; owing to a number of members exhibiting in more than one breed it had become difficult to hold a successful meeting. Rule 7 was to be altered to read: 'The AGM of the club shall be held at some convenient venue before the end of March'.

1969

The AGM was held at Holme Farm, West Willoughby, Grantham, Lincolnshire, the home of Miss Adams and Mr Orton. At this meeting Mr Orton proposed that the committee number be increased to six members; this was carried. Mr Orton proposed that some form of award should be given to honour the memory of the late Mrs Johnstone. This was agreed and Mr Jack Freer was to make some enquiries with a view to purchasing a salver, which would be called the Queenie Johnstone Memorial Salver. Hove was the obvious choice of show for it to be allocated to, but it was felt that it was not an ideal location as regards exhibitors. The secretary was instructed to write to Three Counties, asking if they would put classes on for the breed; these would be fully guaranteed.

Mr Freer said that ground had been offered to the association to hold a field trial; two trophies were also offered for competition. The meeting felt that there were not enough working Sussex to hold a full-scale trial. Mr Freer said the donor would be agreeable to a working test and this was agreed.

Mr Freer proposed that bona fide gamekeepers be admitted to membership of the association for half the fee, i.e. 10s.6d. (about 52p); this was agreed.

1970

Mrs Freer resigned from the committee. Mr Freer was approved as the breed representative to the Kennel Club Liaison Council.

Three Counties had approved four classes at their show for an experimental period; members were asked to give their support.

The Cocker Spaniel Council had written asking for two delegates to attend the forthcoming European Spaniel Congress on behalf of the breed. Mr Golding donated the expenses for the delegates; Mrs Munday and Mrs Lancaster were nominated.

1971

Mr W. Graham Golding resigned as chairman; Miss Daphne Dodson was elected in his place. Mr Freer also relinquished his position as the breed representative to the Kennel Club Liaison Council. The Kennel Club had written to say that although Mr Freer was the nominee for Sussex Spaniels, he was, in fact, the representative for all the spaniel breeds. The appointment of a replacement would therefore involve a by-election, and the association would be advised of when this could be organised. Mrs Munday suggested that a reply in line with the KC directive in the *Kennel Gazette* of January 1969 should be sent; each breed, as opposed to each variety, should be represented and the association, therefore, would like to nominate its own representative.

A letter from Dr Rickards, the convenor of the European Spaniel Congress, had been received, asking that the association should send delegates to an inaugural meeting of the proposed United Spaniel Association. It was decided that two delegates should be sent with a watching brief; the committee would decide who would attend.

1972

A letter was received from the Kennel Club regarding the Kennel Club Liaison Council; they had agreed that each spaniel breed should have its own representative.

1976

The death of Mrs R. Paull was recorded.

1978

An open show was to be organised; Mr Reg. Gadsden was to be invited to judge.

1979

A rescue scheme was proposed and put into effect. £50 was donated from association funds.

1981

Miss Adams's death was recorded.

1982

Miss Dodson retired as chairman and was elected as a life member.

1984

Miss Scarr and Miss Harris were elected as life members. Diamond Jubilee events were organised. The first year book was to be published to coincide with the Diamond Jubilee.

1985

Mrs J. Freer's death was recorded. Miss Scarr was elected president and Mr G. Lancaster was elected as chairman.

APPENDIX

List of Pedigrees

Pedigree   Name
Number

 1 Bebb 2101
 2 Bachelor 6287
 3 Ch. Bachelor III 11617
 4 Ch. Baryta 12690
 5 Rosehill Romulus 24757
 6 Ch. Bridford Mocky 745D
 7 Bridford Giddie 26957
 8 Rosehill Ruler II 36391
 9 Ch. Newbarn Billy 1011M
10 Ch. Rosehill Rattler 901R
11 Harviestoun Pedro 854Q
12 Harviestoun Beau 753AA
13 Broadhurst Brush 1395DD
14 Primax Judy 975FF
15 Langrish Bruno 83GG
16 Westmark Belle 1317MM
17 Ch. Agrivista Beta 1940LL
18 Ch. Okimat of Fourclovers 1316MM
19 Agrivista Helios 93AH
20 Pontiac of Fourclovers 94AH
21 Shataukok Spandax
22 Sh.Ch. Penruddocke Evelyn 1068AQ
23 Sh.Ch. Haiwatha of Fourclovers
24 Sh.Ch. Chesara Chervil 1579AY
25 Sh.Ch. Sharland Sussex Wine 3087BH
26 Sh.Ch. Creswelshaw Hannibal
27 Sh.Ch. Topjoys Sussex Harvester
28 Sh.Ch. Quintic Joby 672BN
29 Sh.Ch. Harvest Glow of Oldfield 1094BU
30 Sh.Ch. Creswelshaw Oriel of Daelyb
31 Sh.Ch. Oldholbans Lesanlea Paperchase
32 Novacroft Thyme

BEBB 2101
Date of birth 1866

DOG	PARENTS	G PARENTS	GG PARENTS	GGG PARENTS
	SIRE			
Bebb 2101 (liver) Br. P. Bullock	P. Bullock's Old Bebb	S. Lord Derby's breed		
		D. (thought to be English Water Spaniels)		
	DAM	S. G. Jones of Oscott's Bob 2110 (black Cocker)	S. Bob 2107 (Cocker)	S. Burdett's Frank — (black and tan)
				D. Mousley's — (liver and white)
	FLIRT		D. G. Jones's Flo (Cocker)	S. Frank
				D. —
		D. Nellie 2226 (black Cocker)	S. Bob 2110	S. Bob 2107
				D. Flo
			D. G. Jones of Oscott's — (Cocker)	S. Bob
				D. Jones's Chloe (Cocker)

BACHELOR 6287

Litter brother to Rover III and Duchess III. (Bred by Dr H.B. Spurgin, whelped May 1875. Bought by Saxby, and sold to Langdale, who sold him to Jacobs.)

DOG	PARENTS	G PARENTS	GG PARENTS	GGG PARENTS
Bachelor 6287	**SIRE** Buckingham 4400	S. Marchant's Rover	S. Sir P. Micklethwaite's Dash	S. — D. —
			D. Weston's Fanny	S. Marchant's Rover II D. Marchant's Duchess II
		D. Saxby's Fan	S. —	S. — D. —
			D. —	S. — D. —
	DAM Dr H.B. Spurgin's Peggie 5255 Br. Mr Hine Wh. 1875	S. Bebb 2101	S. Old Bebb	S. Lord Derby's breed[1] D. —
			D. —	S. — D. —
		D. Ruby	S. Salter's Chance 2119	S. Lightfoot's Bounce D. Bradfield's Spot
			D. Bowers's Pop (black)	S. Jobling's Rap D. Floss

[1]Thought to be English Water Spaniels

CH. BACHELOR III 11617

Owner: Moses Woolland, breeder: T. Jacobs, whelped 1881. Also pedigree of Dolly 14205, liver and tan.

PARENTS	G PARENTS	GG PARENTS	GGG PARENTS	GGGGG PARENTS
SIRE: Bachelor II	SIRE: Bachelor 6287 Wh. 1875	S. Buckingham 4400 Wh. 1871	S. Marchant's Rover	S. Sir P. Micklethwaite's Dash
				D. Weston's Fanny
			D. Saxby's Fan	S. —
				D. —
		D. Dr H.B. Spurgin's Peggie 5255	S. Bebb 2101	S. Old Bebb
				D. Flirt
			D. Salter's Ruby	S. Chance 2119
				D. Bowers's Pop
	DAM: F.C. Barton's Countess 9269 Br. H. Hawkins; Wh. 1878 (golden liver)	S. T.B. Bowers's Rover III 5249 Br. Dr. H.B. Spurgin; Wh. 1875	S. Buckingham 4400	S. Marchant's Rover
				D. Saxby's Fan
			D. Peggie 5255	S. Bebb 2101
				D. Salter's Ruby
		D. T.B. Bowers's Duchess III 5252 Br. Dr H.B. Spurgin	S. Buckingham 4400	S. Marchant's Rover
				D. Saxby's Fan
			D. Peggie 5255	S. Bebb 2101
				D. Salter's Ruby
DAM: Brunette 15906 Wh. Jan. 1880	SIRE: Bachelor 6287 Wh. 1875	S. Buckingham 4400	S. Marchant's Rover	S. Sir P. Micklethwaite's Dash
				D. Weston's Fanny
			D. Saxby's Fan	S. —
				D. —
		D. Peggie 5255	S. Bebb 2101	S. Old Bebb
				D. Flirt
			D. Salter's Ruby	S. Chance 2119
				D. Bower's Pop
	DAM: T. Jacobs's Ladyship[1] (late Russet) 6302 Br. Martin Pate; Wh. Apr. 1875 (golden liver)	S. Rev. Shields's Rex 2163 Wh. 1872	S. Bebb 2101	S. Old Bebb
				D. Flirt
			D. Fuss 2213; Wh. 1867 20lbs	S. Shields's Bill[2]
				D. Shields's Fan[2]
		D. T.B. Bowers's Ruby 6301 Br. Mr Handy; Wh. 1872 (liver)	S. Salter's Chance 2119	S. Lightfoot's Bounce
				D. Bradfield's Spot
			D. Bowers's Pop	S. Rap
				D. Floss 2209

[1] Used extensively to breed Field Spaniels

[2] This pedigree goes back to Burdett's Frank, Mousley's Venus and Bullock's Bob 2108

CH. BARYTA 12690

Sussex Spaniel dog, whelped January 1882. Owned by Messrs Holley, Laurel Cottage, Sherfield, Basingstoke. Also pedigree of Holleys' Horatio 13265 and Aurelia 13778.

PARENTS	G PARENTS	GG PARENTS	GGG PARENTS	GGGG PARENTS
SIRE	**SIRE**	**GG PARENTS**	**GGG PARENTS**	**GGGG PARENTS**
T. Swaby's Bounce	H. Saxby's Bachelor 6287 Br. Dr H.B. Spurgin	S. Buckingham 4400 Wh. 1871	S. Marchant's Rover [1]	S. Sir P. Micklethwaite's Dash
				D. Weston's Fanny [2]
			D. Saxby's Fan [1]	S. –
				D. –
		D. Dr H.B. Spurgin's Peggie 5255	S. Bebb 2101	S. Old Bebb (Lord Derby's breed)
				D. Flirt
			D. Salter's Ruby	S. Salter's Chance 2119 (Wh. 1865)
				D. Bowers's Pop (black)
	DAM			
	T. Jacobs's Smutty 7385 Br. Mr Lang; (black Field Spaniel)	S. W. Boulton's Rolfe 5264 (black Field Spaniel)	S. Boulton's Beaver 4408 (black Field Spaniel) Wh. Feb. 1874	S. Buccleuch 4413 [4]
				D. Nellie [1]
			D. Boulton's Runic 4434 (black Field Spaniel)	S. Rex (Cocker Spaniel)
				D. Fan (Old English Cocker)
		D. W. Boulton's Belle 2184 Wh. 10 Aug. 1873 (black Field Spaniel)	S. Langdale's (black Field Spaniel)	S. Powley's Ben (Wh. 1869, blck, br. unknwn)
				D. Boulton's Ferry [6]
			D. Nellie 2221	S. –
				D. –
DAM	**SIRE**			
Duchess IV	T.B. Bowers's Rover III 5249 Litter brother to Duchess III; Wh. approx. 1875	S. T.B. Bowers's Buckingham 4400 Br. H. Saxby; Wh. 1871	S. Marchant's Rover	S. Sir P. Micklethwaite's Dash
				D. Weston's Fanny
			D. Saxby's Fan	S. –
				D. –
		D. Peggie 5255	S. Bebb 2101	S. Old Bebb
				D. –
			D.	S. Chance 2119
				D. Bower's Pop
	DAM			
	T.B. Bowers' Duchess III 5252 Litter sister to Rover III; Wh. approx. 1875 (golden liver)	S. Buckingham 4400	S. Marchant's Rover	S. Sir P. Micklethwaite's Dash
				D. Weston's Fanny
			D. Saxby's Fan	S. –
				D. –
		D. Peggie 5255 1874	S. Bebb 2101	S. Old Bebb
				D. –
			D. Ruby	S. Chance 2119
				D. Bowers's Pop [1]

[1] Saxby lived at Lewes, Sussex. It is assumed Marchant and Saxby had Fuller's strain, but there is no written evidence of this, only claims.

[2] By Marchant's Rover II ex Duchess II.

[3] By Jobling's Rap ex Handy's Floss 2209.

[4] By Bouton's Old Bruce, brother to Boss 4412.

[5] By Bainton's Sussex ex Cocker bitch.

[6] By Rufus 2167 (Cocker Spaniel) ex Jet 2216, who was by Prince's dog ex Chloe.

ROSEHILL ROMULUS 24757

Sussex Spaniel dog; liver. Date of Birth: 7 April 1887. Bred by owner: Campbell Newington of Ticehurst, Sussex. Also pedigree of Rosehill Ross 24758 and Rosehill Reine 24768

PARENTS	G PARENTS	GG PARENTS	GGG PARENTS	GGGG PARENTS
SIRE	**SIRE**	S. Buckingham 4400 Wh. 1871	S. Marchant's Rover	S. Sir P. Micklethwaite's Dash
	Bachelor 6287		D. Saxby's Fan	D. Weston's Fanny
H. Green's Caistor 9265 (late Guess) Wh. 27 Sept. 1877 (whole golden liver)				S. —
				D. —
		D. Dr H.B. Spurgin's Peggie 5255	S. Bebb 2101	S. Old Bebb
				D. Flirt
			D. Salter's Ruby	S. Salter's Chance
				D. Bowers's Pop (black)[2]
	DAM	S. Chance 2119	S. Lightfoot's Bounce	S. Eyton's Tippo Sahib
				D. Lightfoot's Belle
	H. Green's Chloe 5251[1] (own sister to Chancellor 5247) Wh. 23 May 1875		D. Bradfield's Spot (from Mr Cox, Berkshire)	S. —
				—
		D. Salter's Chloe	S. —	S. —
				D. —
			D. —	S. —
				D. —
DAM	**SIRE**	S. Bachelor 6287	S. Buckingham 4400	S. Marchant's Rover
				D. Saxby's Fan
C. Newington's Countess of Rosehill 20598 Br. H. Sutton	Chance II 12691		D. Peggie 5255	S. Bebb 2101
				D. Salter's Ruby
		D. Chloe 5251	S. Chance 2119	S. Lightfoot's Bounce
				D. Bradfield's Spot
			D. Salter's Chloe	S. —
				D. —
	DAM	S. —	S. —	S. —
				D. —
	T.B. Bowers's Bustle 4404 Wh. 1869 (unknown pedigree)		D. —	S. —
				D. —
		D. —	S. —	S. —
				D. —
			D. —	S. —
				D. —

[1] Green was of Fincham, Sussex.

[2] By Jobling's Rap ex Floss 2209

CH. BRIDFORD MOCKY 745D

Whelped 3 July 1897; litter brother to Bridford Bibelot.

PARENTS	G PARENTS	GG PARENTS	GGG PARENTS	GGGG PARENTS
SIRE Bridford Prince 796C Wh. 1895	**SIRE** Bridford Bredaboy 671M Wh. 1892	S. Bridford Giddie 26957	S. Bridford Victor 20589	S. Bridford Dallian 18486 D. Bridford Battle 19249
			D. Bridford Naomi 20596	S. Guy 8352 D. Bridford Battle 19249
		D. Bridford Brida II 22535	S. Bridford Dallian 18468	S. Horatio 13625 D. Belle of Bradley
			D. Bridford Brida 11623	S. Rover III 5249 D. Brida I
	DAM Rosehill Rita 38397	S. Rosehill Ruler II 36391	S. Young Wallace 20594	S. Caistor 9265 D. Flirt
			D. Wanda 18291	S. Quince 12695 D. Cyprus (by Bachelor)
		D. Rosehill Ruby	S. Rosehill Ruler 33934	S. Young Wallace 20594 D. Wanda 18291
			D. Rosehill Russet 29111	S. Candidate 22548 D. Rosehill Reine (by Caistor)
DAM Bridford Minnie 33937	**SIRE** Bridford Giddie 26957 Wh. 1888	S. Bridford Victor 20589	S. Bridford Dallian 18486	S. Horatio 13625 D. Belle of Bradley
			D. Bridford Battle 19249	S. Chance II 12691 D. Sutton's Bustle
		D. Bridford Naomi 20596	S. Guy 8352	S. Bachelor 6287 D. Chloe 5251
			D. Bridford Battle 19249	S. Chance II 12691 D. Sutton's Bustle
	DAM Bridford Brida 11623	S. Rover III 3249	S. Buckingham 4400	S. Marchant's Rover D. Saxby's Fan
			D. Peggie 5255	S. Bebb 2101 D. Ruby
		D. Brida I	S. Bebb 2101	S. Old Bebb D. Flirt
			D. Ruby	S. — D. —

BRIDFORD GIDDIE 26957

Sussex Spaniel dog. Date of birth: 21 July 1888. Breeder/owner: Marcus Woolland.

PARENTS	G PARENTS	GG PARENTS	GGG PARENTS	GGGG PARENTS
SIRE Bridford Victor 20589 Br./owner: M. Woolland	SIRE Bridford Dallian 18486 Wh. 1884 Br./owner: M. Woolland	S. Horatio 13625	S. Swaby's Bounce	S. Bachelor 6287 D. Smutty 7285 (black Field)
			D. Duchess VI	S. Rover III 5249 D. Duchess III 5252
		D. Belle of Bradley	S. Hooker's Sport	S. — D. —
			D. Hooker's Flirt	S. — D. —
	DAM Bridford Battle 19249 Br. H. Sutton; Wh. 1883	S. Chance II 12691	S. Bachelor 6287	S. Chance 2119 D. Salter's Chloe
			D. Chloe 5251	S. — D. —
		D. Sutton's Bustle (or bitch with similar name)	S. —	
			D. —	
DAM Bridford Naomi 20596 Wh. 1885	SIRE Guy 8352 Wh. 1877	S. Bachelor 6287	S. Buckingham 4400	S. Marchant's Rover D. Saxby's Fan
			D. Spurgin's Peggie 5255	S. Bebb 2101 D. Salter's Ruby
		D. Chloe 5251	S. Chance 2119	S. Lightfoot's Bounce D. Bradfield's Spct
			D. Salter's Chloe	S. — D. —
	DAM Bridford Battle 19249	S. Chance II 12691	S. Bachelor 6287	S. Buckingham 6287 D. Peggie 5255
			D. Chloe 5251	S. Chance 2119 D. Salter's Chloe
		D. Sutton's Bustle	S. —	S. — D. —
			D. —	S. — D. —

ROSEHILL RULER II 36391

PARENTS	G PARENTS	GG PARENTS	GGG PARENTS	GGGG PARENTS
SIRE	SIRE	S. Caistor 9265	S. Bachelor 6287	S. Buckingham 4400
				D. Spurgin's Peggie 5255
	Young Wallace 20594		D. Chloe 5251	S. Salter's Chance 2119
				D. Salter's Chloe
		D. Flirt	S. —	S. —
				D. —
			D. —	S. —
				D. —
Rosehill Ruler II	DAM	S. Quince 12695	S. Boscoe (Field Spaniel)	S. —
36391				D. —
Br. T. Newington;			D. Fan VII	S. Bachelor 6287
Wh. 15 July 1889				D. —
(golden liver)	Wanda 18291	D. Cyprus	S. Bachelor 6287	S. Buckingham 4400
				D. Peggy 5255
			D. Bustle	S. —
				D. —

CH. NEWBARN BILLY 1011M

PARENTS

DOG

Ch. Newbarn Billy 1011M
Wh. 3 Feb 1906

G PARENTS

SIRE

Bridford Bobs 1193KK
Ch. 1899

DAM

Newbarn Momie 1012M

GG PARENTS

S. Ch. Bridford Mocky 745D

D. Ch. Bridford Queenie 693A
Wh. 1892

S. Ch. Bridford Mocky 745D

D. Rolyat Rose
(Field Spaniel)

GGG PARENTS

S. Bridford Prince 796C
Wh. 1895

D. Bridford Minnie 33937
Wh. 1888

S. Bridford Giddie 26957
Wh. 1885

D. Bridford Dolly 26967

S. Bridford Prince 796C

D. Bridford Minnie 33937

S. Ch. Bridford Tommy
(Field Spaniel)

D. Ch. Bridford Gypsy
(Field Spaniel)

GGGG PARENTS

S. Bridford Bredaboy 671M (Wh. 1892)
D. Rosehill Rita 38397

S. Ch. Bridford Giddie 26957
D. Bridford Brida 11632[1]

S. Bridford Victor 20589
D. Bridford Naomi 20596

S. Bachelor III 11617 (Wh. 1888)
D. Bridford Brida II 11555

S. Bridford Bredaboy 671M
D. Rosehill Rita 38397

S. Ch. Bridford Giddie 26957
D. Bridford Brida 11623[1]

S. Ch. Bridford Shah[2]
D. Bridford Dolly II[3]

S. —
D. —

[1] By Rover III 5249 ex Brida I.
[2] By Bachelor III (Sussex) ex Ch. Squaw (black).
[3] By Ch. Bridford Shah (Field Spaniel) ex Bridford Dolly (Sussex).

CH. ROSEHILL RATTLER 901R

Whelped 27 October 1908; litter brother to Rosehill Reason 8R and Rocca 903R. (This mating was repeated in 1909 and resulted in Rosehill Rip 1138T.)

PARENTS	G PARENTS	GG PARENTS	GGG PARENTS	GGGG PARENTS
SIRE Rosehill Radium 1066N	**SIRE** Ch. Rosehill Rashleigh 1194K	S. Ch. Bridford Mocky 745D	S. Bridford Prince 796C	S. Ch. Bridford Bredaboy 671M
				D. Rosehill Rita 38397
			D. Bridford Minnie 33937	S. Ch. Bridford Giddie 26957
				D. Bridford Brida 11623
		D. Rolyat Rose (Field Spaniel)	S. Ch. Bridford Tommy (Field Spaniel)	S. Ch. Bridford Shah
				D. Bridford Dolly II
			D. Ch. Bridford Gypsy (Field Spaniel)	S. —
				D. —
	DAM Rosehill Reda	S. Ch. Rosehill Ranji 839H	S. Rosehill Rush 40626	S. Rosehill Rebel 38595
				D. Futurity 33940
			D. Rosehill Rhonda	S. —
				D. —
		D. Carntyne Jessie	S. Heather Glen	S. Ch. Bridford Victor
				D. Bridford Bustle
			D. Carntyne Nell	S. Young Wallace
				D. Peggie
DAM Rosehill Rossa	**SIRE** Ch. Rosehill Ranji 839H	S. Rosehill Rush 40625	S. Rosehill Rebel 38595	S. Rosehill Ruler II 36391
				D. Rosehill Ruby
			D. Futurity 33940	S. Dick of Arvon 29104
				D. Bridford Infidelty (Field)
		D. Rosehill Rhonda (unreg.)	S. —	S. —
				D. —
			D. —	S. —
				D. —
	DAM Rosehill Rosie 839H	S. Ch. Rosehill Rock 856G	S. Ch. Bridford Bibelot 770E	S. Bridford Prince 796C
				D. Bridford Minnie 33937
			D. Rosehill Rhonda	S. —
				D. —
		D. Rolyat Rose	S. Ch. Bridford Tommy	S. Ch. Bridford Shah
				D. Bridford Dolly II
			D. Ch. Bridford Gypsy	S. —
				D. —

HARVIESTOUN PEDRO 854Q

Born: 8 August 1909.

PARENTS	G PARENTS	GG PARENTS	GGG PARENTS	GGGG PARENTS
SIRE	**SIRE**			
Ch. Newbarn Billy 1011M	Bridford Bobs 1193K	S. Ch. Bridford Mocky 745D	S. Bridford Prince 796C	S. Ch. Bridford Bredaboy 671M
				D. Rosehill Rita 38397
			D. Bridford Minnie 33937	S. Bridford Giddie 26957
				D. Bridford Brida 11623
		D. Ch. Bridford Queenie 693A	S. Ch. Bridford Giddie 26957	S. Ch. Bridford Victor 20589
				D. Bridford Naomi 20596
			D. Bridford Dolly 26967	S. Bachelor III 11617
				D. Bridford Brida II 22555
	DAM			
	Newbarn Momie 1012M	S. Ch. Bridford Mocky 745D	S. Bridford Prince 796C	S. Bridford Bredaboy 671M
				D. Rosehill Rita 38397
			D. Bridford Minnie 33937	S. Bridford Giddie 26957
				D. Bridford Brida 11623
		D. Rolyat Rose	S.	S. —
			All-Field Spaniel	D. —
			D.	S. —
			Breeding	D. —
DAM	**SIRE**			
Sunny Jane 876P	Ch. Rosehill Rock 856G	S. Bridford Bibelot 770E	S. Bridford Prince 796C	S. Bridford Bredaboy 671M
				D. Rosehill Rita 38397
			D. Bridford Minnie 33937	S. Bridford Giddie 26957
				D. Bridford Brida 11623
		D. Rosehill Rhonda (unreg.)	S. —	S. —
				D. —
			D. —	S. —
				D. —
	DAM			
	Sultana 1068N	S. Bridford Bobs 1193K	S. Ch. Bridford Mocky 745D	S. Bridford Prince 796C
				D. Bridford Minnie 33937
			D. Ch. Bridford Queenie 693A	S. Bridford Giddie 26957
				D. Bridford Dolly 26967
		D. Rosehill Regalie 138IJ	S. Ch. Rosehill Ranji 839H	S. Ch. Rosehill Rush 40625
				D. Rosehill Rhonda
			D. Rosehill Rummie (formerly Brownie) (unreg.)	S. —
				D. —

HARVIESTOUN BEAU 753AA
Wh. 12 April 1919.

PARENTS	G PARENTS	GG PARENTS	GGG PARENTS	GGGG PARENTS
DOG				
Harviestoun Beau 753AA				
SIRE	Harviestoun Jimmy	S. Harviestoun Sam 668W	S. Harviestoun Pedro 854Q²	S. Ch. Newbarn Billie 1011M
				D. Sunny Jane 876P
			D. Harviestoun Daisy²	S. —
				D. —
		D. Rona of Wilts (Field Spaniel)	S. —	S. —
			D. —	D. —
DAM	Harviestoun Bruno	S. Harviestoun Rufus	S. Rosehill Romeo	S. Rosehill Rashleigh
				D. Rosehill Rags
			D. Rosehill Rip	S. Rosehill Radium
				D. Rosehill Rossa
		D. Harviestoun Bell¹	S. Harviestoun Pedro 854Q	S. Ch. Newbarn Billy 1011M
				D. Sunny Jane 876P
			D. Harviestoun Polly (Field Spaniel)	S. —
				D. —

¹ Harviestoun Bell must not be confused with Harviestoun Belle, born in 1908 and of mainly Bridford breeding.

² Brother and sister.

Pedigree 13

BROADHURST BRUSH 1395DD

Wh. 2 June 1922.

DOG	PARENTS	G PARENTS	GG PARENTS	GGG PARENTS	GGGG PARENTS
Broadhurst Brush 1395DD	SIRE	Rosehill Reaper	S. Rosehill Raper	S. Rosehill Ruce 578V	S. Ch. Rosehill Rock[1]
					D. Peggy (unreg.)
				D. Rosehill Ruth	S. —
					D. —
			D. Nell (unreg.)	S. Dash	S. —
					D. —
				D. Floss	S. —
					D. —
	DAM	Broadhurst Bokra 91BB	S. Rosehill Rector	S. Rosehill Ruce 578V	S. Ch. Rosehill Rock[1]
					D. Peggy (unreg.)
				D. Rona of Wilts (black Field Spaniel)	S. —
					D. —
			D. Broadhurst Bee	S. Langrish Bang	S. —
					D. —
				D. Langrish Buzz	S. Ch. Rosehill Rattler
					D. Langrish Bud

[1] By Bridford Bibelot out of Rosehill Rhonda; breeder, pedigree and date of birth unknown.

PRIMAX JUDY 975FF

Whelped 15 September 1928. Foundation bitch of Miss Scholefield (Mrs Freer).

PARENTS	G PARENTS	GG PARENTS	GGG PARENTS	GGGG PARENTS
SIRE Harviestoun Marshall 857BB	**SIRE** Harviestour Sam 668W Wh. 1912	S. Harviestoun Pedro 854Q	S. Ch. Newbarn Billy 1011M	S. Bridford Bobs 1193K D. Newbarn Momie 1012M
			D. Sunny Jane 876P	S. Rosehill Rock 856G D. Sultana 1064N
		D. Harviestoun Daisy 851Q	S. Ch. Newbarn Billy 1011M	S. Bridford Bobs 1193K D. Newbarn Momie 1012M
			D. Sunny Jane 876P	S. Rosehill Rock 856G D. Sultana 1064N
	DAM Daisy McMeechen Wh. 18 Feb. 1916	S. Harviestoun Rufus (unreg.)	S. Rosehill Romeo	S. Ch. Rosehill Rashleigh D. Rosehill Rags
			D. Rosehill Rip	S. Rosehill Radium D. Rosehill Rossa
		D. Harviestoun May	S. Harviestoun Pedro 854Q	S. Ch. Newbarn Billy 1011M D. Sunny jane 876P
			D. Harviestoun Bell	S. Harviestoun Pedro 854Q D. Harviestoun Polly 847P (Field)
DAM Primax Beauty	**SIRE** Harviestoun Malloch 134Z Wh. 1917	S. Harviestoun Rufus	S. Rosehill Romeo	S. Ch. Rosehill Rashleigh D. Rosehill Rags
			D. Rosehill Romeo	S. Ch. Rosehill Radium D. Rosehill Rossa
		D. Harviestoun May	S. Harviestoun Pedro 854Q	S. Ch. Newbarn Billy 1011M D. Sunny Jane 876P
			D. Harviestoun Bell	S. Harviestoun Pedro 854P D. Harviestoun Polly 847P (Field)
	DAM Harviestourn Delphine	S. Harviestoun Sam 668Q	S. Harviestoun Pedro 854Q	S. Ch. Newbarn Billy 1011M D. Sunny Jane 876P
			D. Harviestoun Daisy 851Q	S. Ch. Newbarn Billy 1011M D. Sunny Jane 876P
		D. Brussels II (unreg.)	S. —	S. — D. —
			D. Brussels I	S. — D. —

LANGRISH BRUNO

Sussex Spaniel Dog; whelped 16 February 1923.

PARENTS	G PARENTS	GG PARENTS	GGG PARENTS
SIRE	SIRE		
Paxhill Buckle	Punch of Heaton	S. Shot	S. Willington Tony
			D. Willington Floss
		D. Ruby	S. Denne Orwith
			D. Topsy
	DAM		
	Rattle	S. Dandy	S. —
			D. —
		D. Langrish Buzz	S. Roschill Rattler
			D. Langrish Budd
DAM	SIRE		
Broadhurst Bexie	Roschill Rector	S. Roschill Ruce	S. Roschill Rock
			D. Peggy
		D. Rona of Wilts 9565 (Field Spaniel)	S. Carnfield Marquis (Field Spaniel)
			D. Ch. Ynysowen Iris (Field Spaniel)
	DAM		
	Bee	S. Langrish Bang	S. —
			D. —
		D. Langrish Buzz	S. Roschill Rattler
			D. Langrish Budd

WESTMARK BELLE 1317MM

Whelped 6 July 1927. This bitch was also used to produce Field Spaniels.

PARENTS	G PARENTS	GG PARENTS	GGG PARENTS	GGGG PARENTS
SIRE Ladbroke Beau 296GG	Langrish Bruno 83GG	S. Paxhill Buckle (unreg.)	S. Punch of Heaton	S. Shot D. Ruby
			D. Rattle	S. Dandy D. Langrish Buzz[1]
		D. Broadhurst Bexie 93BB	S. Rosehill Rector 30X	S. Rosehill Ruce 578V D. Rona of Wilts (Field)
			D. Broadhurst Bee	S. Langrish Bang D. Langrish Buzz[1]
	DAM Earlswood Mafalda 80FF	S. Harviestoun Marshall 857BB	S. Harviestoun Sam 668W	S. Harviestoun Pedro 854Q D. Harviestoun Daisy 851Q
			D. Daisy Meacham (or McMeechin)	S. Harviestoun Rufus D. Harviestoun May
		D. Nona of Leetside 1452EE	S. Harviestoun Malloch 134Z	S. Harviestoun Rufus D. Harviestoun May
			D. Restless of Leetside	S. Harviestoun Beau 753AA D. Harviestoun Sadie
DAM Steep Nell	Harviestoun Derek 589CC	S. Harviestoun Dirk 754AA	S. Harviestoun Sam 668W	S. Harviestoun Pedro 854Q D. Harviestoun Daisy 851Q
			D. Daisy Meacham (or McMeechin)	S. Harviestoun Rufus D. Harviestoun May
		D. Brussels II (unreg.)	S. Harviestoun Sam 668W	S. Harviestoun Pedro 854Q D. Harviestoun Daisy 851Q
			D. Brussels I	S. — D. —
	Westmark Ruth (unreg.)	S. Rosehill Reaper Wh. 1921	S. Rosehill Raper	S. Rosehill Ruce 578V D. Rosehill Ruth
			D. Nell (unreg.)	S. Dash D. Floss
		D. Westmark Jet	S. —	S. — D. —
			D. —	S. — D. —

[1] Ch. Rosehill Rattler x Langrish Budd

CH. AGRIVISTA BETA 1940LL

Sussex Spaniel dog; golden liver; whelped 10 September 1929.

PARENTS	G PARENTS	GG PARENTS	GGG PARENTS	GGGG PARENTS
SIRE Soutar Johnny 1791HH Br./owner: R. Menzies	**SIRE** Broadhurst Bob 1296FF	S. Broadhurst Brush 1395DD	S. Rosehill Reaper	S. Rosehill Raper (unreg.)⁹ / D. Nell (unreg.)⁹
			D. Broadhurst Bokra 91BB Wh. 1921	S. Rosehill Rector 30X (Wh. 1915)⁹ / D. Broadhurst Bee
		D. Broadhurst Dolly 1119CC	S. Harviestoun Beau 753AA	S. Harviestoun Jimmy (unreg.) / D. Harviestoun Bruno (unreg.)¹
			D. Harviestoun Gem (unreg.)	S. — / D. —
	DAM Nona of Leetside 1452EE	S. Harviestoun Malloch 134Z	S. Harviestoun Rufus (unreg.)	S. Rosehill Romeo² / D. Rosehill Rip³
			D. Harviestoun May	S. Harviestoun Pedro 854Q / D. Harviestoun Belle⁴
		D. Restless of Leetside	S. Harviestoun Beau 753AA	S. Harviestoun Jimmy (unreg.) / D. Harviestoun Bruno (unreg.)¹
			D. Harviestoun Sadie	S. — / D. —
DAM Agrivista Asteria	**SIRE** Ch. Brosse 77FF	S. Broadhurst Brush 1395DD	S. Rosehill Reaper	S. Rosehill Raper (unreg.) / D. Nell (unreg.)
			D. Broadhurst Bokra	S. Rosehill Rector 30X (Wh. 1915)⁹ / D. Broadhurst Bee
		D. Broadhurst Brora	S. Punch of Heanton (unreg.)	S. Shot⁵ / D. Ruby⁶
			D. Rattle (unreg.)	S. Dandy / D. Langrish Buzz⁷
	DAM Tehana of Fourclovers 80HH (late Primax Sally) Owner: Mrs Bower Breeder: S.C. Mitchell	S. Langrish Bruno 83GG	S. Paxhill Buckle (unreg.)	S. Punch of Heanton / D. Rattle
			D. Broadhurst Bexie 93BB	S. Rosehill Rector 30X⁹ / D. Broadhurst Bee⁸
		D. Primax Beauty	S. Harviestoun Malloch 134Z	S. Harviestoun Rufus (unreg.) / D. Harviestoun May
			D. Harviestoun Delphine	S. Harviestoun Sam 668W / D. Brussels II (unreg.)

¹ By Harviestoun Rufus ex Harviestoun Belle.
² By Rosehill Rashleigh ex Rosehill Rag.
³ By Rosehill Radium ex Rosehill Rossa.
⁴ By Willington Tony ex Willington Floss.
⁵ By Denne Orwith ex Topsy.
⁷ By Rosehill Rattler ex Langrish Budd.

CH. OKIMAT OF FOURCLOVERS 1316MM

Sussex Spaniel dog; golden liver; whelped 30 June 1930. Bred and owned by Miss J. Scholefield (Mrs Freer).

PARENTS	G PARENTS	GG PARENTS	GGG PARENTS	GGGG PARENTS
SIRE Sihoun of Fourclovers 2002KK Wh. 10 Mar. 1929	**SIRE** Ch. The Sagamore of Fourclovers 1616HH	S. Ch. Brosse 77FF	S. Broadhurst Brush 1395DD	S. Rosehill Reaper / D. Broadhurst Bokra 91BB (Wh. 1921)
			D. Broadhurst Brora	S. Punch of Heanton / D. Rattle
		D. Primax Judy 975FF	S. Harviestoun Marshall 857BB	S. Harviestoun Sam 668W / D. Daisy McMeekin
			D. Primax Beauty	S. Harviestoun Malloch / D. Harviestoun Delpine
	DAM Sandra	S. Ch. Brosse 77FF	S. Broadhurst Brush 1395DD	S. Rosehill Reaper / D. Broadhurst Bokra 91BB
			D. Broadhurst Brora	S. Punch of Heanton / D. Rattle
		D. Treyford Jessica 1014FF	S. Peter of Earlswood	S. Napoleon / D. Marie
			D. Cleopatra	S. Gyp / D. Mildred
DAM Kahana of Fourclovers	**SIRE** Ch. Dash of Ianmohr 1792HH Wh. 19 Feb. 1926	S. Broadhurst Bob 1296FF Wh. 14 Sept. 1924	S. Broadhurst Brush	S. Rosehill Reaper / D. Broadhurst Bokra 91BB
			D. Broadhurst Dolly 1119CC	S. Harviestoun Beau 755HH / D. Harviestoun Gem
		D. Nona of Leetside 1452EE Wh. 9 Aug. 1922	S. Harviestoun Malloch 134Z	S. Harviestoun Rufus (unreg.) / D. Harviestoun May
			D. Restless of Leetside	S. Harviestoun Beau 753AA / D. Harviestoun Sadie
	DAM Kisha of Fourclovers	S. Bruan	S. Ch. Brosse 77FF	S. Broadhurst Brush 1395DD / D. Broadhurst Brora
			D. Nan	S. — / D. —
		D. Bebrhos of Fourclovers	S. Ch. Brosse 77FF	S. Broadhurst Brush 77FF / D. Broadhurst Brora
			D. Treyford Jessica 1014FF	S. Peter of Earlswood / D. Cleopatra

AGRIVISTA HELIOS 93AH

Whelped 31 December 1946. Note that Okimat appears five times in the fourth generation and once in the third, making six direct lines to him in four generations.

PARENTS	G PARENTS	GG PARENTS	GGG PARENTS
SIRE Wabun of Fourclovers	SIRE Tamenund of Fourclovers	S. Sachem of Fourclovers 2033QQ	S. Ch. Okimat of Fourclovers 1316MM
			D. Talula of Fourclovers 1779KK
		D. Lilluar of Fourclovers	S. Ch. Okimat of Fourclovers 1316MM
			D. Langrish Bangle
	DAM Ahmeek of Fourclovers 64AR	S. Ch. Okimat of Fourclovers 1316MM	S. Sihoun of Fourclovers 2002KK
			D. Kananhaha of Fourclovers
		D. Pocahontas of Fourclovers	S. Ch. Agrivista Beta 1970LL
			D. Westmark Belle 1317MM
DAM Hatorask of Fourclovers	SIRE Wabun of Fourclovers	S. Tamenund of Fourclovers	S. Sachem of Fourclovers
			D. Lilluar of Fourclovers
		D. Ahmeek of Fourclovers 64AR	S. Ch. Okimat of Fourclovers 1316MM
			D. Pocahontas of Fourclovers
	DAM Kago of Fourclovers 2079UU	S. Kwasind of Fourclovers 359UU	S. Ch. Okimat of Fourclovers 1316MM
			D. Talula of Fourclovers
		D. Chickamin of Fourclovers	S. Ch. Okimat of Fourclovers 1316MM
			D. Langrish Belle

PONTIAC OF FOURCLOVERS 94AH

Whelped 19 May 1948. Note that Pontiac has eight lines to Okimat.

PARENTS	G PARENTS	GG PARENTS	GGG PARENTS	GGGG PARENTS
SIRE	SIRE			
Wabun of Fourclovers	Tamenund of Fourclovers	S. Sachem of Fourclovers 2033QQ	S. Ch. Okimat of Fourclovers 1316MM	S. Sihoun of Fourclovers
				D. Kenawa of Fourclovers
			D. Talula of Fourclovers 1779KK	S. Ch. Brosse 77FF
				D. Primax Judy 975FF
		D. Lilluar of Fourclovers	S. Ch. Okimat of Fourclovers 1316MM	S. Sihoun of Fourclovers
				D. Kenawa of Fourclovers
			D. Langrish Bangle	S. Daleshill Ray[1]
				D. Inca of Fourclovers
	DAM			
	Ahmeek of Fourclovers 64RR	S. Ch. Okimat of Fourclovers 1316MM	S. Sihoun of Fourclovers	S. Ch. The Sagamore of Fourclovers 1616HH
				D. Sandra
			D. Kanawa of Fourclovers	S. Ch. Dash of Ianmohr
				D. Kisha of Fourclovers
		D. Pocahontas of Fourclovers	S. Ch. Agrivista Beta 1940LL	S. Soutar Johnny 1791HH
				D. Agrivista Asteria
			D. Westmark Belle 1317MM	S. Ladbroke Beau 1296GG
				D. Steep Nell
DAM	SIRE			
Mahngotay of Fourclovers	Wendigo of Fourclovers	S. Tamenund of Fourclovers	S. Sachem of Fourclovers 2033QQ	S. Ch. Okimat of Fourclovers 1316MM
				D. Talula of Fourclovers
			D. Lilluar of Fourclovers	S. Ch. Okimat of Fourclovers 1316MM
				D. Langrish Bangle
		D. Kago of Fourclovers 2079UU Wh. 1937	S. Kwasind of Fourclovers 359UU	S. Ch. Okimat of Fourclovers 1316MM
				D. Talula of Fourclovers
			D. Chickamin of Fourclovers	S. Ch. Okimat of Fourclovers 1316MM
				D. Langrish Bangle[2]
	DAM			
	Nenemoosha of Fourclovers	S. Chipawyn of Fourclovers	S. Tamenund of Fourclovers	S. Sachem of Fourclovers
				D. Lilluar of Fourclovers
			D. Montana of Fourclovers	S. Ch. Earlswood Pete
				D. Goldilocks of Oakerland
		D. Ahmeek of Fourclovers 64RR	S. Ch. Okimat of Fourclovers 1316MM	S. Sihoun of Fourclovers
				D. Kanawa of Fourclovers
			D. Pocahontas of Fourclovers	S. Ch. Agrivista Beta 1940LL
				D. Westmark Belle

[1] By Ch. Dash of Ianmohr and Wendy of Oakerland
[2] By Daleshill Ray and Inca of Fourclovers

SHATAUKOK SPANDAX

Interbred line with Clumber undertaken in 1964.

PARENTS	SIRE	G PARENTS	GG PARENTS	GGG PARENTS		GGGG PARENTS
DOG		Weiden Alexander of Creswelshaw (Sussex)	S. Sedora Noel	S. Sh.Ch. Hiawatha of Fourclovers 2535AU	S. — D. —	
				D. Kate of Tarbay	S. — D. —	
			D. Tasmin Tess	S. Sh.Ch. Hiawatha of Fourclovers 2535AU	S. — D. —	
				D. Lorna of Tarbay	S. — D. —	
Shataukok Spandax KC Reg. No. 106042/68 DAM		Weiden Daisy May (Interbred)	S. Weiden Bronze (Interbred)	S. Thornville Snowstorm (Clumber)	S. — D. —	
				D. Weiden Jhansi of Patmyn	S. — D. —	
			D. Weiden Dawn	S. Sh.Ch. Hiawatha of Fourclovers 2535AU	S. — D. —	
				D. Muskoka of Fourclovers	S. — D. —	

SH.CH. PENRUDDOCKE EVELYN 1068AQ

Whelped 28 May 1955. (Note that only three bitches in this pedigree do not go back to Ch. Okimat of Fourclovers (Talula of Fourclovers, Langrish Bangle and Pocahantas of Fourclovers); all dogs go back to him.

PARENTS	G PARENTS	GG PARENTS	GGG PARENTS	GGGG PARENTS
SIRE	SIRE			
Kenau of Fourclovers 95AH	Wendigo of Fourclovers	S. Tamenund of Fourclovers	S. Sachem of Fourclovers 2033QQ	S. Ch. Okimat of Fourclovers 1316MM
				D. Talula of Fourclovers 1779KK
			D. Lilluar of Fourclovers	S. Ch. Okimat of Fourclovers 1316MM
				D. Langrish Bangle
		D. Kago of Fourclovers 2079UU	S. Kwasind of Fourclovers 359UU	S. Ch. Okimat of Fourclovers 1316MM
				D. Talula of Fourclovers 1779KK
			D. Chickamin of Fourclovers	S. Ch. Okimat of Fourclovers 1316MM
				D. Langrish Bangle
	Hatorask of Fourclovers	S. Wabun of Fourclovers	S. Tamenund of Fourclovers	S. Sachem of Fourclovers 2033QQ
				D. Lilluar of Fourclovers
			D. Ahmeek of Fourclovers 64AR	S. Ch. Okimat of Fourclovers 1316MM
				D. Pocahantas of Fourclovers
		D. Kago of Fourclovers 2079UU	S. Kwasind of Fourclovers 359UU	S. Ch. Okimat of Fourclovers 1316MM
				D. Talula of Fourclovers 1779KK
			D. Chickamin of Fourclovers	S. Ch. Okimat of Fourclovers 1316MM
				D. Langrish Bangle
DAM	SIRE			
Penruddocke Edita 166AN	Piah of Fourclovers	S. Wendigo of Fourclovers	S. Tamenund of Fourclovers	S. Sachem of Fourclovers 2033QQ
				D. Lilluar of Fourclovers
			D. Kago of Fourclovers 2079UU	S. Kwasind of Fourclovers 359UU
				D. Chickamin of Fourclovers
		D. Hatorask of Fourclovers	S. Wabun of Fourclovers	S. Tamenund of Fourclovers
				D. Ahmeek of Fourclovers 64AR
			D. Kago of Fourclovers 2079UU	S. Kwasind of Fourclovers 359UU
				D. Chickamin of Fourclovers
	Jeneca of Fourclovers	S. Wabun of Fourclovers	S. Tamenund of Fourclovers	S. Sachem of Fourclovers 2033QQ
				D. Lilluar of Fourclovers
			D. Ahmeek of Fourclovers 64AR	S. Ch. Okimat of Fourclovers 1316MM
				D. Pocahantas of Fourclovers
		D. Hatorask of Fourclovers	S. Wabun of Fourclovers	S. Tamenund of Fourclovers
				D. Ahmeek of Fourclovers 64AR
			D. Kago of Fourclovers 2079UU	S. Kwasind of Fourclovers 359UU
				D. Chickamin of Fourclovers

SH.CH. HIAWATHA OF FOURCLOVERS
Whelped 28 April 1958

PARENTS	G PARENTS	GG PARENTS	GGG PARENTS	GGGG PARENTS
SIRE Montour of Fourclovers 158AR	**SIRE** Sh.Ch. Kenabeck of Fourclovers 421AN	S. Pontiac of Fourclovers 94AH	S. Wabun of Fourclovers	S. Tamenund of Fourclovers D. Ahmeek of Fourclovers 64AR
			D. Mahngotay of Fourclovers	S. Wendigo of Fourclovers D. Neenemoosha of Fourclovers
		D. Kemsdale Silk	S. Kenau of Fourclovers 95AH	S. Wendigo of Fourclovers D. Hatorask of Fourclovers
			D. Kemsdale Brownie	S. Tamenund of Fourclovers D. Montana of Fourclovers
	DAM Keeko of Fourclovers	S. Noohneeds of Fourclovers	S. Chipawyn of Fourclovers	S. Tamenund of Fourclovers D. Montana of Fourclovers
			D. Ahmeek of Fourclovers 64AR	S. Ch. Okimat of Fourclovers D. Talula of Fourclovers
		D. Unaga of Fourclovers	S. Pontiac of Fourclovers 94AH	S. Wabun of Fourclovers D. Mahngotay of Fourclovers
			D. Kemsdale Silk	S. Kenau of Fourclovers 95AH D. Kemsdale Brownie
DAM Cadillac of Fourclovers 680AQ	**SIRE** Noohneeds of Fourclovers	S. Pontiac of Fourclovers 94AH	S. Wabun of Fourclovers	S. Tamenund of Fourclovers D. Ahmeek of Fourclovers
			D. Mahngotay of Fourclovers	S. Wendigo of Fourclovers D. Neenemoosha of Fourclovers
		D. Wawonaissa of Fourclovers	S. Wendigo of Fourclovers	S. Tamenund of Fourclovers D. Kago of Fourclovers 2079UU
			D. Hatorask of Fourclovers	S. Wabun of Fourclovers D. Kago of Fourclovers 2079UU
	DAM Unaga of Fourclovers	S. Pontiac of Fourclovers 94AH	S. Wabun of Fourclovers	S. Tamenund of Fourclovers D. Ahmeek of Fourclovers
			D. Mahngotay of Fourclovers	S. Wendigo of Fourclovers D. Neenemoosha of Fourclovers
		D. Kemsdale Silk	S. Kenau of Fourclovers 95Ah	S. Wendigo of Fourclovers D. Hatorask of Fourclovers
			D. Kemsdale Brownie	S. Tamenund of Fourclovers D. Montana of Fourclovers

SH.CH. CHESARA CHERVIL 1579AY
Whelped 1964

PARENTS	G PARENTS	GG PARENTS	GGG PARENTS	GGGG PARENTS
SIRE	SIRE	S. Kenau of Fourclovers 95AH	S. Wendigo of Fourclovers	S. Tamenund of Fourclovers
				D. Kago of Fourclovers 2079UU
Chesara Pride 452AX	Sh.Ch. Penruddocke Evelyn 1063 AQ Wh. 1955		D. Hatorask of Fourclovers	S. Wabun of Fourclovers
				D. Kago of Fourclovers 2079UU
		D. Penruddocke Edita 166AN Wh. 1950	S. Piah of Fourclovers	S. Wendigo of Fourclovers
				D. Hatorask of Fourclovers
			D. Seneca of Fourclovers	S. Wabun of Fourclovers
				D. Hatorask of Fourclovers
DAM	DAM	S. Sh.Ch. Bobbie of Tarbay	S. Byrony of Tarbay 294AM	S. Agrivista Helios 93AN
				D. Hornshill Bangle 292AM
Chesara Joy 451AX (litter brother and sister)	Gayle of Tarbay		D. Sh.Ch. Hornshill Elizabeth 153AP	S. Kenau of Fourclovers 95AH
				D. Hornshill Celandine 583AM
		D. Hornshill Meg	S. Kenau of Fourclovers 95AH	S. Wendigo of Fourclovers
				D. Hatorask of Fourclovers
			D. Hornshill Celandine 583AM	S. Wendigo of Fourclovers
				D. Nenemoosha of Fourclovers

SH.CH. SHARLAND SUSSEX WINE 3087BH

Born 2 September 1972; breeder: Mrs J. Munday.

PARENTS	G PARENTS	GG PARENTS	GGG PARENTS	GGGG PARENTS
SIRE Sh.Ch. Sunreef Harvest Brew 453BG	**SIRE** Sunreef Rich Harvest 1558BD	S. Sedora Noel	S. Sh.Ch. Hiawatha of Fourclovers 2535AU	S. Montour of Fourclovers / D. Cadillac of Fourclovers 680AQ
			D. Kate of Tarbay 1578AY	S. Sh.Ch. Kenabeek of Fourclovers / D. Sh.Ch. Hornshill Elizabeth 53AP
		D. Sunreef Twigtree of Fourclovers	S. Chesara Pride 452AX	S. Sh.Ch. Penruddocke Evelyn 1068AQ / D. Gayle of Tarbay
			D. Minnihaha of Fourclovers	S. Sh.Ch. Hiawatha of Fourclovers 2535AU / D. Muskoka of Fourclovers
	DAM Sunreef Tinamou of Fourclovers 1735BA	S. Montour of Fourclovers 158AR	S. Sh.Ch. Kenabeek of Fourclovers 1121AN	S. Pontiac of Fourclovers 94AH / D. Kemsdale Silk
			D. Keeko of Fourclovers 64ARU	S. Pontiac of Fourclovers 94AH / D. Hatorask of Fourclovers
		D. Minnihaha of Fourclovers	S. Sh.Ch. Hiawatha of Fourclovers 2535AU	S. Montour of Fourclovers / D. Cadillac of Fourclovers 680AQ
			D. Muskoka of Fourclovers 159AR	S. Pontiac of Fourclovers 94AH / D. Kemsdale Brownie
DAM Sh.Ch. Treherne Sharland Sussex Mead 48BF	**SIRE** Sh.Ch. Chesara Chervil of Sedora 1579AY	S. Chesara Pride 452AX [1]	S. Sh.Ch. Penruddocke Evelyn 1068AQ	S. Kenau of Fourclovers 95AH / D. Penruddocke Edita 166AN
			D. Gayle of Tarbay	S. Sh.Ch. Bobbie of Tarbay 135AQ / D. Hornshill Meg
		D. Chesara Joy 451AX [1]	S. Sh.Ch. Penruddocke Evelyn 1068AQ	S. Kenau of Fourclovers 95AH / D. Penruddocke Edita
			D. Gayle of Tarbay	S. Sh.Ch. Bobbie of Tarbay / D. Hornshill Meg
	DAM Sharland Sedora Aniseed	S. Sedora Noel [2]	S. Sh.Ch. Hiawatha of Fourclovers 2535AU	S. Montour of Fourclovers / D. Cadillac of Fourclovers 680AQ
			D. Kate of Tarbay 1578AY	S. Sh.Ch. Kenabeek of Fourclovers / D. Sh.Ch. Hornshill Elizabeth 153AP
		D. Sedora Christmas Rose [2]	S. Sh.Ch. Hiawatha of Fourclovers 2535AU	S. Montour of Fourclovers / D. Cadillac of Fourclovers 680AP
			D. Kate of Tarbay 1578AY	S. Sh.Ch. Kenabeek of Fourclovers / D. Sh.Ch. Hornshill Elizabeth 153AP

[1] Litter brother and sister.
[2] Litter brother and sister.

SH.CH. CRESWELSHAW HANNIBAL
Whelped 28 March 1976

PARENTS	G PARENTS	GG PARENTS	GGG PARENTS	GGGG PARENTS
SIRE Sh.Ch. Oakmoss Ruff 434BK	**SIRE** Teal of Creswelshaw	S. Uncas of Fourclovers	S. Montour of Fourclovers 158AR	S. Sh.Ch. Kenabeek of Fourclovers / D. Keeko of Fourclovers
			D. Minnihaha of Fourclovers	S. Sh.Ch. Hiawatha of Fourclovers 2535AU / D. Muskoka of Fourclovers
		D. Weiden Alexandra of Creswelshaw	S. Sedora Noel	S. Sh.Ch. Hiawatha of Fourclovers 2535AU / D. Kate of Tarbay 1578AY
			D. Tasmin Tess 1516BA	S. Sh.Ch. Hiawatha of Fourclovers 2535AU / D. Lorna of Tarbay 2843AH
	DAM Oakmoss Meg	S. Teal of Creswelshaw	S. Uncas of Fourclovers	S. Montour of Fourclovers 158AR / D. Minnihaha of Fourclovers
			D. Weiden Alexandra of Creswelshaw	S. Sedora Noel / D. Tasmin Tess 1516BA
		D. Saba of Fourclovers 1315BC	S. Montour of Fourclovers 158AR	S. Sh.Ch. Kenabeek of Fourclovers / D. Keeko of Fourclovers
			D. Muskoka of Fourclovers 159AR	S. Pontiac of Fourclovers 94AH / D. Kemsdale Silk
DAM Sh.Ch. Discreet of Creswelshaw 2129BE	**SIRE** Sh.Ch. Sedora Comfrey 2910AZ	S. Sh.Ch. Chesara Silk of Sedora 1579AY	S. Chesara Pride 452AX	S. Sh.Ch. Penruddocke Evelyn 1068AQ / D. Gayle of Tarbay
			D. Chesara Joy 451AX	S. Sh.Ch. Penruddocke Evelyn 1068AQ / D. Gayle of Tarbay
		D. Sedora Christmas Rose	S. Sh.Ch. Hiawatha of Fourclovers 2535AU	S. Montour of Fourclovers 158AR / D. Cadillac of Fourclovers 680AQ
			D. Kate of Tarbay 1578AY	S. Sh.Ch. Kenabeek of Fourclovers / D. Sh.Ch. Hornshill Elizabeth 153AP
	DAM Tasmin Tess 1516BA	S. Sh.Ch. Hiawatha of Fourclovers 2535AU	S. Montour of Fourclovers 158AR	S. Sh.Ch. Kenabeek of Fourclovers / D. Keeko of Fourclovers
			D. Cadillac of Fourclovers 680AQ	S. Noohneeds of Fourclovers / D. Unaga of Fourclovers
		D. Lorna of Tarbay 2843AN	S. Sh.Ch. Bobbie of Tarbay 135A	S. Byrony of Tarbay 294AM / D. Sh.Ch. Hornshill Elizabeth 153AP
			D. Maggie of Tarbay 2278AQ	S. Pontiac of Fourclovers 153AP / D. Hornshill Meg

SH.CH. TOPJOYS SUSSEX HARVESTER
Whelped 12 August 1977

PARENTS	G PARENTS	GG PARENTS	GGG PARENTS	GGGG PARENTS
SIRE Sh.Ch. Oakmoss Ruff 434BK	**SIRE** Teal of Creswelshaw	S. Uncas of Fourclovers	S. Montour of Fourclovers 158AR	S. Sh.Ch. Kenabeek of Fourclovers 1121AN D. Keeko of Fourclovers
			D. Minnihaha of Fourclovers	S. Sh.Ch. Hiawatha of Fourclovers 2535AU D. Muskoka of Fourclovers 159AR
		D. Alexandra of Creswelshaw	S. Sedora Noel	S. Sh.Ch. Hiawatha of Fourclovers 2535AU D. Kate of Tarbay 1578AY
			D. Tasmin Tess 1516BA	S. Sh.Ch. Hiawatha of Fourclovers 2535AU D. Lorna of Tarbay
	Oakmoss Meg	S. Teal of Creswelshaw	S. Uncas of Fourclovers	S. Montour of Fourclovers 158AR D. Minnihaha of Fourclovers
			D. Alexandra of Creswelshaw	S. Sedora Noel D. Tasmin Tess 1516BA
		D. Saba of Fourclovers 1315BC	S. Montour of Fourclovers 158AR	S. Sh.Ch. Kenabeek of Fourclovers D. Keeko of Fourclovers
			D. Minnihaha of Fourclovers	S. Sh.Ch. Hiawatha of Fourclovers 2535AU D. Muskoka of Fourclovers 159AR
DAM Sh.Ch. Penygader Hannah of Topjoys 340BL	**DAM** Sharland Sussex Mayday	S. Mattawin of Fourclovers 449BD	S. Caribou of Fourclovers	S. Chesara Pride 452AX D. Minnihaha of Fourclovers
			D. Tanosay of Fourclovers 451BD	S. Montour of Fourclovers 158AR D. Minnihaha of Fourclovers
		D. Kilcoram Adelma	S. Sh.Ch. Chesara Chervil of Sedora 1579AY	S. Chesara Pride 452AX D. Chesara Joy 451AX
			D. Chesara Golden Dream	S. Chesara Pride 452AX D. Minnihaha of Fourclovers
	Sh.Ch. Sharland Sussex Wine 3087BH	S. Sh.Ch. Sunreef Harvest Brew 453BG	S. Sunreef Rich Harvest 1558BD	S. Sedora Noel D. Sunreef Twigtree of Fourclovers
			D. Sunreef Tinamou of Fourclovers 1735BA	S. Montour of Fourclovers 158AR D. Minnihaha of Fourclovers
		D. Sh.Ch. Treherne Sharland Sussex Mead 48BP	S. Sh.Ch. Chesara Chervil of Sedora 1579AY	S. Chesara Pride 452AX D. Chesara Joy 451AX
			D. Sharland Sedora Aniseed	S. Sedora Noel D. Sedora Christmas Rose

SH.CH. QUINTIC JOBY 672BN
Whelped 30 November 1977

PARENTS	G PARENTS	GG PARENTS	GGG PARENTS	GGGG PARENTS
SIRE Oldholbans Flashlight 2899BK	**SIRE** Fourclovers Shiki 1478BJ	S. Uncas of Fourclovers	S. Montour of Fourclovers 158AR	S. Sh.Ch. Kenabeek of Fourclovers 1121AN D. Keeko of Fourclovers
			D. Minnihaha of Fourclovers	S. Sh.Ch. Hiawatha of Fourclovers 159AR D. Muskoka of Fourclovers 159AR
		D. Kittimat of Fourclovers	S. Uncas of Fourclovers	S. Montour of Fourclovers 158AR D. Minnihaha of Fourclovers
			D. Petulama of Fourclovers	S. Caribou of Fourclovers D. Tamosay of Fourclovers 451BD
	DAM Oldholbans Rowena	S. Sharland Kilcoram Andross 194BE	S. Sh.Ch. Chesara Chervil of Sedora 1579AY	S. Chesara Pride 452AX D. Chesara Joy 451AX
			D. Chesara Golden Gleam	S. Chesara Pride 452AX D. Minnihaha of Fourclovers
		D. Sh.Ch. Treherne Sharland Sussex Mead 48BP	S. Sh.Ch. Chesara Chervil of Sedora 1579AY	S. Chesara Pride 452AX D. Chesara Joy 451AX
			D. Sharland Sedora Aniseed	S. Sedora Noel D. Sedora Christmas Rose
DAM Penygader Dorcas 1592BL	**SIRE** Sh.Ch. Oakmoss Ruff 434BK	S. Teal of Creswelshaw	S. Uncas of Fourclovers	S. Montour of Fourclovers 158AR D. Minnihaha of Fourclovers
			D. Weiden Alexandra of Creswelshaw	S. Sedora Noel D. Tamsin Tess 1516BA
		D. Oakmoss Meg	S. Teal of Creswelshaw	S. Uncas of Fourclovers D. Weiden Alexandra of Creswelshaw
			D. Saba of Fourclovers	S. Montour of Fourclovers 158AR D. Muskoka of Fourclovers 159AR
	DAM Sh.Ch. Sharland Sussex Wine 3087BH	S. Sh.Ch. Sunreef Harvest Brew 453BG	S. Sunreef Rich Harvest 1558BD	S. Sedora Noel D. Sunreef Twigtree of Fourclovers
			D. Sunreef Tinamou of Fourclovers 1735BA	S. Montour of Fourclovers 158AR D. Minnihaha of Fourclovers
		D. Sh.Ch. Treherne Sharland Sussex Mead 48BP	S. Sh.Ch. Chesara Chervil of Sedora 1579AY	S. Chesara Pride 452AX D. Chesara Joy 451AX
			D. Sharland Sedora Aniseed	S. Sedora Noel D. Chesara Joy 451AX

SH.CH. HARVEST GLOW OF OLDFIELD 1094BU

Whelped 24 August 1983

PARENTS	G PARENTS	GG PARENTS	GGG PARENTS	GGGG PARENTS
SIRE Sh.Ch. Creswelshaw Idris 671BN	**SIRE** Sh.Ch. Elmbury Pevensey Hero 341BI	S. Sunreef Rich Harvest 1558BD	S. Sedora Noel	S. Sh.Ch. Hiawatha of Fourclovers / D. Kate of Tarbay
			D. Sunreef Twigtree of Fourclovers	S. Chesara Pride / D. Minnihaha of Fourclovers
		D. Oakmoss Spice 1478BD	S. Teal of Creswelshaw	S. Uncas of Fourclovers / D. Alexandra of Fourclovers
			D. Saba of Fourclovers 1315BC	S. Montour of Fourclovers 158AR / D. Minnihaha of Fourclovers
	DAM Creswelshaw Hannah 2002BM	S. Sh.Ch. Oakmos Ruff 434BK	S. Teal of Creswelshaw	S. Uncas of Fourclovers / D. Alexandra of Fourclovers
			D. Oakmoss Meg	S. Teal of Creswelshaw / D. Saba of Fourclovers 1513BC
		D. Sh.Ch. Discreet of Creswelshaw 2129BE	S. Sh.Ch. Sedora Comfrey 2910AZ	S. Sh.Ch. Chesara Chervil of Sedora / D. Sedora Christmas Rose
			D. Tamsin Tess 1516BA	S. Sh.Ch. Hiawatha of Fourclovers / D. Lorna of Tarbay 2843AH
DAM Scotshill Felicity Brown	**SIRE** Sh.Ch. Topjoys Sussex Harvester 102BN	S. Sh.Ch. Oakmoss Ruff 434BK	S. Teal of Creswelshaw	S. Uncas of Fourclovers / D. Alexandra of Fourclovers
			D. Oakmoss Meg	S. Teal of Creswelshaw / D. Saba of Fourclovers 1513BC
		D. Sh.Ch. Penygader Hannah of Topjoys 340BL	S. Sharland Sussex Mayday	S. Mattawin of Fourclovers / D. Kilcoram Adelma
			D. Sh.Ch. Sharland Sussex Wine 3087BH	S. Sh.Ch. Sharland Sussex Brew 453BG / D. Sh.Ch. Tr'hn Sharland Sussex Mead 48BP
	DAM Sh.Ch. Creswelshaw Isadora 2278BM	S. Sh.Ch. Elmbury Pevensey Hero 341BI	S. Sunreef Rich Harvest 1558BD	S. Sedora Noel / D. Sunreef Twigtree of Fourclovers
			D. Oakmoss Spice 1478BD	S. Teal of Creswelshaw / D. Saba of Fourclovers 1513BC
		D. Creswelshaw Hannah 2002BM	S. Sh.Ch. Oakmoss Ruff 434BK	S. Teal of Creswelshaw / D. Oakmoss Meg
			D. Sh.Ch. Discreet of Creswelshaw 2129BE	S. Sh.Ch. Sedora Comfrey / D. Tamsin Tess 1516BA

SH.CH. CRESWELSHAW ORIEL OF DAELYB 4335BU

Sussex Spaniel bitch; golden liver; whelped, 29 September 1984. Breeders Mesdames Lancaster and Brookes.

PARENTS	G PARENTS	GG PARENTS	GGG PARENTS	GGGG PARENTS
SIRE	**SIRE**			
Sh.Ch. Nordahl Sea Otter of Oakmoss 1503BQ	Sh.Ch. Quintic Joby 672BN	S. Oldholbans Flashlight 2899BK	S. Fourclovers Shiki 1478BJ	S. — / D. —
			D. Oldholbans Rowena	S. — / D. —
		D. Penygader Dorcas 1592BL	S. Sh.Ch. Oakmoss Ruff	S. — / D. —
			D. Sh.Ch. Sharland Sussex Wine 3087BH	S. — / D. —
	DAM	S. Sh.Ch. Oakmoss Ruff 434BK	S. Teal of Creswelshaw	S. — / D. —
	Creswelshaw Hannah 2002BM		D. Oakmoss Meg	S. — / D. —
		D. Sh.Ch. Discreet of Creswelshaw 2129BE	S. Sh.Ch. Sedora Comfrey 2910AZ	S. — / D. —
			D. Tamsin Tess 1516BA	S. — / D. —
DAM	**SIRE**	S. Sh.Ch. Oakmoss Ruff 434BK	S. Teal of Creswelshaw	S. — / D. —
Creswelshaw Melanie 0214BT	Sh.Ch. Brytonian Aelwyn 0074BR		D. Oakmoss Meg	S. — / D. —
		D. Creswelshaw Isobel 575BP	S. Sh.Ch. Elmbury Pevensey Hero 341BI	S. — / D. —
			D. Creswelshaw Hannah 2002BM	S. — / D. —
	DAM	S. Sh.Ch. Quintic Joby 672BN	S. Oldholbans Flashlight 2899BK	S. — / D. —
	Lorna of Creswelshaw 1105BS		D. Penygader Dorcas 1592BL	S. — / D. —
		D. Creswelshaw Hannah 202BM	S. Sh.Ch. Oakmoss Ruff 434BK	S. — / D. —
			D. Sh.Ch. Discreet of Creswelshaw 2129BE	S. — / D. —

SH.CH. OLDHOLBANS LESANLEA PAPERCHASE 4301BU

Whelped 1 September 1984

PARENTS	G PARENTS	GG PARENTS	GGG PARENTS	GGGG PARENTS
SIRE Oldholbans Walnut 2204BT	**SIRE** Sh.Ch. Risdene Albatross of Shipden 4360BR	S. Sh.Ch. Tibeash of Fourclovers 2982BG	S. Uncas of Fourclovers	S. Montour of Fourclovers 158AR / D. Minnihaha of Fourclovers
			D. Ch. Sahoni of Fourclovers 1529BG	S. Uncas of Fourclovers / D. Petulama of Fourclovers
		D. Shipden Harnser 0347BR	S. Fourclovers Maco 1000BM	S. Ch. Shipden Ambassador 1813BG / D. Ch. Sahoni of Fourclovers
			D. Elmbury Pevensey Belle 1142BL	S. Sunreef Rich Harvest 1558BD / D. Oakmoss Spice
	DAM Sh.Ch. Oldholbans Flashpoint 2980BK	S. Fourclovers Shiki 1478BJ	S. Uncas of Fourclovers	S. Montour of Fourclovers / D. Minnihaha of Fourclovers
			D. Kittimat of Fourclovers	S. Uncas of Fourclovers / D. Petulama of Fourclovers
		D. Oldholbans Rowena	S. Sharland Kilcoram Andross 3194BE	S. Sh.Ch. Chesara Chervil of Sedora 1579AH / D. Chesara Golden Gleam of Sedora
			D. Sh.Ch. Treherne Sharland Sussex Mead 48BF	S. Sh.Ch. Chesara Chervil of Sedora / D. Sharland Sedora Aniseed
DAM Oldholbans Saintley Sorrel at Adurni	**SIRE** Corraline Bumble 3197BL	S. Sh.Ch. Oakmoss Ruff 434BK	S. Teal of Creswelshaw	S. Uncas of Fourclovers / D. Alexander of Creswelshaw
			D. Oakmoss Meg	S. Teal of Creswelshaw / D. Saba of Fourclovers 1315BG
		D. Oldholbans Rosolio	S. Fourclovers Shiki 1478BJ	S. Uncas of Fourclovers / D. Kittimat of Fourclovers
			D. Oldholbans Rowena	S. Sharland Kilcoram Andross 3194BE / D. Sh.Ch. Tr'hn Sharland Sussex Mead 48BF
	DAM Quintic Primrose 3664BS	S. Sh.Ch. Quintic Joby 0672BN	S. Oldholbans Flashlight 2899BK	S. Fourclovers Shiki / D. Oldholbans Rowena
			D. Penygader Dorcas	S. Ch. Oakmoss Ruff / D. Sh.Ch. Sharland Sussex Wine 3087BA
		D. Corraline Pippin 0075BR	S. Penygader Exodus	S. Sh.Ch. Oakmoss Ruff 434BK / D. Sh.Ch. Sharland Sussex Wine 3087BA
			D. Oldholbans Rosolio 2279BM	S. Fourclovers Shiki / D. Oldholbans Rowena

NOVACROFT THYME

Whelped 1 August 1986. Note that Mrs Gardner's Novacroft line is the only link with the Clumber outcross.

PARENTS

SIRE: Sh.Ch. Topjoys Sussex Passtime 1188BU

DAM: Novacroft Herself 0876BT

G PARENTS

SIRE (of Sire): Sh.Ch. Quintic Joby 0672BN
DAM (of Sire): Sh.Ch. Topjoys Sussex Nutmeg 0880BP

SIRE (of Dam): Sh.Ch. Novacroft Major 2633BP
DAM (of Dam): Sh.Ch. Novacroft Hello Holly 2001BM

GG PARENTS

Under Sh.Ch. Quintic Joby 0672BN:
- S. Oldholbans Flashlight 2899BK
- D. Penygader Dorcas 1592BL

Under Sh.Ch. Topjoys Sussex Nutmeg 0880BP:
- S. Sh.Ch. Creswelshaw Hannibal 1140BL
- D. Sh.Ch. Penygader Hannah of Topjoys 340BL

Under Sh.Ch. Novacroft Major 2633BP:
- S. Fourclovers Maco
- D. Novacroft Wisteria of the Whitegrounds

Under Sh.Ch. Novacroft Hello Holly 2001BM:
- S. Sh.Ch. Creswelshaw Hannibal 1140BL
- D. Novacroft Wisteria of the Whitegrounds

GGG PARENTS

Under Oldholbans Flashlight 2899BK:
- S. Fourclovers Shiki
- D. Oldholbans Rowena

Under Penygader Dorcas 1592BL:
- S. Sh.Ch. Oakmoss Ruff 434BK
- D. Sh.Ch. Sharland Sussex Wine 3087BH

Under Sh.Ch. Creswelshaw Hannibal 1140BL:
- S. Sh.Ch. Oakmoss Ruff
- D. Sh.Ch. Discreet of Creswelshaw 2129BE

Under Sh.Ch. Penygader Hannah of Topjoys 340BL:
- S. Sharland Sussex Mayday
- D. Sh.Ch. Sharland Sussex Wine 3087BH

Under Fourclovers Maco:
- S. Ch. Shipden Ambassador 1813BG
- D. Ch. Sahoni of Fourclovers 1529BG

Under Novacroft Wisteria of the Whitegrounds:
- S. Teal of Creswelshaw
- D. Shautaukok Looby Loo (Interbred)

Under Sh.Ch. Creswelshaw Hannibal 1140BL:
- S. Ch. Oakmoss Ruff 434BK
- D. Sh.Ch. Discreet of Creswelshaw 2129BE

Under Novacroft Wisteria of the Whitegrounds:
- S. Teal of Creswelshaw
- D. Shautaukok Looby Loo (Interbred)

GGGG PARENTS

Fourclovers Shiki:
- S. Uncas of Fourclovers
- D. Kittimat of Fourclovers

Oldholbans Rowena:
- S. Sharland Kilcoram Andross
- D. Sh.Ch. Tr'hn Sharland Sussex Mead 48BP

Sh.Ch. Oakmoss Ruff 434BK:
- S. Teal of Creswelshaw
- D. Oakmoss Meg

Sh.Ch. Sharland Sussex Wine 3087BH:
- S. Sh.Ch. Sunreef Harvest Brew 453BG
- D. Sh.Ch. Tr'hn Sharland Sussex Mead 48BP

Sh.Ch. Oakmoss Ruff:
- S. Teal of Creswelshaw
- D. Oakmoss Meg

Sh.Ch. Discreet of Creswelshaw 2129BE:
- S. Sh.Ch. Sedora Comfrey 2910AZ
- D. Tasmin Tess 1516BA

Sharland Sussex Mayday:
- S. Mattanin of Fourclovers
- D. Kilcoram Adelma

Sh.Ch. Sharland Sussex Wine 3087BH:
- S. Sh.Ch. Sunreef Harvest Brew
- D. Sh.Ch. Tr'hn Sharland Sussex Mead 48BP

Ch. Shipden Ambassador 1813BG:
- S. Uncas of Fourclovers
- D. Sedora Broom

Ch. Sahoni of Fourclovers 1529BG:
- S. Uncas of Fourclovers
- D. Petaluma of Fourclovers

Teal of Creswelshaw:
- S. Uncas of Fourclovers
- D. Alexandra of Creswelshaw

Shautaukok Looby Loo (Interbred):
- S. Weiden Alexander of Creswelshaw
- D. Weiden Daisy May (Interbred)

Ch. Oakmoss Ruff 434BK:
- S. Teal of Creswelshaw
- D. Oakmoss Meg

Sh.Ch. Discreet of Creswelshaw 2129BE:
- S. Sh.Ch. Sedora Comfrey 2910AZ
- D. Tasmin Tess 1516BA

Teal of Creswelshaw:
- S. Uncas of Fourclovers
- D. Alexandra of Creswelshaw

Shautaukok Looby Loo (Interbred):
- S. Weiden Alexander of Creswelshaw
- D. Weiden Daisy May (Interbred)